The Crusaders
Love - Peace - Drugs - Friendship

D1557563

JOHN
O'MELVENY
WOODS

The Crusaders
Final Version 21W

©2015 John O'Melveny Woods

ISBN: 978-1502574473

Cover Design: John O'Melveny Woods

Cover artwork: Michael Ilaqua
www.cybertheorist.com

Published by

Waterfront Digital Press

2055 Oxford Avenue
Cardiff, California 92007
www.Waterside.com

www.TheCrusadersBook.com

Dedication:

To those who also screwed up and thought there was no hope...

there is.

Table of Contents

Introduction

Part One: 1963-1967

- The Bridge
- Beatles Versus Stones
- Skateboards
- Chase I
- Coke Versus Crusaders
- Goodness Gracious
- Caper I
- School Incident Part I
- School Incident Part II
- Smoking
- Kim
- Mini-Caper
- Hitchhiking I
- Chase II
- Stamp Books
- Cool and Uncool
- Garage Dance
- Trick or Treat
- The Flood
- Sunday Night, 1964
- Bands
- Stan the Man
- Initiation I
- Playing Music

Table of Contents

Table of Contents

Table of Contents

The Crusaders
Love - Peace - Drugs - Friendship

Crusaders

Allan   John   Kenny

Kim   Stanley   Paul

Crusaderette:

Billy   Sandy

Introduction

Born in 1952, I was truly a baby boomer.

I was in the age group that was to experience the mainstreaming of rock and roll (The Beatles and Stones), the pill and free sex (not that it helped *me* at all), the Vietnam war and its protests, the race to space, the Civil Rights Movement, the murders of two Kennedys and Martin Luther King, the introduction of "recreational" drugs (which did help me - at first), and a host of other profound and unique events that were birthed in the late 1950's and came to fruition throughout the 1960's.

Growing up within this timeframe, neither I nor any of my friends developed any true awareness or understanding of the times we were living in. That came in hindsight. Many others found deep and profound meaning growing up during those years.

Not The Crusaders.

Even though the events of the 60's were truly historic, at the time they were simply events; we were aware of them; they weaved around and through our lives, but were not really of any great significance to us. Rather than being objective participants, trying to make sense of the times, we were simply too busy growing up and having fun.

We didn't actually make a conscious choice to have fun; rather, we simply did -- instead of despairing in the angst that was supposedly appropriate for the times we lived in, and expressed á la Bob Dylan protest songs.

The stories you are about to read (I know, it sounds like a Jack Webb TV program - also a product of the 1960's) are *mostly* true. Being one of the participants, I found it somewhat difficult to be objective. However, I have confirmed most of these tales with my friends who were there, and between us we reached a consensus of what "really" happened.

This is what I've written.

There are a few hazy parts. The reasons for this will become obvious as you get nearer the end of the book. "*If you remember the sixties, you really didn't participate in them*" wasn't just a colloquialism.

In our case, it was, to a great extent, a fact.

There is a recurring thread that weaves its way throughout these adventures that I hope to adequately convey to the reader: the deep, unyielding, loyal friendships that were formed and have endured to present day, almost fifty years later.

This is the story of best friends, The Crusaders, and our growing up together in a small "*Leave It to Beaver*" bedroom community called La Puente in Southern California. It is a tribute to these friends, who, with the exception of one, are still around to kid and reminisce with.

These stories share how we got through those tumultuous times in our own little cocoon with humor, friendship, and "creative" approaches to problems. They celebrate and offer another view of those years, told from a different perspective than in other popular books about that era.

Those free spirited years were not without problems, however, even for The Crusaders. They are shared with the reader as well.

I did not write this as a *mea culpa* condoning our behaviors, or to hold ourselves up as role models. We were anything but that, in both thoughts and deeds. This is simply our story. It was a special time in a special universe, unlike any time before or since.

Heck, it was the 1960's.

We were impressionable, budding, pubescent teenagers. Drugs, rock and roll, few or no consequences for actions, girls on the pill, and "make love not war" slogans were everywhere.

What could possibly go wrong under those circumstances?

Crusader John

Map of Neighborhood

The Crusaders
Part One

1963-1966

*"You were a little hard on the
Beaver last night, Ward."*

John O'Melveny Woods

The Bridge

I'm not sure when we started our little "gang," seems like it was the summer of '63.

My family moved from a temporary home in Los Angeles to the 'burbs, twenty-five miles east of Los Angeles in the San Gabriel Valley – a bedroom community called La Puente. It was partially undeveloped when I arrived. Large swaths of orange groves dotted the land between budding housing developments. The air was clear and fresh.

It was a community of immigrants, mostly third generation, with a smattering of first and second. A cosmological gathering of the future faces of America: Italians, Irish, Mexicans, Poles, and Jews. All living together and no one noticing what type they were or caring. Only that they were good people and everyone seemed to like one another.

Our physical neighborhood was very unusual in that all of the streets were laid out ninety degrees to the main street, Puente Avenue, and they dead-ended into it. At the end of each street was a large circle of asphalt to allow fire trucks to turn around. They now call these types of streets cul-de-sacs, a fancy name for a dead-end street. In any event, I lived in the second house from the end of the cul-de-sac.

The day we moved was long and tiring. My dad was so excited about being in our new house that he promised us all a big home-cooked spaghetti dinner our first night there.

The movers weren't privy to that promise.

They took longer than expected, and by about six o'clock they finally finished. Huge boxes littered every room of the house. There would be no home-cooked meal that evening. My dad had thin graying hair, blue eyes, a slightly bulbous nose and a perpetual smile. No smile that night. He was crestfallen, resigned to getting some hamburgers from the local Gigi burger joint the movers had told him about.

Knock, knock. "Hello?"

We answered the door and were met by our new neighbors, the Adamos, who lived directly across the street. Mrs. Adamo, a demure and slightly shy woman of perhaps forty with pulled-back black hair and dark eyes, stood outside the screen door holding a nine-by-twelve-inch pan covered by tin foil. Her son Joey and daughter Josie were with her.

"Welcome to the neighborhood," she said with a strong Italian accent, smiling. "We thought you would like this since you were moving all day."

My dad grabbed the tray and peeked under the foil. Thank-you's abounded as we followed the metal tray and the intoxicating aroma into the kitchen.

He looked at all of us kids. "Remember my promise?"

"Yes!" we five munchkins replied in synchronous anticipation.

Dad peeled back the foil to reveal the biggest mound of spaghetti and meatballs I'd ever seen.

We quickly learned that's the way it was in La Puente. Everyone was friendly. And boy, was that pasta meal tasty. The last things I remember about that night were an empty pan and falling fast asleep with a full stomach.

The next day my little sister Kathy left the back door open and our cat Nicky escaped. *Crap.* My mom was beside herself, holding back the tears. I quickly volunteered to find the little guy (I think it was a guy), grabbing my Stingray bike and riding around the neighborhood, calling for the cat. I worked my way up two streets and thought I saw Nicky dart into a garage. I pedaled toward the driveway that led to the garage.

A boy I later learned was Stanley stood at the end of the driveway. I stopped. He was a foot shorter than me and gangly, almost as if his bones didn't fit his body. Like a newborn foal trying to get his footing. His light brown hair, parted in the middle, crowned dark brown eyes set within an egg-shaped face.

"Hey, I think that's my cat that ran into your garage."

He replied tersely, "The fuck it was."

I'd heard that word before. Wasn't sure what it meant.

"I'm telling you, it was my cat." I wasn't positive at that point, but I wasn't going to back down.

"What does your cat look like?"

"Like the cat I just saw run into your garage."

"Well, it's not yours."

"Look, dick-head," I started. This was a term I heard older kids say one time or another when they were mad. Didn't know what it meant either. But it seemed to get people's attention. "We just moved here and our cat ran away." I pointed toward the garage. "And that is our cat."

"What did you call me?"

"Dick-head, that's what. And if you don't give me my cat back, I'm gonna kick your butt." Another quote from some kids I heard from my time in LA.

"You and whose army?"

"I don't need any army."

"Get the fuck outta here," he replied with a dismissive gesture of his arm.

"I told you, that's my cat, and I'm getting it." I set the bike down on its side and walked toward him.

He met me more than halfway, and with a wicked left slugged me in the stomach followed by a right slamming into

5

my mouth. I fell back over my bike and landed in the street. The shock of it all paralyzed me.

"I told *you*, dick-head, that's my cat. Now get the fuck out of here before I really kick your ass."

I jumped up almost crying and rode the Stingray back toward my house, unsure as to why I didn't continue the fight. The knuckle sandwich was something I had never experienced before. Fist fighting. It just never happened. At least to me. Returning home, I made up some excuses for the redness of my face and washed up. We never did find that cat. But I had been introduced to one of my future best friends.

Kenny was my next-door neighbor. My height, sandy-blond hair, blue eyes, soft features. Infectious smile. We became fast friends. He was a year older and was friends with Stanley. Kenny and I walked to school together the first year I was there (he was in sixth grade – I was in fifth), and also later when we were in junior high and high school. Paul was Kenny's best friend. He soon became mine too.

We started at Tonopah Elementary. That's where I eventually met the whole gang – Stanley, Kim, Billy (through Stanley), and Allan, who lived on Barrydale, which was right on the way to and from school. Funny enough, Stanley never mentioned the one-sided fight when we initially met, as though it never happened.

Without knowing or planning it, everything was falling into place. Like some pre-ordained karmic path that we neither created intentionally, nor in any meaningful way guided. The genesis of The Crusaders was being born.

And... we would spend the next seven years together.

Beatles Versus Stones

Getting up in the morning was one of my least favorite things to do - except on Christmas morning. Then, I always woke up when it was still dark, lying in bed thinking about what I would get. Man, was that exciting.

It'd gotten worse since I'd left parochial school (Catholic school for those too young to recognize that term), and entered the public school system. I had to get up earlier than my brother and sisters because my school started earlier. By the way, did I say "left" parochial school? That's not entirely correct, and a whole different story best saved for later. That was just another one of the myriad of events that seemed totally unfair in my life.

That particular morning my mom walked into my war-torn room – her description, not mine – looked around in disgust and decided to play a trick on me. This was generally not in her nature, as she was pretty anal retentive even on her best days. But I guess she overrode those tendencies and went ahead anyway. Not that it was clever in any way. It just caught me off guard.

By the way, my Mom was always on my case about my room being a mess. I never understood why. I had the lower half of a bunk bed shared with my little brother Patrick, and we also shared a desk and closet. As far as I was concerned, he was just as messy as I was. Maybe even more so. But because I was the big brother, I was held to some higher standard; one that I could never get a satisfactory answer from her as to what, exactly, that higher standard was. No matter. I could always be sure that whatever *I* thought was good enough, wasn't. So I could never win.

Purely subjective BS from my mom.

She quietly closed the hollow-core wooden door, waited a few moments, and then pounded on it.

"Johnny. Johnny. Time to get up. Now!"

She opened the door and popped her head around as I tried to hide mine under the drool-covered pillow.

"You need to get up now or you'll be late for school," she said.

School? Crap.

Now, I admit it took me a few minutes to fully understand where I was in the morning, let alone what day it was. I'd been that way ever since I could remember. But this didn't sound right. Then Patrick ran into the room as my mom left and yelled at me to get out of bed for school and scrambled back out as I threw the pillow at him. He slammed the door with a vengeance. *That little shit.*

So up I got, being careful not to bang my head and increase the almost permanent dents already there from the hundreds of other times my cranium actually did hit the bottom of the open bunk bed.

On one hand, I really hated school. Not that it was hard. On the contrary, it was quite easy. It was just the authoritarian rules and attitudes of the teachers that I had to get through every day, like getting my hair cut, no smoking on campus, crap like that. It seemed as though I was constantly in trouble with the pinheads who were in charge.

On the other hand, I loved school. It's where I got to hang out with my friends and be a part of something. That was the only thing I looked forward to. Except for one incident I will discuss later.

The Crusaders

On went my white Dewey Weber t-shirt. *Okay, that's a good start.* I jumped into my Levis, pulled on my white socks with the different colored striped tops, that surprisingly matched that day, and slipped into my Vans. "That wasn't too hard," I said aloud, pretending I was having fun with the morning ritual. I dragged myself out of the bedroom to the bathroom I shared with Patrick and my sisters, Debby and Kathy.

Strange. They're not in there. I guess I won't have to yell at them to hurry up. Too bad. I kinda looked forward to that part of our morning hazing.

I combed my hair ever so perfectly – "Kookie" style -- to look as though I hadn't combed it, using the exact amount of Brylcreem to accomplish that amazing task. Did a zit check. *Okay, no new eruptions.* Then I brushed my teeth.

Suddenly I noticed it. That smell. That truly amazing smell. Percolated coffee. I loved how it filled up the house in the morning. Not that I would ever drink it. I'd tried, and it tasted like, well, like mud strained through a jock strap. In case you're wondering, no, I never tried that either. But the aroma from that percolating pot floated throughout the house, and I really treasured it.

Then I smelled more. *Could that be... bacon? Wait a second. We never had bacon except on weekends.* And then my mind kicked in and I got it.

Tricked.

I ran out and through the front room where Dad was reading the paper, then into the kitchen. Mom was standing over the stove cooking breakfast: bacon, eggs, pancakes. The works. She looked over with a grin as I skidded to a stop.

"Are we up already, sleepy head?"

My kiss-ass of a little brother, Patrick, was sitting at the table, smirking. Giving me the evil eye.

9

"I knew it was Sunday," I lied.

"Is that why you're dressed for school?" Patrick chimed in. And rather like a smart ass, too.

"Shut up, you little twerp."

Mom turned and lectured with the spatula in hand. "Johnny, that's enough. Stop it right now."

"M-o-m," Patrick pleaded and whined as if his feelings were hurt.

"Knock it off out there," Dad shouted from behind the newspaper in the front room.

"Johnny, apologize to your brother right now," Mom demanded. "There's no talking like that in this house."

Silence. *I'll be damned if I'll apologize to that little-*

"Right now," she shouted, shaking the spatula again for emphasis.

So I did my usual - a sing-song version that I knew would piss him off. "I am soooo soo-rrr-yyy."

"Mom, he doesn't mean it."

"You little . . ."

"John-ny!" Mom shouted in her terse way without ever moving her lower lip. The 'ny' part always ended on a higher octave.

That was it. Game over. Once my name was used in that tone of voice, it was time to retreat. If not, a backhand across the face was sure to follow.

"Okay, okay. I'm sorry, all right?"

I followed this with mouthing "you little twerp." He got all bent out of shape but knew he couldn't milk this situation any more either, so it was a truce.

"Now, go and clean your room before breakfast," Mom ordered.

I walked back through the living room and stopped near my dad. Like I mentioned, he was reading the paper. He always kept up on current events, although I think it was more to be able to participate in the neighborhood conversations with his friends and at work with coworkers. I'd heard him say on more than one occasion that it didn't matter what was happening in the world, you couldn't do much about it anyway. Especially since those "dang Republicans" were starting to control everything. I think this attitude may have started after President Kennedy had been assassinated the previous year. My dad really loved him; he was a fellow Democrat and Irish Catholic to boot.

He peeked over the paper. "What's going on in school today, Johnny?"

Then he winked and smiled.

Okay, you guys got me this time. But there is going to be a payback. And payback is a bitch.

I went to my room and performed the usual cleaning ritual: everything under the bed, including anything I could find of Patrick's. Then I pulled the blanket over the rumpled bed, tossed all the papers into a desk drawer, and voila. A clean room.

After breakfast I decided to meet the guys at our usual hangout – in the field behind Kim's house. It was an old dirt field sandwiched between a convalescent hospital on one side and apartments on the other. It went from the street to Kim's backyard block wall fence, about a quarter mile, and offered all kinds of opportunities to do what we wanted in complete privacy. That's where we always went when nothing else was happening.

I grabbed my homemade skateboard and pushed off through the neighborhood. It always reminded me of *Leave it to Beaver's* first home and neighborhood, not the new two-story house the characters moved into the previous season on TV.

I scooted past rows upon rows of houses all looking pretty much the same, except it seemed some had upside down or reverse plans of others. For instance, Kenny's house was identical to ours except instead of going left into the kitchen, you went right. The exterior paint jobs and gardening touches differentiated them enough to keep the neighborhood from looking like a Monopoly board.

When I finally hopped the fence and landed in the field, I could see Kenny, Stanley, and Kim sitting on the wooden boxes we'd snatched from Alexander's Market and set up as our special area to hang out. They were smoking away and arguing, hardly seeming to notice my arrival.

"They rule," Kim said.

"They do not," Stanley contended.

"Do too."

"Do not."

"You are so full of crap."

"You are." Stanley turned to me. "You tell him."

I squinted and tipped my head. "Tell who what?"

"The Stones rule, man, that's what."

I nodded. "Of course they do."

"You are such an asshole, John," Kim said. "The Beatles rule, and that's it."

"Stones rule, dude, period," Stanley dismissively said.

"Listen," Kim continued. "The Beatles are cooler because their songs rock. And besides, they have the coolest album cover ever."

"What?"

"Yeah, when you steam off the cover to *Yesterday and Today*, there's dead babies and other cool stuff under it."

"That's why they're such pussies," I said. "They tried to be cool and then hid it."

Kim shouted. "They didn't hide it. The record company made them do it."

"That's the point, Kim," Kenny said. "The Stones wouldn't have let them hide *their* cool cover."

"That's because the Stones are too untalented to even think of a cool album cover," Kim retorted.

"There ain't a better song than '*Satisfaction*'," Stanley said.

"*Day Tripper*?" Kim suggested.

"Well, okay. That's cool. But the rest of their songs are for pussies."

"I swear to God, The Beatles rule," Kim said.

"You can't use a swear to God for that, Kim," I said. "It doesn't work."

"Does too."

"You're an idiot."

"Swear to God I'm not."

Time to take a rest. This sort of loop was hard to get out of and got tiring very quickly.

"And besides," Kim finally asked. "Who's better looking? The Beatles or Stones?"

"Better looking? What are you, some kind a queer?" Stanley questioned.

I sang in a sing-song voice ... Kenny joined in. "Kim is a quee-er."

"Kiss my ass, hatchet head," Kim shouted. I was nick-named that because they thought my head was thinner than most. I didn't.

"Hard to find, Kim, since you're a total ass," I replied.

Another lull in the conversation.

Kim lit a cigarette, slapped the lighter shut and started again.

"I don't understand how you guys can be for such three-chord no-talent idiots like the Stones."

"Because the Stones tell it like it is," I said. "Not some pussy songs like '*Michelle Ma Belle*'." I used air quotes for emphasis. "What is that all about?"

"It's about talent and taking chances," Kim replied.

"Kim, you're an idiot," Kenny stated.

"No I'm not."

"You are," Stanley and I agreed.

"Swear to God I'm not."

Being all argued out for the moment, we decided to light up some more smokes. We pulled out our Marlboro hard packs and extracted the cigarettes. We had to light them with lighters. They were cool. Matches were definitely for low lifes. Uncool. That was a rule we came up with for no apparent reason other than we must have heard it somewhere and decided to adopt it as part of The Crusaders' rules. Kim lit another one and after a few drags asked me why I didn't play more Beatles songs on the guitar.

"Because they are too hard to play, man. I can't figure out all the chords they're using."

"See what I mean?" Kim said.

"What do you mean see what I mean?"

"Beatles have talent. They rock."

"Beatles suck, and so do you."

"Drop dead."

"I tell you, Kim, Stones rule and *you* suck," Stanley said.

"Take that back," Kim yelled.

"No," Stanley said.

"Fuckin' A, you better."

14

The Crusaders

Kim and Stanley started getting in each other's faces, which was a common occurrence among us Crusaders. It never amounted to anything. We'd never had a real fight among us. But it was part of the game of being and looking tough. If one of us backed down, he'd be in the kiss-ass pussy department and would really get the whole can of ribbing from the rest of us for a long time. So it was easier to get in each other's faces, and then let someone break it up - always in the nick of time.

Paul jumped over the fence and joined us.

"Okay you guys, knock it off," Kenny shouted to Kim and Stanley. "Let's shoot over to Dairy Delight and get some food."

Dairy Delight was a little stand-alone ice cream and hamburger joint a few blocks away.

"You're fuckin' A lucky," Kim snorted.

Stanley shot back, pointing. "You're the lucky one, Kim."

"What's this all about?" Paul asked.

"Beatles and Stones," I said. He nodded knowingly.

"Hey, who has any money?" Kenny asked.

"I do," Paul answered.

That's how it was with us. Sometimes we'd be arguing for hours. But it was playful. We really didn't care. It really didn't matter to me – I liked both The Stones and The Beatles. Most of the time when we argued we'd be pretty evenly split. No matter what side anyone took, we usually had to have an equally opposing opinion, and split 50/50 between the guys. It's just the way we did it.

However, with Stones versus Beatles, all were against Kim. We just happened to like the Stones better.

I said 'guys'. That's not correct.

We were The Crusaders.

A few years back we were walking and talking about all sorts of inconsequential things when one of us, I forget who, suggested that since we were always together, we might as well be a gang. And, if we were a gang, well, we'd need to have a name. We'd all noticed there were a couple of older guys with really bitchin' cars in the neighborhood, and in the back windows of their cars were these neat metal sculpture things that had the name of the car clubs to which they belonged. Like the Hessians or some other exotic-sounding name. They also wore jackets with the club name on the back. That was really cool.

So, since we decided we were a gang, we focused our attention on coming up with a name for the gang so we could be cool too. And it wasn't lost on us that these older guys in the car clubs always had girls in their cars.

That is where it gets a little cloudy.

Kenny says he came up with it first. I really don't remember. But Kim "swears to God" that he came up with it first. And Kim never got caught in a swear to God, except once, so I think maybe he was right. In any event, the name that stuck after many variations was "The Crusaders."

The inspiration was Crusader Rabbit, a colorful little runt of a cartoon creature on television at the time, and *not* the 12th century warriors that the name could also reference. All of us agreed that the name Crusaders was the coolest and that was how we'd refer to ourselves from then on. We thought about that blood brother thing, but decided against it because some pain might be involved, and pain was not cool.

We did decide we would all wear Saint Christopher medals, since they were pretty bitchin' looking, came in multiple colors, and were available at the local record shop near Food Giant. They also seemed to have something to do with surfing, although, being raised a Catholic, I couldn't imagine there really was a patron saint of surfing. I mean, there wasn't even surfing back in the day when they were making saints. But somehow, the saint thing stuck, and we all went and got a Saint Christopher.

So we officially became The Crusaders.

We sat around and smoked a couple more Marlboros before starting for the Dairy Delight. By the way, we were smoking Marlboros from the hard-pack boxes, not those pussy soft packs. The hard packs had hidden numbers you found when you lifted the little inside flaps, and somehow we thought that if you got the right set of numbers you'd get a prize of some sort. What prize? We hadn't a clue.

The fact was, we didn't even know what the right numbers were, and couldn't guess what to do with the little tabs if we did get the right one. But boy, try and tell Kenny his number was crap and you'd really piss him off. He said he knew the right numbers, and his were the right ones, and furthermore, he wasn't going to tell us what they were, because then we'd get the prize, or reward.

"Where's Billy?" I asked.

"He'll meet us there later," Kenny said.

"Let's book," Stanley motioned as we got up and headed to our second favorite food place.

Of course, I wasn't exactly hungry, having just finished that wonderful breakfast at home. Still, a couple of deep fried, grease-dripping taquitos with that weird green sauce that substituted for guacamole sounded pretty good. We checked our funds on the way. They were low. Luckily for us, Paul had just gotten his allowance.

I think Paul was the only Crusader to get an allowance, because his parents were pretty well-off. Their entire household was purchased from Sears, including a brand-new washer and dryer. So we had enough scratch for everyone. I knew I would cut the grass later at my house and make a dollar, so I could pay Paul back. And he was a bit of a stickler about being paid back. Not that it mattered much, because I or one of the other Crusaders would just borrow it again and promise to pay it back later. It went on and on like that forever.

I think I may still owe him some dough.

Stones versus Beatles came up again as we were trucking over toward Dairy Delight. Same arguments and counter-arguments were shouted back and forth. Only this time Paul got to join in. He was a Stones guy too.

It wasn't going to be solved any time soon.

If ever.

Skateboards

We'd heard about skateboarding. Pictures were in all the surf magazines. Although we had not surfed yet, we still considered ourselves surfers. But in reality, we were surfer wannabes. So the next best thing? Skateboards. Problem was, how to get one?

There were none in production, anywhere.

We needed to create our own.

Billy's Catholic school friend Guy had a dad who owned a hardware store in town We found wood there about the right size. Six inches wide. We had it cut to about two and a half feet in length. It was a guess at that point. One of us, I forget who, came up with the idea of using metal roller skates for the wheels. The skates were the kind you slipped over your shoes, adjusted for length and then strapped on. The coolest part was, the skates pulled apart in two pieces, a pair of wheels on each.

My sisters Debby and Kathy each had a set of these skates, so theirs were the first ones we used. Unfortunately, the skates didn't lie flat on the bottom of the board. However, a vigorous pounding with a hammer to flatten the ridges that normally wrapped around the shoe solved that problem. Then we used nails to attach them to the front and rear of the piece of wood.

Our first skateboard.

Stanley grabbed it, set it on the asphalt street in front of my house and pushed off, promptly falling on his ass while the skateboard flew out in front of him. Never discouraged, he jumped up and pushed off again. He went about five feet before a little rock in the street met the metal wheel of the former roller skate and abruptly stopped the board, causing Stanley to fly forward and hit the pavement.

Paul tried it next, and he rode about ten feet before the inevitable skid to a stop and fall off the skateboard. Undeterred, we built a second one and hurried to the corner where there was a sidewalk. Each one of us tried his balance, and luck, on the two skateboards, and after a few days we became very proficient. Except for those darn rocks. When the metal wheels hit them, you skidded to a stop.

Quickly.

Flying off and hitting the pavement.

Ouch.

Blood and scrapes.

Stanley grabbed a pair of skates from his house. Billy liberated two pairs from his sister and little brother. Soon, we all had multiple skateboards, and we were tearing around the neighborhood like a pack of, well, skateboarders. It was new. No one had ever seen them before.

We were the bee's knees, so to speak.

When our parents saw what we were doing, the first thought they appeared to have was... *where did you get those skate wheels?* It didn't take long for them to figure it out. I was cutting lawns for a couple of weeks to buy my sisters another pair from Western Auto.

But we had our skateboards.

We were cool.

We were officially surfers.

At least on land.

Between the skateboards and our Stingray bikes, we were mobile. Many times we would strap the skateboards to the back of the banana seat roll bars and ride our bikes to a suitable location where we could skate. Edgewood Junior High had an outdoor basketball court and long hallways that served us well. Unless there was someone like a janitor on duty. In that case, we would go to the mall, where we could skate until security chased us away.

After that, we would trek over to Bishop Amat High School and ride through their hallways. And parking lot. Sometimes it took hours before the priests found us and shooed us away.

We were free and doing what we wanted. Going where we wanted. At least as far as our bikes would take us. But... we also wanted to become "real" surfers. And that meant we needed to get surfboards and get to the beach.

Thirty miles away.

And then, learn to surf.

No small task.

That would require a whole new creative approach.

The Crusaders were up to the task.

Chase I

"Hey, fuck you guys!"

It came out so quickly, I just stood there, stunned. *Did Stanley really just scream that out?* The object of this taunt, two jocks about eighteen years old in white shirts, blue jeans, white socks and black shoes, were about thirty feet in front of us, walking and talking. I say jocks because their hair was clipped short, military style, a requirement to participate in sports of any kind. Their shoulders, at least from our perspective, were way wider than their hips, and their biceps looked like sledge hammers. Perfectly timed with this outburst was Stanley's racing toward the front door of a Thom McAn shoe store directly to our right.

The jocks stopped dead in their tracks and quickly turned around. Their incredulous looks seemed to convey, "What the fuck could that skinny-ass long-haired surfer be thinking, shouting at us like that?"

And I couldn't blame them. I was five foot eleven, weighed maybe one-hundred and twenty-five pounds wet, and had shoulder-length sandy blond hair. My Dewey Weber t-shirt, tan blue jeans and black Vans completed my surfer wannabe look. The closest you could get to anti-jock apparel imaginable.

Stanley completely disappeared from their view through the door, stopped, turned around and laughed.

"What the fuck?" I wondered aloud.

The jocks were past being momentarily stunned. "What did you say, punk?" the taller of the two finally asked.

"I didn't say anything."

"The fuck you didn't," the other replied as they both started walking toward me, fists clenched, eyes narrowing.

Double fuck. My heart was pounding. Adrenaline raced through my body, and before I was even conscious of it, my feet took flight. I was haulin' ass in the opposite direction.

"We're going to kick your ass, you little surfer prick," I heard them shout behind me. But I didn't care. All I wanted to do was put some distance between me and two big guys who would surely beat the crap out of me and brag later to their friends about how they kicked some surfer kid's ass. Right then I wasn't even mad at Stanley for doing it, although I should have been. No. Only one thing occupied my mind -- my entire being.

Getting the hell away and living through it.

I reached a parking lot and started running between the cars. I passed two lanes and raced down the parking aisle until I could cut through another couple of cars, all the while keeping an eye on a residential neighborhood about a quarter mile away. I dodged two cars moving in the parking lot and kept running. Like I said, I was a skinny runt of a guy but one thing I could do was run like hell. In Edgewood Junior High I was the fastest at the 100 yard dash and pretty decent on the half mile. But I also had a bit of asthma, and knew that if I didn't ditch these assholes soon, I would be out of breath and in some deep shit.

Using every bit of muscle and determination I could muster, I raced for the fence that divided the houses from the parking lot. I had no idea where those guys were, and was afraid to turn around and see. It didn't matter. That fence separated me from them, and nothing was going to stop me from reaching it. Leaping from the asphalt, I grabbed the six-foot wall's cinder block top. My Vans gripped the side, and I pushed and leaped over it, plopping unceremoniously onto the asphalt on the other side. Hands scraped and bloody, I pushed up and started running down the street.

Where was I? Shit. I'd never been in that neighborhood before.

Halfway down the street, I turned toward one of the houses and headed for the wooden fence that defined the backyard. I skidded to a stop, shakily lifted the black gate latch and ran into the backyard, shutting the gate behind me. I scanned for dogs and then squatted down low. Deep breaths were heaving out of my lungs. My head hurt, and my legs were burning. After about five minutes I figured I had ditched those two assholes, and that I'd better get out of there.

I knew I would have to walk about two miles until I reached Willow Avenue, which ran north and south. It would intersect with Francisquito Avenue. Then I could cut through to Cagliero and get home.

Suddenly, I realized how tired and achy I was. And now I was plenty mad.

That fucker Stanley. Wait till I get hold of him.

After going home and eating, I walked two blocks over to Stanley's house to give him the big what-for. I spied him standing in his garage telling Kenny, Paul, and Billy about the whole incident. They were laughing like hell. It escalated when they saw me walking toward them and saw the look on my face.

"Hey, hatchet head," Paul started. "Heard you got chased by some jocks today."

"No shit, Sherlock," I replied, pointing to Stanley. "Thanks to you, asshole."

"It was so cool," Stanley said.

24

"What?" I shouted. "I almost got killed."

"You should have seen the looks on their faces," Stanley continued. "It was funny as heck. Like a deer in headlights." They all laughed.

"It's not funny," I protested.

"Dude," Billy laughed. "Stanley says you hauled ass through cars and everything."

"All I saw after they passed me was assholes and elbows," Stanley said.

"I was scared shitless, man," I said. "They coulda kicked my ass but good."

"But they didn't," Kenny piped in. "And that's way cool."

I lit a Marlboro and took a long drag.

"Those damn jocks were pissed as hell, man," Stanley said. "I followed them out to the parking lot, and it looked like they might catch you. But that jump over the wall... shit man." He started laughing. "That was one fucking close call, dude."

"Yeah. What the fuck were you thinking?"

"How funny it would be seeing you get chased," Stanley said.

"Real fuckin' funny, asshole."

I took another drag from the cigarette.

Kenny thought for a minute. "Let's get some more 'chase.'"

"What are you talking about?" I asked.

"That is so cool," Paul added. "We flip off jocks and have them chase us."

"Think so? It's not so damn fun when they're chasing you," I said. "They were pretty fast."

"Yeah, but not as fast as The Crusaders," Billy said.

"Fuckin' A right," said Paul.

"Chase, huh?" I said. Then I laughed. "It was pretty cool... the getting away part."

"See," Stanley said, lighting a cigarette. "I got you some 'chase,' dude."

"Well, Taxi Cab, next time give me a little notice before you do it." That was Stanley's nick name, because his ears stuck out like two doors of a taxi cab. He didn't think so.

Stanley laughed, winking at Paul, Kenny, and Billy. "Wouldn't be as much fun if I did."

"Yeah?" I said. "Well guess what, Stanley? Payback's a bitch." I took another drag from my cigarette and pointed at him with it between my fingers.

"And you're fucking number one on my shit list."

I realized pretty quickly that my shit *and* payback list was growing rapidly.

Coke Versus Crusaders

There was no Pepsi versus Coke in the sixties. No rock stars or sports figures hawking the virtues of one or the other. That was unheard of.

There was RC Cola, You could get it in a big bottle for about half the price of Coke, and our parents would usually opt for that rather than the "real thing." Economics dictated the choice. There was not much difference in taste. And bottles were bottles as far as returning them for cash was concerned.

Coke machines - containing real Coca-Cola - were everywhere in our vicinity: gas stations, apartment complexes, and outside supermarkets. The mechanical machines that held them varied in style and utility. Some held them in stacks atop one another. You opened the door, put in your money and pulled one straight out. Other dispensing machines were like a big three-by-six-foot freezer. The bottles stood straight up. You lifted the thick white lid, put in your money, slid the bottle to the end and pulled it out. Many of them contained Orange Fanta as well as root beer.

"What do you think?" Paul said.

"I think it will work." Stanley said.

"Of course you'd say so," Paul said. "You thought up the damn thing. Trouble is, will we get caught?"

"Nobody is going to catch us," I said. "Hell . . . we run pretty fast."

Stanley's lips got thin, his eyebrows furrowed as he thought about it. Finally, he shrugged his shoulders. "If we go at night, we should be okay."

"What's the point?" Kim said.

Stanley, Paul, and I looked at him, half grinning. "The point, Kim," I said, "is that we'll get all the free Coke we can drink and pull off a really cool caper."

"Where will we get the stuff we need?" Kim asked.

"Least of our problems," Paul said. "Worst case, we steal them from Dairy Delight."

"Makes sense," Stanley said.

Stanley stood up from the orange wooden crates we had stolen from Alexander's Food Markets and now used for chairs in the dirt field next to the convalescent hospital, our official Crusaders club area.

"Paul," Stanley said, "you and John go to Dairy Delight. We'll meet back here tonight and start with the Villa Capri apartments to test it out."

"What will you two do?" I said.

"We'll get the bottle openers."

"And tape," Kim said.

"Tough job," Paul said.

"Someone's got to do it," Kim shot back.

Paul shook his head and motioned for me to follow him. We agreed to meet back about seven that evening.

We approached the Coke machine located in an open courtyard at the Villa Capri apartments. Heads darted about looking for anyone who might try to stop us. No one around. Billy had joined us. Stanley opened the glass door on the right side, reached in with his left hand, pulled the bottle out until it stopped, positioned the bottle opener over the metal cap with his right hand and motioned for Paul to hand him a paper cup.

He held it under the bottle's neck, popped off the cap and the fizzy caramel liquid poured into the cup. When it stopped, he wiggled his eyebrows a couple of times, smiled and poured it down his throat.

"Man, that is good," he smiled.

"Let me go next," I said.

There were two rows of bottles twelve deep that were exposed by the glass door. Since the Cokes laid on their sides, they only gave up half their contents, but that was enough. Within twenty minutes, we had emptied them all, and were pulling each other's fingers, burping, farting and laughing.

"That was so cool," Billy said. "Where to next?"

We were off to the gas station our friend Guy worked at, about four blocks away.

That machine presented more of a challenge. It also promised more of a reward. There were perhaps forty or fifty bottles in the freezer-style machine. They were in rows standing straight up with metal bars close together to limit the bottles' upward movements. You had to pay and slide them to the left, and then pull them out, one at a time.

Our plan?

Straws.

Each of us taped three of them together end to end. They were about two feet long. We lifted the lid, reached in and started popping the caps off the bottles. Straws pierced through the small openings and then we sucked the liquid out. It must have taken about a half hour, and by the end there were a dozen bottles that, although already opened, were still full. Our tummies distended, we could barely control our burping and farting, and... we'd had enough.

The lid to the Coke machine slammed closed, and we walked home, discarding our burglar straws and cups along the way.

"What do ya think, guys," Stanley said, pushing his hair back out of his eyes. "There's still a lot of machines around we can hit tomorrow night."

Paul ejected a loud belch, and we laughed. "Maybe we could skip a night."

We nodded unanimously at the suggestion.

Goodness, Gracious...

"Watch this," Allan said as he sat on the curb in front of our house. He spread apart his denim Levi covered legs and smirked. Out from his shirt pocket came a book of matches.

Stanley, Paul, Kenny, Billy and I watched as he pulled a match out, lit it and held it near his butt. It burned down to his fingertip, causing him to toss it while shaking the pain out of his hand.

"What are you doing?" Stanley asked.

"Just watch for a moment, Stanley."

He took out another match, struck it, held it close to his butt, and grimaced. Suddenly a huge flame shot out, accompanied by the loud trumpeting sound of escaping gas.

"Holy crap, man," Paul said. "Did you just light your fart on fire?"

"I did. Pretty cool, huh?"

"Let's try it," Kenny suggested, motioning us to sit on the curb.

Sitting down spread-eagle, we took out some matches, except for Paul who used a lighter, and tried to ignite the escaping gas. I didn't have any. Stanley always had a fart or two waiting for an unsuspecting Crusader to be nearby when he released it. Paul, Billy, and Kenny were hit and miss as far as gas was concerned.

Stanley let out a beauty - it looked like a flamethrower and traveled about a foot out. We oohed and aahed at the feat. I finally forced out what could only be described as a minor eruption, and Paul and Kenny skunked out. Nothing.

31

Allan continued showering us with his prowess for releasing gas. He and Stanley were definitely the more adept.

During the next week, when the mood hit us, we would try lighting those gaseous eruptions again. But the rest of us were amateurs compared to Stanley and Allan. They could light them up at will. They always seemed to have a judicious supply of gas available.

Allan came over in shorts the following week. It was twilight, and none of the neighbors were around. He took off his shorts and had his skivvies on - JCPenney stretchy whites. He said that the Levi's stopped the flow of gas and that he could light bigger and better ones without the interference.

He positioned himself, legs apart, matches in hand. Striking one, he looked up, gave a thumbs-up with one hand and held the match in the other. The escape began, and a flame shot out about a foot and a half.

Unfortunately, the skivvies were loose fitting, and when the gas expanded it also went around his pubic hair and frizzed everything. He jumped up screaming, slapping his groin area.

We were in a state of suspended animation - for about two seconds - before the hysterical laughter began. Allan was jumping around like a bronco bucking in a rodeo, slapping his nuts. We were pointing and laughing, while Allan was swearing at us to knock it off.

Finally, his underwear stopped smoking. He sat back down, dejected and, I guess, a little bit embarrassed.

"Didn't you try that before now?" Paul asked, still chuckling over the incident.

"Not really. Thought it would work," Allan said.

"What the fuck," I said. "You could have burned your whole dick off, Allan."

He started laughing. "No kidding." Smiling from ear to ear, he looked up at us. "Glad I didn't too."

From then on, we decided that lighting farts only worked when you were wearing Levi's.

Just to be on the safe side.

Caper I

Paul, Kenny, Kim, Billy and I were in front of my house smoking and shooting the breeze, when Stanley sauntered up to us, animated with excitement.

"Guys, you'll never guess what I saw," he started.

Paul smirked. "Joanie naked?"

"I wish," he winked. "No. So I'm walking home from Alexander's Market and decide to cut through the convalescent hospital and went by that little building in the back. Then I saw this orderly dude walking out with a case of empty Coke bottles. So I stopped and watched him. He went inside the building, and then I heard him go into the little courtyard and plop them there. Unbelievable man. Ran here fast as I could."

"What are you sayin,' Stan?" Kenny asked. "There's Coke bottles in that little courtyard?"

"I'm saying the 'mother fucking lode' of coke bottles is there, just waiting to be liberated."

Wow. A potential Crusaders' caper. You could feel the energy of our minds churning upon learning this info - a caper *and* potential riches. The ideal combination.

"Were they the big bottles or the smaller ones?" I asked.

"The smaller ones, I think. But we could still get two cents each for them."

Kenny squinted his brows. "How many are there?"

"Don't know. We'd have to check it out."

"Let's go see," Billy motioned, already walking in that direction. We followed him, smoking our Marlboros incessantly along the way.

The Crusaders

We hopped over the block wall that separated the dirt field from the neighborhood, and walked into the field until we were about parallel with the building behind the hospital. We stared at it. The block wall that surrounded the courtyard was about nine feet wide by ten feet long -- and almost six feet high. It guarded the outside area on three sides.

Formidable.

We argued back and forth about who would go take a look, and since I was the tallest I was finally elected to go and peer over the fence. I carefully made my way toward the small building, looking out for orderlies *Mission Impossible* style, and then grabbed the top of the wall and pulled myself up to see over it.

Before me stood the mother lode.

Dozens of rows of wooden cases stacked neatly – maybe five or six high. Each case full of empty coke bottles. I pushed back from the wall and ran over to my fellow Crusaders.

"Un-fucking-believable, man," I stated. "There's maybe fifty, sixty cases of bottles in there."

Billy shook his head, whistling. "No shit?"

"I shit you not."

Paul took a hit off his smoke. "What are we going to do?"

"I'll tell you what we're going to do," Stanley chimed in. "We're going to get those bottles and cash them in. You realize how much scratch that is?"

"Over a thousand bottles?" Paul figured. "Maybe a couple hundred dollars."

"No shit," Kenny exclaimed. 'That's fucking boss."

"Anybody got a plan?" Billy asked.

Stanley smiled, devilishly. "No problem."

For the next forty-five minutes we discussed the pros and cons of how to get those bottles, and, of course, not get caught. We came up with what I considered a way too complicated and elaborate plan. But it sounded cool, and we all liked it. So we put it to the vote and it was unanimous. In two days we would take down the convalescent hospital's little courtyard full of bottles, and make a clean getaway.

But before I go into that, I want to share another ongoing mini-caper we Crusaders came up with. One that was already quite profitable and which helped lead Stanley to his observation.

A year before, we were walking down a street (I think it was Cagliero), and we noticed one of the garage doors up with no cars inside. Being somewhat curious, we went up the driveway and looked inside. Stanley, Paul, Billy and I, if I remember correctly. Anyway, nothing much of interest was in there except, right next to the freezer, sat ten six-packs of empty Coke bottles, stacked in two rows.

"Hey guys, see those bottles?" Stanley said.

"Of course," Paul answered. "What about them?"

"The liquor store will cash those in at three cents a bottle."

Paul quickly calculated the amount. "Shit, we could take them there and continue on to the In-N-Out and get some burgers and fries."

"Think they'll miss them?" I asked.

Billy squinted. "Not really. How the heck would I remember what coke bottles were in my garage? I say we take six of them, leave the rest, and they'll never even realize they're gone."

"You're right, Billy," Paul nodded his head. "I doubt if anyone would know."

36

"Let's do it," I said.

We walked up and grabbed two six-packs each and then calmly walked out of the garage and down the street toward the liquor store. We cashed them in, went to In-N-Out and treated ourselves to hamburgers and fries. While sitting around eating, we plotted.

"How many garages do you think have Coke bottles?" Stanley asked, stuffing his mouth with a burger.

"Probably all of them," Paul answered, fries thick in catsup.

"Damn," Billy said, slurping a coke. "We could do this all day long and no one would be the wiser. I mean, Coke bottles. We'd actually be doing them a favor by taking them off their hands."

"I doubt they'd see it that way," I said. "But sure as shit it would be easy to do, and if we're smart, we could supplement our dough pretty easily. I mean, there are hundreds of houses around here."

Billy burped as he set down his Coke. "And most leave their garage doors open."

"Well," Stanley said. "Let's finish up here and scope out some of those other garages and see what they have."

"Good plan," we all agreed.

So we Crusaders had found a new source of income that involved very little risk and paid out huge rewards. Coke bottles from garages. Almost all of the garages in our neighborhood were left unlocked. You simply had to raise the door and you were inside. They also had a side door, but these were usually behind the backyard fence and, hence, too dangerous to attempt.

After our In-N-Out feast we checked out three garages on the way home. All of them contained bottles we could cash in.

It was like a ready-teller machine. Pick them up, take them to the liquor store, and cash them in.

So now we had discovered the mother lode of all Coke bottle repositories:

The convalescent hospital's little building.

Piece of cake.

We decided that the cover of darkness would help shield our caper and offer some protection from unwanted eyes. We picked two nights after Stanley's discovery, a Friday, and agreed to meet in Kim's backyard, since it was the closest to the hospital and his parents were out that night. We dressed in what now would be considered Ninja style -- totally black clothing -- although back then we didn't even know the term. But it was close enough. In as much black as possible.

I remember Dad asking me where I was planning on going dressed like I was, and I mumbled something about going to a school function. You could do that back then. Nobody, especially our parents, really thought we could do anything to get in very much trouble. So any answer to a question like that was met with an "Okay, but be home before eight."

We met in Kim's backyard – Stanley, Billy, Paul, Kenny, me, and of course Kim. We looked like *Mission Impossible* wannabes, but that was okay. We were dressed for the part.

The plan was pretty simple. We'd divided the different functions among us. Stanley would be helped over the wall and inside the courtyard. Kenny would be sitting on the wall, one leg straddling each side. I would grab the case from Kenny and run back with it to Kim's block wall fence. Paul would do the same. Kim would be sitting on the wall and then hand them over to Billy. I could almost hear "Good Evening, Mr. Phelps" as we made a little diagram in the dirt with a stick and flashlight.

Stanley blew smoke rings, dropped his cigarette and toed it out. "Why do I have to go inside?"

"Because you are the smallest and lightest of us," Billy said, which didn't make sense to me but Stanley seemed okay with the response.

"Any other questions?" Paul asked.

Kenny laughed. "This is one fucking cool caper."

"Yeah," I added.

Paul motioned us to get going. "Let's save it for when we get the money. In the meantime, let's go."

We jumped over the wall, leaving Kim and Billy behind, and snaked over to the field with our backs against the block wall. Then we duck-walked across the field, stopped when we were parallel with the building and laid down on the dirt, listening and watching.

Nothing. No orderlies, no people at all.

"Let's go," Stanley whispered. We pushed up and ran over to the building's wall. I admit, at this point my heart was racing. In truth, I was flat-out scared. But it was too late to do anything about it. I didn't want to be the one who chickened out.

Kenny made a stirrup with his hands and Stanley pulled himself up and over the wall. I made a stirrup, and Kenny sat himself atop the wall. Okay. We were all in position.

I could hear Stanley pick up a case and hold it up for Kenny to grab. He swung it over to my side and handed it down to me. I ran with it over to the wall where Kim sat and handed it up to him, who then handed it down to Billy on the other side.

Geez, that was kinda easy, I thought.

Paul was grabbing the next load from Kenny and running back and past me as I was running back toward Kenny.

"Fuckin' A cool," Paul whispered as he passed.

I reached Kenny as he handed me another case. I ran back again to the wall. *Three cases*, I thought. And pretty quick too. It took a little longer for me to hand it up to Kim, and Paul caught up with me. I decided to wait for Paul, and we both ran back to the courtyard wall.

"Hurry up, assholes," Kenny whispered while holding a case of bottles. He started to reach down to hand it to me when-

"What are you doing back there!" a deep voice shouted from the hospital.

Holy shit!

We froze for a millisecond. What the fuck do we do? It never occurred to us we would get caught. We had no plan of escape. I looked up at Kenny who looked down at Stanley. He started screaming.

"Get me the fuck out of here, Kenny!"

Kenny reached his hand down. Stanley clasped it, and he yanked Stanley up and over the wall in one pull. It's amazing what adrenaline coursing through your body can do when you're scared shitless. And we were. Kenny let the crate full of bottles drop when he reached down for Stanley. They crashed to the ground with a thunderous sound of breaking glass.

Holy shit!

Paul and I turned to run while Kenny hopped off the wall and brought up the rear behind Stanley. We hauled ass full-speed toward Kim's wall. He'd already jumped down into his yard. We could hear yelling and the scuffing of shoes behind us as we neared the wall. I reached it first and dove up to meet the top, swung my legs over and plopped to the ground. Paul followed. Stanley jumped but was too small to make it over.

Kenny grabbed him, pushed him up and over and followed immediately, landing on the grass.

"Grab the bottles," Paul yelled, reaching down to pick up one of the cases.

I picked one up and Kenny followed suit as we ran out of Kim's backyard and into the street. We ran east toward the end of the block, rounded the corner and then two more blocks until we reached the corner of my street.

The house on the corner had a yard completely grown over with ivy, and we instinctively set the cases of bottles in the middle of the ivy where they almost disappeared. We then ran down the street and stopped near the front of my house and caught our breath under the streetlight.

Kim and Billy were nowhere in sight.

"Holy fuck, that was close," I said, catching hard breaths between each word.

Paul was bent over breathing hard too. "No shit."

"You almost left me there," Stanley said.

"The fuck we did," Kenny replied

"Kenny, you were gonna fucking leave me," he continued, breathing hard and angry.

"But I didn't."

"Look at my hands," I said, holding them up. They were bloody from the rough cement cuts I received grabbing the block wall and jumping.

Paul looked at his hands. "Me too."

"What are we gonna do?" Kenny said.

"About what?" I asked.

"About those assholes who saw us."

"They don't know who they saw. Just some kids trying to steal their bottles. We're safe now," Paul replied, looking around. "But I wonder where Billy and Kim are?"

"Those fucks probably lit out the minute they heard those guys… leaving us to get caught," Stanley scoffed, getting ready to light a smoke.

"I seriously doubt it," I lied. Although… *if I had been them I'd have done the same thing.*

"Look, we better get home and work this out in the morning," Paul said, looking at his watch. "We got three cases, and we didn't get caught. I say let's call it a night."

Kenny started laughing. "Got some chase too."

"That was still too fucking close," I said, still feeling my heart beating madly.

"Good idea," Stanley said to Paul. "Let's get home. We'll meet here tomorrow morning."

They left, and I went into my house. After saying goodnight to my parents, I went into my room, got undressed and sank into the lower bunk. The adrenaline rush left me totally drained. I fell asleep within a few minutes. Before I did, however, I went over all that had happened that night. It was fun, exciting, scary, terrifying and exhilarating -- all at the same time.

I wondered if the other Crusaders felt the same way.

Turns out they did.

We cashed in the bottles a week later, waiting that long in case the hospital warned the local stores of our mission. As we suspected, Kim and Billy ran to Billy's house and were hiding in the backyard. It didn't matter. We took the funds and got some fifteen-cent hotdogs at Der Weinershnitzel, although it was totally suspect as to whether they were really hot dogs. As a matter of fact, we weren't even sure what was in those things. Didn't matter. They tasted delicious.

A week later, we went to the field to meet and noticed a new addition to the hospital's bottle repository: a chain link fence screen around and over the top, blocking any access into the area.

All in all, although technically a bust, it was one exciting and fun caper.

School Incident - Part I

Allan and I were walking home after our classes in the seventh grade. Allan was always nicely dressed. Color coordinated clothes. His dark hair was trimmed and combed back in a rake, and matched his dark eyes, which always seemed to be thinking something on their own. Edgewood Junior High had been a completely new experience for both of us. Instead of one teacher, like we had in grades one through six, we now had six. We were forever rushing to and from classes -- and our lockers -- for books.

It was late in the school year.

I noticed that the majority of the school's seventh, eighth and ninth graders were milling about Willow Avenue, the same street where we were walking. Some of them were pointing toward us. At least I thought so.

Usually, when kids were milling around after school that meant only one thing.

"Hey Allan. I think there is going to be a fight somewhere near here," I said. My stomach tightened up for no apparent reason. *Strange*, I thought. *What is this feeling about?*

Allan scanned the scene. "Guess so."

Ahead of us, maybe one hundred feet, stood two big guys on the corner of Willow and Barrydale, the street we were heading toward. They were staring directly at me.

"Allan, I'm getting a bad feeling about this."

"About what, John?"

I pointed with just my hand and whispered. "Those guys up there."

He sized them up. "They aren't waiting for us. Let's just keep going."

My intuition and heart told me otherwise, for it had started racing within my chest. The accelerating pounding resonated throughout my entire body. I looked across the street and noticed the students constantly moving in sync with us toward those two dudes. Craning my neck straight ahead I could still feel them staring at me. I ducked my head down, trying to look small. Allan started to pick up a vibe at that point. I saw it in his demeanor. He slouched and started walking faster.

Inching closer toward those guys, my head and heart pounded louder. Just as we reached and started to pass them, a huge hand grabbed my jacket sleeve and pulled back hard, jerking me to a sudden stop.

"Hey punk. I like your tanker jacket," the taller of the two said.

"Thanks, man."

"Take it off."

"What?"

"You heard me punk, take it off. I want it."

What he meant by my tanker jacket were those thin foam-filled nylon deep-blue jackets found at the army surplus store in San Pedro. We Crusaders all owned one and wore them whenever we could. They weren't officially our jackets. But they were as close as you could get to a club jacket without a name sewn onto them, which was way beyond our limited budgets.

"No way," I replied, digging my fingers into the palms of my hands, whitening the knuckles. Sheer frustration with a healthy dash of fear gripped me. It came out louder than I expected. "It's *my* jacket."

Smash.

Stars flashed in my eyes. Just like in the cartoons. Pain, surprise, shock, and adrenaline all passed through my body as it slammed back onto the concrete sidewalk, my head smacking against it like a piece of ham. I laid there motionless, wondering what actually happened. *Did he just hit me? I guess so.* I could taste a salty liquid pooling in my mouth and dripping down the side of my face. My nose throbbed and oozed blood.

I laid there for a few moments, my mind muddled. Suddenly I remembered the entire school was scattered across the street and watching the whole thing. *What the fuck? What am I going to do?* I couldn't just get up and run, which is what I wanted to do. They would easily catch me. Plus, I'd look like the biggest pussy in school. Which at that moment I was.

"Get up, you little asshole," I heard one of them say in the foggy background. I focused on Allan standing above me staring down, gape-jawed. Holy shit danced in his eyes. He was scared too.

I leaned up on my elbows and wiped my nose. It was gushing blood everywhere. Then, gazing up, I realized the hopelessness of the situation. Before me towered two massively built ninth-graders. One was as tall as I was, the other shorter, but each outweighed me by at least fifty pounds. Their bodies were ripped in tight-fitting Penney's t-shirts, they had short, close-cropped hair, and both were snarling down at me. Jocks. *What the fuck did I do to them?*

When I pushed up off the ground, the shorter one grabbed me by the shoulder and started to pull my jacket off me.

"Hold it," I shouted, clenching my teeth. I angled my arms out of the sleeve while the guy pulled me out of it and yanked the jacket away.

"One more thing, you dirty hippie," the shorter one said.

"John, what's going on here? What happened to you?" a female voice asked from behind me.

I turned to see Kathy B., the older sister of Mike, one of my good friends. She walked toward us with two of her girlfriends. They were in eleventh grade and on their way home from Bassett High School. I started to cry, not giving a shit what the whole school thought.

"This fucker here punched me and took my jacket," I blurted out, pointing at the guys.

"What the hell?" She strode up and faced them. She was maybe five foot six inches – taller than the shorter one and smaller than the other guy.

"Why are you guys picking on my friend here?" She got closer to their faces, her cheeks turning red. "Real tough guys, picking on a seventh grader. Is that all you guys can do?"

"Well no, we just-"

"You know who my boyfriend is?" she shouted, pointing at the taller one. "I'll tell you. Sam McDonald. And I'm going to have him teach you guys a lesson and kick the shit out of you cowards. You're disgusting."

She spit-screamed the rest.

"Now give him his jacket back and get the fuck out of here."

Even though we were outside, with traffic, birds and wind, it got real quiet right then. I looked over and the entire school was staring at the two guys, pointing their fingers and shaking their heads slightly in disbelief.

The shorter guy feebly threw my jacket back to me as I tried to stop the bleeding from my nose.

"You guys better get out of here now, get it?" She screamed with authority, staring them down. Their shoulders slumped. Fear mixed with surprise took over their features.

They slowly backed up and off the curb, and turned to join the other students across the street.

"You okay, John?" she asked.

"I guess so," I replied, wiping the tears away.

"Those punks. Sam will take care of them. Go home and don't worry about it." A caring smile graced her face as she put her hand behind my shoulder and walked Allan and me the few feet toward the corner. Kathy and her two girlfriends said goodbye and continued up Willow while Allan grabbed my arm and pulled me down Barrydale toward his house.

"Fuck, John, what was that about?" Allan asked.

"No idea, Allan. Seriously. I never saw those guys before."

After a few moments I heard a familiar voice.

"Hey you, wait a minute. Stop right there."

"Shit," Allan shouted and stopped. I was still in such a state of shock that I didn't care. I stood right where I was, somewhat dazed. The same two guys were walking toward us.

"Hey, you, come here," they motioned halfway down the block like a traffic cop.

We cautiously walked up to them. I wasn't scared anymore. More dazed than anything else. Kathy had warned them. I knew who Sam McDonald was by reputation. He was legendary. Nobody but nobody could kick his ass. I hoped they knew who he was too.

We finally reached them.

"One more thing, punk," the taller one started. "Get your hair cut. If you don't, we'll cut it off for you after school tomorrow."

And then it just came out.

"Fuck you," I yelled.

"Yeah," the shorter one said, half smiling. "We'll see who fucks who tomorrow."

They turned and swaggered back down the street.

"Holy shit, John, what are you going to do?" Allan shrieked.

"No fucking idea."

I knew my mom would give me the third degree if she saw blood on my clothes. Not that she was sympathetic to my injuries – she never was. It's just that I would have to explain everything to her or lie about it, and I just didn't want to expend the effort to do either one. So, after washing my face and cleaning the blood from my clothes, I laid in my bed and thought. *What had I done to these guys to make them do that shit? Why did he hit me? Was it really just because of my long hair? My clothes?*

At the same time, I ran the scene over and over again in my mind, pretending I had acted differently and it ended with me winning. It made me feel better, but I knew it was an illusion. It hadn't ended up that way. And what was I going to do the next day? My whole body was shaking and cold.

Most of the kids at school had witnessed the entire incident. By tomorrow morning everyone would know what they threatened to do to me. Rumors traveled like scared jackrabbits in junior high. Those assholes couldn't back out - getting their asses kicked later or not. And I sure as hell wasn't going to get my hair cut.

And then there was the fear -- the kind that gripped me by the throat and made it difficult to swallow. The kind that weighed down my chest so much that it was difficult to even take a breath. Paralyzing, frightening fear. I had never experienced it in that form before. I wanted to shrivel up and die.

And worst of all… I could see no way out.

My dad came home around 3:30 that afternoon, and I rushed out of my bedroom to meet him in the front yard.

"What happened to you?" he asked, staring at my nose and lip.

"Got hit in flag football today," I lied.

"Jeez, Johnny. That musta hurt."

"Dad, I want to learn karate," I blurted out.

"What?"

I motioned chop chops with my hands. "Karate, Dad. You know?"

"What for?"

"To protect myself."

"You need protection?"

"No... but... just in case."

"Just in case, huh?" he stared at me for a few moments. "Johnny, you're going to have to learn to get along with people. You can't beat everyone up."

"But what if they don't want to get along?" I almost started crying. "What if they just want to beat you up for no reason?"

"That happening to you?"

"I've seen it happen."

He gave me a reassuring look. "Like I said, Johnny, you can't beat everyone up. I learned that growing up on Staten Island as a kid. There were some pretty tough kids I grew up with. Names you'd recognize today. But we all ended up as friends. You've just got to try."

"Never mind. I'm going over to Stanley's."

"Johnny."

"Yeah, Dad."

"You okay?"

"Yeah, sure Dad. Tell Mom I'll be back for dinner."

I grabbed my skateboard from the front porch and headed over the two blocks to Stanley's house, kicking the asphalt furiously.

My dad really did care about me. He always tried to help. And I loved him dearly. But I don't think he understood the way things worked in my day and age as compared to his. When he was growing up, there was a certain code of ethics among the tough guys, at least on the East coast. He grew up with gangsters like Tommy Lucchese and Joseph Bonanno.

He shared stories all the time about them. But he also noted how they did not pick on weaker guys in school (although sometimes they would shake them down for a nickel a week protection money) and always gave him and his brothers a fair shake. The fact is one of my uncles, Barney, became a pretty-well-respected gangster and was very successful at it.

However, my problem was how to deal with people like those shit-for-brains jocks I just had a run-in with. Guys with no code or honor. Guys who would, for no good reason, pick a fight, beat me up. And why? Because of my hair? My clothes? To impress the other students in school? Was it some kind of macho jock ritual? How was I to deal with that? How was I supposed to just get along with them? I didn't know and was really too scared to try and figure it out.

Stanley, Paul, Kenny, and Billy were at Stanley's when I arrived. From the looks on their faces as I walked up, I could see they had already heard the story from Allan.

"Shit, John," Paul said. "What the fuck. You alright?"

"Not really. I think those assholes broke my fucking nose."

"Goddamn jocks," they all said in unison.

School Incident Part II

We hung around Stanley's garage for an hour or so the day the jocks tried to take my jacket, just shooting the shit and trying to avoid bringing up anything more about the incident. Then Stanley's older brother Paul came home.

"Hey, John, heard you got your ass kicked today."

I shrugged and nodded my head.

"That true?"

"Yeah, and he's threatening to cut off my hair tomorrow after school."

"No kidding?"

"You think I'd make that shit up?"

He shook his head and headed to the house. Allan's brother Marty pulled up in his car, stopped, got out and approached us.

"Jeez, John," he said. "Allan told me what happened."

Jeez, I thought. *Who doesn't know about it?*

Marty walked into the house and we lit up some more smokes. I felt like throwing up. My stomach was in knots, and my hands were shaking. I was doing anything I would normally be doing in order to keep my mind off tomorrow's fate. Two fates, really; facing everyone at school, and then walking home and being confronted by those assholes.

"I've got to get home," I finally said. "Dinner's almost ready."

I had no idea if dinner was ready. I just didn't feel well, and didn't want to pussy out in front of my friends. I skateboarded home, went to my room, laid on the bed and started thinking. Were they really going to help me? What if they didn't show? What was I going to do? I had a very bad habit of focusing only on what could go wrong, and not the other way around. It was the way I was brought up by my mother and her Catholic faith.

My dad was the opposite. He always looked on the positive side. He even gave me a book when I was fifteen called *The Magic of Believing* by Claude Bristol. Still have it. But back then, you could have called what I was doing *The Doom of Worrying About What May Happen* by yours truly. And it was working me up into a frenzy of fear.

I didn't eat much that night. My dad noticed. He stared at me when he thought I wasn't looking. I excused myself after dinner and started to my room.

"Want to throw some balls?" Dad asked as I walked away.

"Not tonight. I've got to study for tomorrow," I lied.

Once in the bed I worried myself to sleep, which was a fitful night, indeed. I must have woken a dozen times and always worried myself back into unconsciousness. In the morning, I was exhausted.

I met up with Allan as we walked to school.

"You going to walk home with me today?"

"Of course, John."

"You aren't scared of those guys?"

"Of course I am."

"Really?"

"They're punks. Marty told me about guys like them. Picking on little guys. If they touch me, Marty will kill them."

"Thanks, Allan."

"You're my friend John."

"Thanks anyway."

That day was one of the worst of my life. Every student I passed looked at me like a doctor before he gave someone a terminal cancer diagnosis. My friends came up and asked what

I was going to do. I shrugged. I planned my entire day around not running into those two guys. Once I went around to the outfield to take a leak for fear of getting caught in the bathrooms with them and their scissors.

As the last two classes dragged on, I became more and more tense. My stomach was shouting. I hadn't eaten lunch – again, I would have been exposed to the school collectively pitying me, and I could perchance have run into those guys.

Finally, the period six bell rang and I knew I would have to walk home. I felt a kindred spirit with those in San Quentin awaiting the electric chair, knowing their appointed time was near. I left everything in my locker, looked around and thought I saw the entire student body heading toward my destination. *News really does travel fast.*

Allan met me at the school's front entrance.

"Come on, John, let's get going."

I wanted to just run away and hide. *Why was I so scared? They said they would meet me, didn't they? Everything would be alright. But would it?* I was shaking so much I was sure everyone could see it. Allan didn't say anything, so I guessed it was all in my mind. Each step from the schoolyard to the street seemed like an eternity. A real lesson on Einstein's theory of relativity. Only I wasn't going the speed of light.

Allan and I ambled silently to the corner and then across to Barrydale Street. I looked back. Nobody was following us. *What the fuck?* I was sure the whole school knew what they threatened to do.

We kept walking.

Still nothing.

"Allan, did you hear anything at school today about those guys?"

"Not really. I'm guessing they believed Kathy when she told them McDonald would kick their ass if they screwed with you again. He's a crazy motherfucker."

"Yeah," I said, pondering that scenario. "You think so?"

Allan nodded.

I thought about it some more. Maybe those guys felt the same way I did. Maybe they laid sleeplessly awake last night wondering what would happen if they did beat up on me again. I had no way of knowing, of course. But somehow, I started to feel a little better.

Fuck them.

I was still scared of running into them at school. However, it never happened. Maybe they were avoiding me too. The school year was almost over, and the following year they would be going to Bassett High School. Maybe they would be out of school by the time I got there. Maybe I would be able to beat the crap out of them by the time I went into ninth grade. Maybe they would even forget about the whole incident.

That night I laid awake in my bed and again went over the whole incident in my mind. *Why was it so difficult for me to stand up for myself? Why did I not fight back when they attacked me? Was I really a pussy? Or just frozen with the fear of the moment? Why was I so damn scared? Why couldn't I have had an older brother like Stanley and Allan had?*

It could have ended a lot worse.

Luckily, it didn't.

Slept a lot easier that night.

I also vowed that night to someday learn karate – probably after I was eighteen since my dad was dead set against it.

Just in case I wasn't able to "just get along" as my dad hoped I would.

Smoking

There was no stigma attached to smoking. All of our parents and neighbors smoked. Our houses were full of cigarettes, and that is how we Crusaders started - stealing cigarettes from our parents.

It was difficult. We'd cough, spew up phlegm, and generally felt bad after smoking - at first. After a while, it was no big deal.

However, stealing cigarettes from our parents could not go on for long, so we came up with another plan: have people buy them for us in front of the liquor store.

That did not go well.

"What are you kids doing smoking?"

"Do your parents know you smoke?"

"You're too young to be doing that."

While walking through the Capri apartments, which were only a few blocks from our houses, Stanley tapped me on the chest and pointed. There, against the wall next to the laundry room, was a brand new cigarette vending machine. *Holy shit.*

We rushed up to it, and there was every major brand, including Marlboro hard packs, which was our smoke of choice. And they were only a quarter.

Suddenly, we had access to cigarettes any time we wanted.

We did not plan a caper to steal them out of the machine. It was agreed that it would be much better to leave it in place and just buy them.

Kim

Alexander's Market was a family-owned affair. The cashiers (who were always women) were in their forties, and the bag boys were all local kids. The store looked tired when it was new, and more so after a few years. Our parents avoided it unless absolutely necessary, choosing to shop at Food Giant on Amar Road, a much more modern store.

By the way, Food Giant had a very cool cake-decorating area where you could watch their frosting artisans create beautiful theme cakes. With tubes of sugary "goo" being squeezed out methodically, they would create intricate borders and mountain scenes. Then they would use an airbrush to spray colors as they spun the cake in circles. Finally, tubes with colored frosting were squeezed to write the name of the recipient in beautiful cursive script. Moreover, they never seemed to make a mistake. A real lost art.

However, Alexander's Market was only a couple of blocks from our house. Kim asked me if I wanted to go with him to get something for his mom. We smoked cigarettes on the way and found what his mom wanted; biscuits and packages of gravy. We chose what appeared to be the shortest line and stood in it. Three women were in front of us, one holding a young girl's hand.

Kim looked around, and then shouted:

"No, you can't kiss me."

"What?" I said.

"I said I won't kiss you, John, and please don't ask again."

Silence reigned as heavy as a lead sheet as everyone - the women in line, the cashier, the box boy, and people from the lines next to us - steeled their gazes at Kim and me, jaws dropped and shaking their heads as if they couldn't believe what they just heard. I know I didn't.

"What the fuck are you talking about, Kim?"

"I said I won't kiss you, and that's the end of it."

My face flushed. My heart raced. I forcefully pushed him into the candy rack, and bolted past the three ladies and out the door of the store, finally slowing down when I reached the end of the plaza. *That asshole. What was that all about? I'm gonna kick his ass when he gets out.*

Kim exited the store holding a paper bag and broke out laughing... so hard that I thought he would spin into an asthma attack.

"What's so funny, Kim?" I asked.

He could barely spit it out. "You should have seen your face in there. Man, it was beet red."

"No shit, asshole. Why'd you do it?" I got up into his face.

"Gotcha," he said. "You gotta admit, it was pretty fucking funny."

I hadn't really thought about it, I was so mad. However, within a few seconds his laughter crept up and grabbed me, and I was laughing too. *It was pretty damn funny, the looks on everyone in there. Wonder what they thought?*

"Okay, Kim, you got me," I laughed as we walked back toward his house. "But there will be payback."

"Expect it," he said, still giggling.

"Damn right."

A new tradition started that day, and Kim was relentless in its execution and perfecting it into a fine art. Sometimes one of us would be with him, and there would be jocks in line.

"No, I don't think you could kick that guy's ass up there, Paul."

A chase would usually follow. And the tradition went on.

"No, I don't think that woman in front of us is fat, Stanley."

"I have no idea if that girl will let you kiss her, Billy."

It became so ubiquitous that we were all cautious about going anywhere with Kim. Paranoid really. *What would he say? Do? Would I have to run? Could I get out of the store in time not to get my ass kicked?*

It was a brilliant twist on the chase routine. No one would chase him, or even get mad at him. After all, he was simply "answering" something "we" had already said.

Creative...

And so Crusader-like.

Mini-Caper

Besides our proclivity for procuring Coke bottles to fund our activities, we knew we needed to get "real" jobs to afford cars and gas to get to the beach, and -- if we were lucky -- date girls. Stanley had stopped by a real estate office and asked if they had any work. He learned they had apartment buildings nearby and hoped they might need some help to clean them. The owner said no he didn't. Since we usually walked by the office every day on the way to In-N-Out, we stopped there as part of our rounds.

"Hello there, sir. Do you have any work for us?" one of us would ask.

"Sorry boys, not today. Check back with me tomorrow."

We'd smile, give a slight shrug and move on.

This continued for a couple of weeks, when one particular day we did not stop in and ask. Forget the reason why. The next day we went to see him.

"Hello there, sir. Do you have any work for us?"

"Hello boys. I'll tell you what. I had a bunch of stuff yesterday for you, but you didn't show up so I had to give it to someone else. Really could have used you."

Stanley listened to this, shook his head and slowly walked behind him. On the wall was a plaque that contained the first dollar he ever made. He motioned with his arm for us to keep the fellow talking.

"Oh, that is a bummer," Kenny said, sincerity dripping from his voice. "We really wanted to work for you."

The Crusaders

"I know, I wanted you too. You'll just have to keep checking in with me and see what is available."

Stanley removed the dollar from the frame and put it in his pocket. We all backed out of the office, thanking him profusely, and then tore out toward In-N-Out.

It bought four hamburgers.

Not a bad day's score.

Never went back into that office, either.

Hitchhiking I

A lot of the time we Crusaders just hung out, with no agenda as to what we should do. That's not to say we had nothing to do. On the contrary, we always had more things to do than we had time to do them: skateboarding, hitchhiking, walking to various malls and shops and exploring, getting chased, playing baseball, swimming – the list was truly endless. We'd get together, see what the majority wanted to do and just spontaneously do it.

One summer day, we met on the corner of my street and decided to hitchhike to the beach. No reason, really. Just something to do. We'd already done it dozens of times that summer. No big deal. We had our "baggies" shorts on, standard gear for us during the summer months. We split into two groups: Paul and Kenny, me and Billy, and started thumbing east on Francisquito. The first ride usually would take us to Hacienda. Going south down Hacienda Boulevard took us over the hills to Whittier Boulevard. A short walk west and we were at the beginning of Beach Boulevard, which ended about twenty miles later in Huntington Beach, our final destination.

Sometimes the smaller groups would split up, such as Paul and Kenny getting separate rides'… but most often not. If you were going to get picked up, it didn't seem to matter if it was one or two people that needed a lift.

The types of people who would pick us up varied. Some were old people, mostly lonely I guessed, looking for the chance to speak with someone. Many times business people would stop and pick us up on their way to work. Often it was families on their way to the beach, a carload of kids in tow. Others, guys like us but older, were looking for gas money, which we usually had.

Kenny and Paul were thumbing near Whittier Boulevard when they were picked up by this guy, maybe thirty years old. Clean-cut. Nice smile. Kenny jumped in the front seat, Paul in the back. After awhile, the guy asked Kenny:

"What happens if you get picked up by someone who wants to hurt you guys?"

"No problem, man," Kenny said, as he pulled out the beautiful six-inch Bowie-style knife he always carried in his pocket and displayed it proudly.

The man held out his hand. "Can I see it?"

"Sure," Kenny responded, pulling the knife from its sheath and handing it to the guy.

Paul, in the back seat, was shitting bricks at this point. *What the fuck is Kenny doing? He just gave a total stranger the frickin' knife.*

"What the fuck?" Paul shouted. Kenny turned around with a "what the fuck do you want" look.

The guy held the knife up and smiled. "What would you do now?"

It suddenly dawned on Kenny what he'd just done. He reached for the knife. The man pulled it away.

"Give me back the knife, man," Kenny demanded.

Smirking, he slowly handed it back.

"Next time, you might think that last move out," he suggested.

Kenny grabbed it and put it back in his pocket. Paul razzed him about it the rest of the day.

However, our rides were not without reward at times. Girls. The mother lode of all thumbing adventures was when girls would pick us up, which did not happen all that often, by the way.

But later that day…

…Paul and Kenny were leaving the beach after all four of us swam, got lathered up with Coppertone and ate too many Jack-in-the-Box tacos along with their fifteen-cent burgers. No rides for awhile. They decided to split up on Beach Boulevard. Kenny walked north toward Main Street, and Paul hung back near Coast Highway. Suddenly, four teenage girls in a convertible turned onto Beach Boulevard and stopped in front of Paul.

"Want a ride?"

"Sure," Paul said.

They opened the door and he climbed in the back between two giggling blonds. He put an arm around each one and leaned back, smiling ear to ear. They pulled away and he saw Kenny ahead. Kenny recognized it was Paul in their car and started waving him over – that was the plan – for the first guy to get a ride and then implore the driver to pick up the other one. Anyway, Paul was in the convertible, Beach Boys blaring on the AM radio, his arms around two beautiful blonds. Kenny started waving frantically.

"That a friend of yours?" one of them asked.

"Nope."

As they cruised toward and then passed Kenny, Paul waved and smiled. Kenny, incredulous, raised both hands flipping Paul and the girls off in stereo. The girls laughed and so did Paul. They gave Paul a ride almost all the way home.

That, by the way, was a major - and classic - Crusader *uncool.*

The beach was at least an hour and a half away from La Puente, thirty-seven miles if we were driving straight there, so it was no small feat to get there and back with total strangers. But it always worked out, although sometimes we got home a little late for dinner. That night was no exception.

Our parents never gave it a second thought. Hitchhiking was normal, and safe.

Most of the time, anyway.

More about that later.

Chase II

Chase could be instigated by any one of us, at any moment. That was the beauty of it. Like musical chairs, only in this case you never knew when the music would start.

Sometimes a car would pass and one of us would stick his arm out and flip it off. If we were lucky, chase. Sometimes we would be walking out of a restaurant and one of us would yell "Fuck you" to some jocks.

One time Paul, Kenny, Stanley, and I were walking through a neighborhood, north of the San Bernardino Freeway, on our way to Bob's Big Boy. We spied some jocks playing football in the street. High-school age. Stanley cupped his hands and yelled "Hey assholes" through them, bullhorn style. When they looked our way, he flipped them off.

The football slammed to the ground, and they came tearing at us, full speed. Six or seven of them.

The chase was on.

We ran down a street and turned the corner. They were behind us, shouting how they were going to kick our asses when they got us. We ran to the end of the block, turned left and ran into a dead end. Block wall.

Shit.

We ran to the block wall and peered over.

The freeway.

Behind us, fifty feet away, were a bunch of muscled and angry jocks hell-bent on kicking our ass. In front was an eight-lane freeway we needed to cross without being killed in order to avoid the beating.

The choice was easy.

Stanley jumped up and over first, then Paul, Kenny and I. We landed on ice plants next to the slow lane of the freeway. Our hearts raced. Adrenaline was gushing through our bodies. We looked left. There was a slight break in the cars. We ran out in front of a slower moving truck. Horns honked and we heard skidding tires. We made it to the center of the median, slid under the chain link fence and looked back. The jocks were throwing rocks at us from atop the block wall.

We couldn't care less. We needed to get across that freeway. The solution to that problem had our full attention.

No break in the cars could be seen. What to do? It was loud. We couldn't hear each other talk. Waiting. Waiting.

Paul tapped my back and pointed. After a station wagon passed we could run and make it. Maybe. We glanced at one another, nodded, watched the station wagon get closer, walked out into the fast lane, then right next to the station wagon as it passed, and ran to the other side.

We scaled the fence, fell to the ground, pushed up, and ran another couple of blocks into a neighborhood. Found a shady spot under a tree and sat on the curb.

Breaths still labored. Nobody spoke a word. Smokes came out and were lit. I saw my hand trembling. Paul's too.

After a few deep drags, Kenny finally spoke.

"That was fucking far out, dudes. Maybe the best chase ever."

Paul took a deep inhale and blew it out in little rings. "That was pretty close. If that had been a real dead end, then...."

"Did you see the look on those guys' faces when we were in the center divider? Fucking couldn't believe it," Stanley said.

"Neither could I," I said.

"Let's go to Bob's and get some shakes," Kenny said, standing up.

"Can you believe we just ran across a fucking freeway?" Paul said.

"And lived to tell about it," I added.

Stamp Books

During that same summer, while hanging out in front of Paul's house, Stanley came up to us. A big shit-eating grin highlighted his tan, oval face.

"Look what I have," he said, pulling out three Blue Chip Stamp books.

"Yeah, so what?" we asked.

He pulled out a Super Shopper, the local free newspaper (which, by the way, I was a paper boy for).

"There's an ad in here that says they'll pay $1.25 per book for these things."

"Where'd you get them?" one of us asked.

"From a house up the street."

"What?"

"No shit. I went into it through the patio door and there they were, inside one of the kitchen drawers."

"You went into someone's fucking house?" Paul remarked.

This was a big revelation, and concerned us greatly.

Although there were many times we would do things that skirted the law, and I'll share them with you throughout this book, breaking and entering a house was not even on our radar. If someone left Coke bottles in their garage, that was considered by us to be fair game. Once, we were walking by a garage and leaning against the back wall was one of those home beer dispensing machines like in a bar – you pulled down the handle and beer came out the tap. A plan started to formulate in our fertile minds. We decided to play a game of football in the street directly in front of the house, and we would each take turns catching the ball. Only in this case, we would *miss it*, the ball continuing into the garage. Naturally, we would have to go in and retrieve it, right?

While there, of course, we would stick our head under the tap and gulp away. This was not my favorite caper. I didn't like the taste of beer. Still don't.

Anyway, so Stanley's breaking into a house -- although I guess technically it was simply entering the house -- was concerning. And big-time illegal.

"It was easy," Stanley continued. "I rang the front door bell. No one answered, so I went around back and walked right in. These books were the only thing I took. They'll never miss them."

We talked about it back and forth. If, and that was a big if, we only took the Blue Chip and S&H Green Stamp books and nothing else, then we decided it was innocent enough. But I didn't like it at all.

"Let's see if they really will buy the darn things," I suggested.

A quick note about the stamp books. Back in the day, there were promotions at all of the supermarkets that gave you either Blue Chip Stamps or S&H Green Stamps whenever you purchased something. You would lick them and put them in books that the stores gave you – maybe twenty-five pages, if memory serves. In any event, when you finished filling up a book with stamps, you could look through a catalog and use it to redeem various things: irons, blenders, silverware – all kinds of ways to spend your "book money" – "chatke" as Allan would say. Of course, you had to get a lot of books to get anything of real value, but it was surprising how quickly they added up. On certain sales days, like at the Food Giant near us, they would often offer double and triple stamps. But if someone bought the books, they could still use them to purchase things. I am guessing it cost much less to pay so much per book than to spend the money on groceries to accumulate them.

We walked down to Temple Street and then west a couple of blocks to the address. Stanley walked up and knocked. After a few minutes he came out with $3.75 - $1.25 per book.

He tossed the three quarters up and down in his hand, pocketing the dollars. "She said she would buy all of them we could bring."

I still didn't like it. And neither did Paul, judging from the expression of concern on his face. But we decided to pick another house... far from home... and see what they had. Stanley walked up to the door, rang the bell. No answer. We walked around to the back, tried the sliding glass door. Locked. Then the back door. Open. We all walked in and crept into the kitchen. My heart was pounding. I thought for sure the other guys could hear it.

Stanley started rummaging through the drawers and suddenly he found four books of green stamps.

"Let's get out of here," I whispered, and started heading for the back door. The others followed.

"Pretty easy, huh guys?" Stanley said as we walked back toward the lady who would buy the books.

"I didn't like it," I said, trying not to sound like a pussy, my heart still pounding.

"Neither did I," Paul added, as he rubbed the sweat from his hands onto his jeans.

"Shit guys, that was easy," Stanley said.

"We've never broken into houses before," Kenny said.

"It's not like breaking in if you don't actually *break* into them."

"Seems the same to me," although I couldn't figure out a way to counter the argument more than that at the time.

Stanley would have none of it, and brushed off our concerns like a horse's tail would a fly. I realized then that Stanley had more nerve than I did, but it would take a while to see the extent to which it was steeled. Paul, Kenny, and I never broke into another house again. It crossed a line we somehow never wanted to cross.

Coke bottles, yes. Seemed innocuous enough, nobody was really hurt, and it was fun. Other scams and plans, yes. But there was an ethical boundary, one that we refused to cross and pretty much kept us in line. Most of us, anyway.

Stanley crossed that line. We wanted no part of it.

Stanley seemed to have a lot of money for the next few weeks. That tapered off immediately, however, after he explained how someone came home while he was in their kitchen. Almost got caught. Realized how dangerous it really was.

We all decided that the little books weren't worth it, and Stanley vowed never to do it again. We started refocusing on coke bottles in open garages.

It was still a good business, and relatively risk free.

Cool and Uncool

An uncool was anything that was not cool. Seems simple enough, but there were distinctions. Didn't matter what the actions were that prompted the comment. The results, or more precisely the effects, were what determined if something were one or the other.

For instance, throwing dirt clods at each other playing "war" in the field was cool. Hiding a rock in the middle of the dirt clod for better accuracy was "uncool." Sharing a cigarette with your fellow Crusaders was cool. Bogarting your cigarettes was "uncool."

Once, Paul invited Debbie Marble over to swim at his house (to see her in a bikini) and didn't invite any of us. On purpose. That was an uncool.

If we were hitchhiking to the beach and got a ride, and passed up another Crusader without picking him up, that was an uncool. If we were eating something and didn't offer one of the others a bite, that was also an uncool.

Being clever and witty was cool. Being negative was an uncool. Unless it was clever and witty. Always a close call. Always subjective as heck.

Seems like the cools negated the uncools, but we never kept score.

Garage Dance

"Are you going?" Danny asked. He and I had been friends since fifth grade.

I furrowed my brow. "Going where?"

He looked around as if someone might hear. "To the dance, dude. It's at Mike Bruno's house Saturday night."

I leaned in closer, licked my lower lip. "Are *you* going?"

"Of course."

"What time is it?"

"I think around six o'clock. Supposedly there will be a lot of chicks there."

I thought about it for a moment. Having never been to a dance, I didn't know what to expect. But the fact that maybe Debra A might be there, along with Bonnie, two girls I had seriously insatiable crushes on, made the answer simple.

"Want me to come over to your house first?"

Danny nodded. "Yeah. Mike's is right down the street. See ya then."

I put it out of my mind until later that evening when I was lying in bed. First off, I didn't know how to dance. But I could watch American Bandstand on Saturday and fix that. Hopefully.

Also, what was I going to wear? I had just gotten a pretty cool Nehru jacket that was a kind of iridescent green that I'd worn the week before when The Crusaders went to a Turtles concert at the Carousel Theater in West Covina. Some black pants. Beatle boots. That should do it. For some reason, though, my heart was palpitating.

Girls.

Debra A was a statuesque blond whom I first met in fifth grade upon moving to La Puente. I said met, but really I just couldn't take my eyes off her. Or more precisely, the two mounds that protruded from her chest. And they were mounds. She was the only girl in the class to have those mysterious protrusions, and, to a pubescent boy like me, they stood out like a neon sign at an all-night diner: "Here we are."

I pretended not to notice, but somehow I got the impression that she not only knew all the guys in class were slack-jawed and drooling, but she also seemed to relish it.

Bonnie, on the other hand, I met in seventh grade. She was from another elementary school that had merged into Edgewood. She had fiery red hair, beautiful green eyes, a freckly face, little button nose and thin red lips. But I seldom looked at her face. Because she had the most luscious and beautifully formed legs I had ever seen. They were a real work of art. And she wore dresses that seemed to beckon and make you want to look at them even more. And by the seventh grade she also had the tiny beginning of those mysterious mounds. She was reserved and studious; seemingly oblivious and uninterested in me or any other guy. I secretly hoped she had a crush on me.

I watched American Bandstand that Saturday, practiced my dance moves and started getting ready in the early afternoon. The big challenge was getting my hair just the right way; combed back with a slight "Kookie" type curl right near the front. My school's principal, "Dead Eye" Purdy, had already warned me about my hair being too long, so I'd had the barber trim it in incremental quarter-inch cuts until it both passed the school inspection and still looked cool.

Dressed and ready to go, I splashed on some Avon something or other 'til I reeked. Or so my mom told me. But I didn't care. Smelled good to me. As I left the house, I picked up the pack of cigarettes I'd hidden in the garden, lit one up and walked over to Laughlin's to pick him up.

Danny was in a jacket too. Dark blue with gold buttons. All slicked up, and reeking of some other Avon scent. They were not complementary,

It was getting dark. We walked to Bruno's house, smoking and not saying a word. I'm guessing he was nervous too.

When we got there, the side garage door was open, and we walked in. There were a couple of dozen people already there, all guys, and we just sort of goofed around and talked for the next half hour. Mike's dad had put a sort of disco ball at the center of the two-car garage, and also a multi-colored light-emitting bar near the stereo. He flipped them on, and then the music started.

Girls started appearing in twos. Pink, blue and green dresses, necklaces, hair pinned up high on their heads. I kept an eye out for Debra or Bonnie. So far, they hadn't shown up. But soon there was a pretty even mix of both sexes.

The first song I remember was *Locomotion* by Little Eva. I scanned the area and noticed that most of the girls were on one side of the garage, and the guys on the other. And separating them was a ten-foot-plus clear area of cement. The zone we would have to cross to ask a girl to dance. The no-man's land that would have to be trekked twice if she should say no when asked. Nobody started dancing, and I was glad. Hadn't practiced that one and didn't know what to do. Then a Beach Boys song, *Fun Fun Fun,* blasted from the speakers. Again, everyone looked around and no one was dancing.

More people had shown up, including a lot of guys and girls I'd never seen before. The garage was turning into a mixture of perfume, hairspray and smoke, By the way, we were in the corner smoking away trying to look inconspicuous until Mike's dad made us go outside - which was pretty cool that he let us smoke at all.

I moved to the end of the guys' section to see the girls clearly, and suddenly I felt myself getting a little self-conscious. *What if one of the girls asks me to dance? Would I want to in front of everyone? What if I fall? What if I got a boner?*

These were serious concerns to me. Most of the girls were in pairs whispering back and forth to each other and smiling. I wondered if they were talking about us. Then it suddenly hit me. *Maybe they were nervous too. Maybe they felt the exact same way I felt. But they were girls, I reasoned. They didn't need to be nervous. Or did they?*

Shaking the thoughts out of my head, *Angel Baby* suddenly came through the speakers and two guys asked a pair of girls to dance, then two more. I let out a breath, shoved my hands in my pockets, gathered up my resolve and walked to a pretty Latina girl and asked her to dance. "Sure," she said.

In the light, the most I could tell was she had shoulder - length brown hair and a clear complexion. Eyes were soft brown. She had an infectious smile, which she tried to hide by bending her head lower. I think she had braces. We wrapped our arms around each other and started moving - left to right - in a sort of rhythmic slow dance. *How close should I hold her to me? What if she gets mad?*

I pulled her a little closer and could smell her perfume. It was... intoxicating. And I could smell *her* too. I can't explain it exactly, it wasn't BO or anything like that. But it was a definite scent. I leaned my head close to her neck and just breathed it in. And then we were holding each other's bodies close together. And I could feel those mystifying mounds. Small, but present never the less. My mind was not on the music, but on her and her body. We danced, and then another song came on, some sort of Motown slow number, and I asked her if she wanted to dance again. She looked deeply into my eyes, smiled with her lips closed, and nodded her head.

We slow-danced three more songs together and then the music sped up. She went back to her girlfriends and I went back and stood with the guys. Kids were dancing now to the faster stuff, but I didn't care. I could still smell her on my hands and face.

Danny and I left early. On the way home, Danny asked me who I was dancing with. Then it hit me.

"I don't know."

"You mean you didn't get her name?"

I shook my head.

He started laughing. "She was pretty hot, dude. I would have gotten her name."

I thought about it a minute. I was so intoxicated by the moment - the music, the environment of low lights, sweaty bodies, close spacing, perfume and my body pressed against hers, that I didn't think to ask. Shoot. I blew it.

"Maybe I'll see her again."

"Dude, she was from St. Louis of France. Unless you go back to Catholic school, that would be highly unlikely."

"You know her?"

"Nah. Just seen her once in a while walking home from there."

"Well, next time you see her. . ."

He held up his hand and laughed. "Dude, I'm not going to get her name for you."

We reached his house and said our good nights.

On the walk home, I searched my whole being to try and understand why I didn't even ask her name. I understood why Danny wouldn't help. He didn't get one dance the whole night. In fact, he didn't even ask anyone to dance. Just hung out with some of the guys and went out to smoke once in a while.

I laid awake in bed for hours trying to understand the feelings I'd had during that dance. Those wonderful, hopeful, exhilarating, mysterious feelings and sensual scents that had literally knocked the sense out of me. I finally tossed and turned myself into a fitful sleep sometime after midnight.

Never did meet her again, or discover her name.

I would always regret that.

Trick or Treat

Six of us walked down the street, pillowcases in hand, half filled with candy. Although we were a little old for trick or treating, it was still fun to go up to the doors and get some candy.

The previous year we scored - we went to a house and the fellow who answered the door, dressed like a ghoul, asked if we wanted a nickel or a candy bar?

Really? A nickel or a candy bar?

We took the nickel, and then changed costumes with each other and went back again. No such bounty found so far that night. Undiscouraged, we continued going door to door collecting goodies.

Part of the fun of Halloween was when all of my family came home and the bartering ensued. Each of us loved certain types of candy - in my case Mars bars and Abba Zabbas. Patrick and my little sister Maureen were the easiest to make deals with. Debby and Kathy were much more experienced negotiators, as far as candy was concerned. Sometimes I'd have to pay two- for-one for a Mars bar.

Down the street I noticed a black El Camino slowly cruising toward us. Not sure why it caught my attention; something about the way the driver was looking around. He was a jock - I could tell from his haircut. When it was parallel with us the car stopped, the driver said something and four more jocks sat up in the back and shouted, "Hey you hippies" at us.

Turning, we were barraged by eggs. A total egg assault. They kept pitching them at us and laughing. Splat, splat, splat. We started running and the eggs followed us until we turned onto the next street.

We stopped and took a visual assessment. Each of us was covered with egg, yolks, and shells.

"Damn those fuckin' jocks," Stanley said, trying to pick the broken shells off his shirt.

Egg white dripped down Paul's forehead. "Yeah... but it was pretty funny."

"Hell," Kenny said. "It could have been us doing it to them, circumstances different."

"Like if we had a car and were fucking brain dead?" I asked.

"Something like that," Kenny replied.

"What are we gonna do?" Allan asked, shaking the goo off his hands.

"Guess we should go home and change. Plenty of candy still to get tonight," Paul said.

"No, I mean about those jocks?" Allan said.

Kenny laughed. "We'll flip off a bunch of them tomorrow and get some chase. That should piss 'em off."

"Good plan, Kenny," Billy said. "But right now I'd settle for some eggs to get them back with."

Next Halloween we carried eggs with us all night. They never showed up again.

The Flood

"Holy shit!"

It just erupted from my mouth as I cautiously crept up the walkway toward my house. Water was covering the front porch and rushing down the walkway. *That's funny,* I thought. *My dad isn't home. At least I thought he wasn't. Where did the water come from?* I had a slight feeling of foreboding, the kind you have when something seems not quite right, but you couldn't put your finger on it.

My parents had been planning a trip all week to visit and have dinner at Uncle Jim and Aunt Helen's on Saturday. They lived in Long Beach. When the time to leave grew closer, I tried to beg out of going. A bunch of us Crusaders were going to get together and ride our skateboards. Not a huge deal, I'll admit. But with school in session and our other extra-curricular activities, we never really planned to go somewhere far on our skateboards. That Saturday we were going to the Western Auto Plaza – a couple of hours round-trip. And it was right near Bob's Big Boy, and I really loved their double-decker hamburgers.

So I whined and protested, finally playing ill with a sore stomach, and my parents relented. However, since I wasn't feeling good, I was told to stay home and feel better.

"But what if I feel better shortly after you leave?"

"Then you should be going with us if you feel you'll start to feel better after-"

"No, no that's okay. I'll stay home."

The Crusaders

Snide looks, razzies with siblings' hands and a tongue snaking in and out of my brother's mouth bid me adios as the rest of the family left in the station wagon. While on the subject, I would like to say something about that particular automobile.

It was a nine-passenger Dodge model, light metallic tan with a 318-cubic-inch engine. Everything was electric – the windows, door locks, everything. It was really cool. What I liked most about it, however, was that the far rear seat faced out toward the back of the car. And that is the seat I always managed to get, along with whoever was lucky enough to sit with me. Why?

Because my parents could not reach the third seat with their back-hands, which they were constantly threatening to do (and oftentimes did) if we didn't settle down and stop fighting. It was a safe zone. Who were they kidding, anyway? Half the fun of going anywhere was fighting with each other. I think it was required if you were a kid in a station wagon.

Anyway, if I got into it with one of my sisters, who almost never sat next to me for obvious reasons, then I could smack one of them on the head in the middle seat and get away with it. The only time I would have to be careful was if my dad said he finally had enough and was going to stop the car and get out and show me a thing or two.

But that happened maybe once or twice that I can remember, so the odds were always in my favor. The only exception to the getting into a fight rule in the station wagon was if we were going to the drive-in theater. We knew we'd have to get along and besides, there was a playground there and we could run, scream, and hit each other all we wanted until the first cartoon started playing.

So there I was, left with the house and effectively grounded – which had not been a part of my original plan.

Stanley came over an hour later.

"Come on, John, let's get going. We need to meet everyone at the corner."

"Can't go, Stanley. My parents said I have to stay here all day until they get back."

"You're kidding me, right?"

I shook my head no.

"When will they be back?"

"I don't know – maybe five or six."

"We'll be back way before then."

"What if they call?"

"Tell them you were outside watering or something. I don't know. We'll figure that out later. Let's go and meet the guys."

It's funny how at the time it all sounded so logical and matter of fact. Of course, we'd be back in time. No one would be the wiser. Would I be breaking my word to my parents? Didn't come up. After all, they were gone, and wouldn't know whether I was here or not. Right? Would I lie to them if they asked? Didn't know. I was hoping they wouldn't ask. So I changed into my Penney's t-shirt, surfer shorts, huarache sandals and grabbed my skateboard. We were off to the mall for an adventure!

Paul, Stanley, Kenny and I ended up at Bob's Big Boy ordering double-decker burgers, fries, and shakes, and after skateboarding the mall and getting chased off by security, we headed home.

As I cautiously walked up to the front door, a sinking feeling in my gut grew, surrounding me. Something I couldn't put my finger on. *It's so odd,* I thought. I reached for the door handle and opened it and whooooosh, water rushes out. Not a little bit, mind you, but gallons and gallons, I'm guessing. *What the heck was going on?*

"Jesus, John, what happened?" Stanley was as dumbfounded as I.

I entered the house and was sandal deep in water. It was everywhere. I looked around in sheer panic.

"Holy shit!"

I rushed to the left, into the kitchen, searching for what, I had no idea. Water was deeper in there, covering all of the tile. I returned to the living room and through the hallway into my parents' bedroom – water everywhere. Then I heard something. Stanley, right behind me, started to say something. I shushed him. I could hear running water. I darted into the bathroom and couldn't see anything. I stopped and listened again. Yes, definitely running water. I stepped back into the hallway and looked at my room. The water was moving out of it. I pushed open the slightly-ajar door and slowly peered around it. There, through one of the window panes where the glass was now broken, was a hose sticking in, dumping water at full pressure.

"Oh my God." I went into panic mode and ran out of the house to the spigot and turned it off. Stanley remained on the other side in my bedroom. I looked in. He was in as much shock as I was. *Who would do this? Worse. Who would do this when I was supposed to be home at the house?*

"Stan, we've got to do something, right away."

"What, John? This is un-fucking-believable."

I darted around the walkway and back into the house.

"Grab a broom and we'll try and start sweeping the water out of the house." Looking around, I saw Stanley had disappeared. I was growing more anxious by the minute. My parents were due home at any time. I had gotten home way

85

later than I thought I would. We had been on a couple of extra good chases that afternoon, and it took longer to get back. Plus, there was a long wait when we stopped at Bob's for lunch.

"Stanley?" I yelled. Nothing.

I ran into the kitchen pantry and grabbed a broom.

"Cowabunga!"

I looked up and observed Stanley running out of the bedroom hallway in his skivvies and plopping on his butt, sliding like a slip and slide toward me in the kitchen. I jumped out of the way as he slid and spun around until he hit the kitchen tile and slammed into the wooden kitchen cabinets. Laughing.

"What the fuck are you doing? I've got to get this place cleaned up, fast."

"Don't worry about it, John. We've got plenty of time before your parents get home." He raced off back to the bedroom hallway, underwear soaked to the skin and dripping wet. Me? I was in full panic mode. There was no way I could get the house cleaned up. The water was was two inches high everywhere. I tried sweeping it out the door, but it was no use. My parents would know I was not there, and I wouldn't have to worry about lying to them. They would kill me.

I closed the front door and started sweeping everything toward the back patio window.

"Far out, man," Stanley shouted as he raced past me again, arms and legs up and spinning around grabbing his legs until he slammed again into the kitchen cabinets.

"Stop fucking around, Stanley," I pleaded. "We've got to get this cleaned up." He was already back to the bedroom hallway when the front door opened.

"What the hell is going on here?" I heard my dad saying. Stanley was already into his next run and on his butt. He saw my dad and couldn't stop his forward momentum. He spun around and hit the cabinets with a large thud. I turned around and the whole family was peering around my dad in total shock.

"Johnny! What happened?" My dad demanded to know.

"I don't know, Dad," I cried out. "We came home and found the house full of water. Someone put a hose in the window and turned it on."

"What the heck," he said as he rushed into my bedroom where the hose was still hanging through it. He went into his bedroom and looked around. Stanley ran into the bathroom and started putting on his clothes.

My entire family - brother, three sisters and Mom, came in - craning around, jaws agape.

"You are in so much trouble, Johnny," my brother Patrick said, scowling.

But he didn't have to. I knew it. My dad was blowing a cork; veins were popping on his neck and forehead, ruby red blood rushed to his face. He was sprinting from room to room around the house in total disbelief.

"Who would do this?" he asked no one in particular.

Stanley was dressed and walked out onto the porch, nudging by the family.

"I've gotta go, John. I'll see you later?" he disappeared within seconds. *Great. Now I really am on my own.*

"Honey," my dad finally said. "Call the police." My mom sloshed to the phone and opened the phone book, looking for the number. She dialed it and spoke to them.

"Johnny, I need to know." Dad looked me straight in the eye, grabbing my shoulders. "You had nothing to do with this, right?"

"I swear to God, Dad. I came home and this is what I found. I'm sorry I didn't stay like you asked."

"We'll talk about that later. Right now, we have to figure out where we are going to spend the night. This place is a soaking wet disaster."

The police came and took a report. They were sympathetic, and very reassuring that they would catch whoever did this to the house. Both my parents were listening when they questioned me, and when I fessed up to how long I was actually gone, their eyebrows rose at the news. Another call went out to the insurance company. They couldn't get to the house until the next day. What were we to do?

Finally, after my dad had gone and got us all Gigi burgers, fries and shakes, we decided that we would sleep in the two station wagons, much like we did at the drive-in near the end of the second movie. And there we did sleep. It was uncomfortable, and I felt like it was, somehow, all my fault. The rest of the family did too, and were quite verbal about it.

Especially my little brother Patrick.

In reflecting back on it, that double-decker Bob's Big Boy hamburger didn't taste all that good.

Turned out the neighbor across the street, a little kid named Michael, was mad at my brother Patrick for something or other and wanted to get back at him.

After he confessed, I was off the hook.

Sunday Night, 1964

"Johnny, Stanley is on the phone."

I rushed and grabbed the receiver from my mom. "Yeah?"

"Hey John," Stanley started. "We're all over here. When are you coming?"

"Soon as I finish getting dressed."

"Bitchin'. The show starts in fifteen minutes."

"I'll be there. But I got to hang up the phone first."

Stanley hung up, missing the joke. I ran back to my room, finished dressing and started to leave the house.

"Where you going, Johnny?" Dad asked.

"I told you, we are all meeting at Stanley's to watch the show tonight."

He was sitting in front of the TV, along with the rest of my siblings. "Be back right after it," he said. "We'll be watching it here."

I said goodbye, grabbed my Stingray and pedaled over to Stanley's. The bike plopped onto the cement entryway as I ran to the door. Stanley's mother was making tacos for us, and all of The Crusaders were there - Paul, Kenny, Billy, Kim, Allan and me.

"Almost starting," Paul said, as he ate a taco. We sat around the Magnavox TV set and stared fixated as the credits rolled, and Ed Sullivan introduced the group.

"Ladies and Gentlemen, The Beatles." He swung his arm toward the stage.

It was one bitchin' night.

Bands

We learned the following quickly:
    Girls liked guys in bands.
    We liked girls.
    Therefore...
    We had to have a band.

Stan the Man

Stanley was always up for something exciting . . . and daring. And we could dare Stanley into just about anything.

"Do you think it will hurt?" Stanley asked.

"Of course not. It just goes around in circles." Paul said.

"And you guys promise to let me out when I've had enough?"

"Stanley. You can just push the door open yourself - it's only held by magnets," I said. Opening and shutting the door, I demonstrated how the door to the commercial dryer located in the laundromat near our house worked. There were about ten of them against a wall. They were pretty big. We'd see people put in two or three loads of clothes at a time. It took a dime to run about thirty minutes.

"Okay. I'll do it."

Paul opened the door and I cupped my hands to make a step. Stanley pulled himself into the dryer, laid back and smiled.

"I'm ready."

We shut the door and put the dime into the little slit and turned the timer to thirty minutes. It started slowly turning and Stanley went round in a three-sixty, holding himself steady with his hands. Paul, Billy and I just stared through the little window as he started going faster. And then he screamed.

"Let me out of here!"

He was going so fast he couldn't open the door. We were laughing hysterically. He started trying to pound the small window, but it wouldn't budge. Then *he* started screaming hysterically.

"It's too fucking hot in here!" he cried out. "Get me out of here, please!"

We hadn't thought of that. The heat. Suddenly Paul reached for the timer to shut it off. It wouldn't move. Shit. I grabbed for the door and yanked it open. The heat gushed out as it started slowing down. Stanley was yelling "get me out of here" and it slowed and came to a stop. Paul reached in and helped pull him out.

"Fuck you guys," Stanley said. He was walking around in a drunken state, trying to stop the spinning that still followed him in his head.

"What, you didn't like it?" I asked.

"You looked like an astronaut," Billy suggested, laughing.

He finally leaned against the wall and slid down to the floor. After a few moments and a few breaths, he looked up and smiled.

"That was pretty cool."

Another time we were hanging out at the wash near our house, catching frogs and goofing around. That wash, by the way, was really a storm drainage system used for water run-off, and it was huge. There were little dirt and grass islands, ponds, and plenty of cement. There was a bridge over the wash and a train trestle.

We had climbed up to the bridge and were halfway over when Paul and Kenny looked at each other, and I believe they psychically communicated another dare for Stanley.

"Hey Stanley," Paul said. "How about we hold you over this bridge by your legs?"

"What?"

"Yeah," Kenny continued, "It will be cool. Hanging over like that."

"You sure you won't let me go?"

"Absolutely," Paul responded. "It will only be for a second."

Stanley looked down. We were about forty feet from the bottom of the cement wash, and he started to have second thoughts.

"Come on Stanley," Paul said nudging him near the edge, "Let's just do it."

Kenny walked over and grabbed Stanley by the ankle, and Paul followed suit. He offered no resistance. They angled him up and over the wash, each one holding him by an ankle.

"Don't let me go," Stanley yelled.

"Hey Kenny, what do you think? Should we let him go?" Paul asked, winking.

"I don't know," Kenny answered with a devilish smile.

They pulled him up higher and let go of his feet -- just for a second -- and then grabbed his ankles again.

"Ahhhhh," Stanley screamed. "What the heck are you guys doing? Stop it."

They let go of his ankles, he fell an inch and then they grabbed them again, laughing.

"Stop it. You promised you wouldn't let me go, assholes."

"Well, who's the asshole hanging over the bridge, huh?" Paul asked, laughing.

"Ahhhhhh."

"Okay, let's bring him in." They pulled him up and over the rail and let him go. Stanley sat there and flipped the both of them off.

"That's for you, assholes," he hollered.

We all started laughing.

Stanley couldn't help himself. He joined in.

Initiation I

"Are you sure this is what I have to do?" Paul S. asked.

Kenny smiled at us and then said, "Don't you want to be a Crusader?"

"Yeah, yeah." Paul S. responded. "But you're sure it's cool?"

"Absolutely, dude," Paul said. "We do it all the time."

"Okay then... I'll do it."

Paul S. had recently moved to our town and lived about six blocks away from us. We would see him around, and when we learned he was a surfer, or at least claimed to be, would talk with him every once in a while. We were about fifteen at the time. He had a funny little crooked smile, was tall and thin and always wore surfer clothes.

When he finally broached the subject of The Crusaders, we told him there had to be an initiation in order for him to join. We were just making that shit up, goofing on him. But he agreed, and so we had to come up with something. Liberating Coke bottles from garages was one of our main sources of income, so we naturally thought of teaching him about our enterprise, and watching if he had the cojones to do it.

We were walking down Barrydale and saw an open garage with a choice amount of Coke bottles stacked up inside in six-packs, and chose it as the initiation location.

"So Paul," Stanley started. "You go in there, grab the bottles and run out and we'll meet you down the street. Be sure and grab two six-packs."

He cautiously walked up to the garage, looked back and gave us the okay sign and crept in. Once he was inside, we ran up to the garage, reached up together and slammed the door shut. Kenny was near the lock and slipped it into place.

Then we banged on the garage door with our fists and screamed "Coke bottle thief, Coke bottle thief," and tore out of there.

Paul S. found us about a half-hour later, and we still hadn't stopped laughing.

"How'd you get out of there?" Paul asked.

He didn't want to talk about it.

We didn't let him join The Crusaders, but thought up more and better initiations for later.

Playing Music

Christmas 1965 was the most important Christmas I'd ever had.

For one thing, my dad woke me up at what I thought was the middle of the night, and asked me to help him put together bikes for everyone. I was pretty handy with tools, so it was easy to do. It took some time to get them out of the boxes, yet a few hours later they were leaning up against their kickstands, encircling the tree. One each for my brother and three sisters. Included among the group was my very own five-speed deep-blue metallic Electro-flyer. Wow.

But that's not the only reason it was so special a day.

By the way, we always put out cookies and milk for Santa and his helpers, and every Christmas morning when we awoke we would rush out and look at the table we'd left them on – we found the glass would be half empty and all that remained of the cookies were crumbs.

Later that evening, after I had put the bikes together, my dad asked if I wanted one of the cookies. Sure. I munched it down, and watched him toss half the milk out of the glass into the sink. One thing Dad always bragged about – he never drank milk – not since he was a little kid in Staten Island.

"Our little secret, eh Johnny?"

Trying not to fall asleep after all the work putting the bikes together, my eyes grew heavy quickly. Struggle as I might, I could not stay awake. I was hoping something else was going to be greeting me in the morning – something other than the shiny new bike and much more dear to me.

"Wake up Johnny, wake up now!"

It was my little brother Patrick shaking me and then running out the door. For a moment I was unsure why he was waking me. Then I remembered.

"Come see what we got," he shouted excitedly from the front room.

I dressed and walked out. Little sandmen were still caking my eyes. Rubbing them out I could see the whole family – Debby, Kathy, Patrick and Maureen looking at their new bikes glistening in the blinking star lights of the angel-hair-covered Christmas tree. I rubbed my eyes again. Then I focused and a huge grin spread across my face.

There, beneath the tree, was a new box guitar. *Holy shit.* I ran over, knelt down and gently stroked it. *This is the most beautiful guitar I've ever seen.* I looked up at Mom and Dad sitting on the sofa, tears running down my cheeks. They both smiled.

I'd been bugging them for a guitar for the past year -- ever since I didn't get one the previous Christmas. They were always telling me "Someday, Johnny, someday." That was a long year.

And finally that someday had came.

"Look at my bike, Johnny," Patrick exclaimed proudly, ringing the bell on the handlebars. I barely heard him. I picked up my guitar and held it. *My guitar.* I ran my fingers gently across the strings. It sounded good.

My grandparents had a beautiful upright piano in their home. Before we moved from Los Angeles to La Puente, we lived right across the street from them on Middleton Place. When I first walked into their house when I was seven and saw it, I sat right down and started plunking keys. It sounded great to me. My grandparents thought otherwise. I was immediately enrolled in a music program at Transfiguration School, which was the Catholic school I attended. The music lessons were given by nuns. In their convent.

For years I took lessons, gave recitals at school, and became a rather accomplished pianist, at least for my age. Those music lessons halted immediately after an incident just before a recital while in fourth grade. I was in the convent, up the stairs on the second floor, practicing the piece I would be playing, when I missed a note in the middle of it. Before I knew what had happened, a wooden ruler came into view attached to a nun's arm and whacked me on the right hand. Unfortunately, the ruler turned. It was metal edged, and a cut appeared, gushing blood on me, on the perfectly white ivory keys, and on the floor. I screamed, grabbed my hand and looked up at the bulbous red face of sister "scary as shit" snarling at me, veins popping and pulsing, anger raging in her eyes.

I panicked.

Quickly pushing back the bench I was sitting on, I jumped up, pushed her aside and ran down the stairs and out the rectory door. The convent faced Roxten Avenue and I ran down it, up Arlington Avenue and then toward my house. The bleeding stopped with the pressure I placed on my hand, and I guess the small cut must have coagulated by the time I got home. I washed it off, put a band-aid on it and thought about what I had done. *What I had done? I'd done nothing. It was that damn nun.* However, I knew my mom would blame me, because in her world the Catholic nun could do no wrong. I found out a little later why that was.

I made a resolution right then. There would be no going back. No lessons with her. That was it. For weeks I pretended to continue going, hanging out after school studying for lessons. I assumed my parents thought I was still going. Fortunately, we were getting ready to leave Los Angeles.

When we moved to La Puente, my grandparents' beautiful walnut piano went with us, and I was able to play it every day.

The music scene was changing then. No longer was it The Kingston Trio, The Hollys, the Lettermen, and groups like that. Suddenly, we started to hear different musical groups on the radio. The Beach Boys, The Ventures, The Safaris, and Little Eva.

And then everything changed – The Beatles and The Rolling Stones appeared.

What did most of these newer groups have in common – besides the long hair? They had guitars in the bands. Not pianos. And so, from the time I realized what the potential of the guitar was, I wanted one. Desired one. Coveted owning one. And then, that Christmas, I finally got one.

It came with a little booklet that showed how to tune it, and had some rudimentary chords you could learn – E, A D, G and C. I picked it up, read the book from cover to cover (it was pretty short) and then took it into the piano room and tuned the first string to lower E on the piano. When my guitar was in tune, I tried to play a chord. It took a while, but I figured it out.

The guitar itself was a low-cost entry-level model, so pushing the strings hurt my fingers at first. I didn't care. I kept playing it, strumming it, for days on end. Calluses started forming on my fingers, and my comfort level grew. Finally, I could pick out a song, and man was I proud. *Walk Don't Run* by The Ventures. I would play it over and over again, until my parents, mainly my dad, told me to "Knock it off, already, Johnny."

I wasn't sure what having it would lead to, but I knew my life would change because of that guitar.

As for my metallic-blue five-speed bike I also got that Christmas? That was stolen about two weeks later. Never recovered, but I didn't care. I kept playing that guitar. I could live without the bike.

Billy lived three blocks away on Donaldale, the same street as Kim. His family was Mexican, and they were very religious. Hence, Billy was sent to Catholic school. St. Louis of France. But he was always with us after school. And he was an original founder of The Crusaders. Later Christmas Day I ran over to his house to share with him that I had gotten a guitar, and he was very excited. We both went back to my house and I showed him what I learned. He picked up the guitar and started playing the same thing, right away. I was floored.

"Where did you learn to play, Billy?"

"I didn't. I just followed what you did."

"Really?"

He was like that. Very talented. Although his family was Mexican, we never referred to Billy or his little brother Michael as beaners. Nor his super-sexy older sister, Sylvia. They weren't beaners. In fact, Billy was a surfer like us. Beaners was a term we used to denote cholos in the neighborhood. They didn't even have to be Mexican. Just guys who took on the ways of a low-riding cholo – khaki-colored cuffless pants belted high up around the waist, a checkered pattern Pendleton shirt, a white t-shirt beneath it, and slicked back hair. And a certain shuffling walk that must have taken hours to learn. For instance, Danny L, who was as Irish as a shamrock, became a cholo. Billy wasn't like that at all.

Billy started to come over to my house more often, and we would learn things together – first by me working it out on the piano and then transferring the tune and chords to the guitar, Then Billy would learn it. As I said, he was very talented.

I've already mentioned that we knew *Walk Don't Run* by The Ventures. We then learned *Surf City* by Jan and Dean. Billy came over and worked out *Wipe Out* and then *Gloria*, a cool song by a band called Them – which was really a front group for a young Van Morrison.

Four songs.

"Maybe we should start a band?" we both suggested.

The Beatles and Stones were all the rage. *Meet The Beatles* had been released, and then *High Tides and Green Grass* by the Stones was rising on the charts. We bought them and listened over and over.

Stanley's house was the place to be to see The Beatles on the Ed Sullivan Show, and after that we knew what we wanted to do. Rock and roll, baby. And it was not lost on us that there were hundreds of screaming girls either.

Groupies.

Mike came over to my house one day and noticed the guitar. He was an interesting guy. Reserved. Quiet mostly. Pock-marked face from a severe case of acne, yet good looking as far as girls were concerned. He spent a lot of time alone at his house. His dad drove big-rig trucks and was gone for weeks at a time. He wasn't officially a Crusader, and never became one. But he was a good friend to us, and we considered him a sort of quasi-Crusader whenever we met up or did anything together.

"I didn't know you played guitar, John. My dad has one in his closet. An electric one."

We quickly hurried over there and opened the closet door. There it was. A beautiful red hollow-body Telecaster – two gold pickups, pearl inlaid fret markers, and a twelve-inch amp. I picked it up reverently, sat down on the bed and played it. It was almost inaudible. However, it felt fantastic. We figured out how to plug it into the amp, and turned it on. Ouch. Total feedback – the gain knob was turned all the way up to ten. Finally, with all the technical issues resolved, I played the four songs I knew, and they sounded like the real deal on this setup. I resolved then and there to get an electric guitar and amplifier.

Mowing lawns, stepping up our Coke bottle business, my paper route and anything else I could think of all went into my savings for a guitar. Within a couple of months I had enough and went to the music store and bought it: a black-edged, tan inside (violin style) solid-body Fender Stratocaster, with three magnetic pickups. I couldn't afford the model with the "wah wah" bar, so prevalent in surf songs, but I didn't care. The guitar went home with me (thanks to my dad driving me there), and I slept with it.

Then it dawned on me. *No amp.*

Billy, meanwhile, had talked his dad into getting him a guitar, and that included an amp. His guitar was a solid-body Fender, metallic blue, with three pickups. The amp was a small Fender with four inputs – one for a microphone.

Stanley said he could play the drums. *Really? How is that?*

A spontaneous version of *Wipe Out* ensued on our box guitars, and when the time came for the drum solo Stanley played it on the bottom of a large, cast iron pot -- the kind you used for cooking spaghetti noodles. It was fantastic. "Okay, Stan, you're in." He talked his dad into getting a snare, bass drum, tom tom, and one cymbal, with a seat thrown in.

So we had two guitars and a drummer. We needed a singer. And my voice was not strong enough. Maybe it was hormones or something. I could sing pretty well as a kid. Maybe it was also the fact that a priest threw me out of choir class by my right ear – literally grabbing it, dragging me and then tossing me through the door. The "supposed" crime? Covering up the large wall clock with spit wads when Father "Dick-Head" wasn't looking. I don't know. I suppose it traumatized the hell out of me. And by the way, I did do it.

Kenny stepped up.

"I can sing," he said.

When I thought about it, I remembered hearing him singing next door to our house in the shower – Dean Martin songs like *Everybody Loves Somebody, Sometime.* And it did sound pretty good. So we agreed to let him try out and sing. We rushed to the music store again and bought a used microphone and stand, and brought it all to Stanley's garage, since he had the drums and it would be a pain in the ass to move them around.

We were just barely fourteen and fifteen years old, and ready to see if we could become a band.

"What a bullshit name," Paul said to no one. "Whoever heard of a band name like that? Makes you sound like, well… fucking retards or pussies."

"I think it's pretty bitchin," I said, chuckling.

"Look, we need to come up with a name, let's at least start with this?" Kenny suggested.

"Yeah," Stanley said.

"Let's just move on with the name." Billy agreed.

All of the equipment was in Stanley's empty garage. Stanley's mom found an old carpet, and we used it as our first gig rug. Stanley set up the drums about midway in the center of the two-car enclosure. The amp was to his left, slightly forward. Billy had his fender guitar and stood to the left. In the center, Kenny perched before the mike stand. I was right of center with my Western Auto brand guitar.

Through a vote we decided that *Gloria* would be the first song we learned as a band.

I started playing the chords, and then Billy joined in. Stanley hit the snare and started drumming, using his foot on the bass drum to give the song a bottom. Kenny pulled the mike close, and started to sing: "Let me tell you 'bout my baby…"

We got through the song with only a few wrong chords, but the timing or beat of the song was way too fast. Not sure why, but half our battle in playing music seemed to be in playing it too fast. Almost wanting to rush through it – maybe so we wouldn't forget something before the song was over. Anyway, we got through that one song and it felt like electricity running through my body.

"How about *Wipe Out?*" Billy asked.

I went into the regressive chord progression of A, sliding down to G, F, and E. Stanley started the drums, and Billy flew into the lead. Started out well, but we lost it sometime after the second go round. But the fact was, we started.

We were an official garage band.

The Chiquita Bananas.

Maybe we'd have to work on that name.

Girls

To say we were naive would be an understatement. When we were twelve years old, Billy came over to my house and told me that he heard his parents talking about Bob Simmons' parents. They were getting a divorce.

"What's that?" I asked.

"No idea, dude, but my parents must have thought it was bad. They were whispering."

We got on our Stingrays and pedaled over to Bob's house and parked across the street, staring and waiting. For what? We had no idea. Maybe we thought it was a disease, or something you could have happen to you? We didn't rationalize it. We just went there to check it out.

Both of our families being Catholic, the word never even came up in our households. As if it didn't exist. Totally off our radar. After about an hour, we decided nothing was going to happen then, so we pedaled back home. That night I asked my mom what it was, and with a horrified look she asked me why? I explained about Bob's parents, and she sat me down and did her best to get me to understand.

Those same sensibilities extended to our first relationships with girls.

We knew nothing.

Billy's first experience I will go into later. In my case, it was Janet.

Janet wasn't my first girlfriend. In fact, I am not sure she was technically my girlfriend. We liked each other. And hated each other.

Janet was my sister Debby's best friend, and was always visiting our house. I would tease her about her glasses, and she would dish it back in spades, usually referring to me pejoratively by one of my Crusader nicknames, traitorously supplied by her brother Allan, such as "hatchet head" or "fish face." Didn't matter to me -- I liked her and thought she was pretty cute.

I had a crush on my neighbor across the street, Josie. But it was unrequited. I am guessing it was that way because she didn't know I had a crush on her.

Janet qualified as my first girlfriend who *knew* I liked her, although I never told her so. But she knew. I knew she knew. She knew that I knew that she knew.

She spent the night at my house with Debby all the time, and Debby at hers.

One night she joined me in the backyard while I was smoking a cigarette. We talked about nothing important. She wasn't wearing her glasses. She smelled clean and fresh.

Grinding out the cigarette on the grass with my huarache sandal, I looked into her eyes, leaned over and kissed her. Just a push on the lips. She held the kiss. I was fourteen, she thirteen. Finally, she pulled away with a slight look of embarrassment, smiled and walked back into the house.

Did she like it? Why did I do that? To my sister's best friend? I felt exhilarated and scared at the same time. *What about Allan? What would he think? Hitting on his little sister.* I vowed to tell no one about it.

Next day I shared what happened with Paul, Kenny, Stanley, and Billy.

Discussions ensued about what I should do next. Most of them were the fantasies of young pubescent boys, mine included. We didn't really know much about sex; in fact, not much at all.

We did have a "movie" with explanations at school that included cartoon drawings of the various sexual areas and how they worked. Could have been about cars for all we could figure out.

Little fish swimming happily into a pond. What did fish have to do with anything?

And, of course, I had three sisters, so I knew there were physical differences. But exactly what to do, how to do it, and more importantly when to do it, were mysteries to us all. Even the *Playboy* magazine's we found at Mike's house hidden in the closet by his dad didn't help much.

Except to titillate.

Which, by the way, they did very well.

Fighting

Kenny, Billy and I were at the stop light at the corner of Francisquito and Puente Avenue, waiting for it to turn green. Opposing cars slowed down and stopped when the signal changed from amber to red.

Three guys on the opposite side of the crosswalk stood waiting for the light to change also.

When the light finally turned green in the opposite direction, we walked toward the middle of the intersection. Both sides of this busy street had dozens of stopped cars on each side, watching us amble along.

As we passed the three guys coming in the opposite direction, one of them pushed me and shouted:

"Watch it, punk."

I pushed him back. "Fuck off, asshole."

He swung a right uppercut and nicked me on the chin, knocking me backwards. I quickly steadied myself with my left foot and raised my fists. Kenny swung a right at another of them and missed completely, causing him to fall into a wicked left uppercut directly into his gut.

Horns started blasting. Headlights flashed their high beams on and off. Shouts of: "break it up" echoed all around us.

Billy swung at one of them, and it looked like a direct hit to the side of the head. He followed up with another punch and pushed him back. A wild swing caught Billy on the side of his face and caused him to momentarily flinch. I was swinging wildly, hitting one of them in the windpipe and another on the shoulder. Kenny had knocked one of them down and was on top of him delivering rapid-fire punches to his chest and face.

Horns continued blaring as the light turned green and we were still in the middle of the intersection, punching it out.

Suddenly, we heard a siren starting to blare and a voice through a loudspeaker:

"You guys. Stop that fighting right now!"

I looked up and over and could see red lights flashing atop a black and white Ford stuck behind two cars across the street, honking its horn for the cars in front to move while trying to get around traffic.

Startled, we stopped fighting and started running toward the convalescent hospital that occupied the corner nearest us, weaving our way around the buildings. We could hear the police car get through the intersection and the familiar roar of the large 390-cubic-inch engine as it made its way to the driveway entrance beside the hospital.

We raced out back of the rear building into a parking lot and toward the chain link fence covered by ivy that separated it from the houses. The police car skidded as it bounced from the driveway into the parking lot and made its way toward us.

"Halt right there," the loudspeaker blared at us, red lights flashing against our escape route.

Like hell we would.

I made it to the metal fence first, grabbed it near the top and pulled myself over. The others reached it seconds later and did the same. The police car came to a screeching stop. We could hear doors slam open and feet running toward us from the other side of the fence as we gave wings to our feet and continued hauling ass through the yard and out around the front of the house into the street.

We ran two blocks to Stanley's yard and slipped in between his and the corner house and stopped to catch our breath. My legs were aching. My lungs were painfully trying to replenish themselves. Two of the guys fell to the ground and laid there, panting.

"Everyone here?" Paul asked.

"Yeah," replied the five voices in the dark.

We practiced the "art" of fake fighting all the time. I say art, because it took us a long time to make it look real. But perfect it we did. We had to learn how to throw a punch so that the recipient not only looked as though he received it, moving his head or body just the right way, but also made a slapping noise with his hands at the same time he grunted or made a guttural sound. If the punch was to their head, then they would move their entire face around so it looked like a hit but out of view. Body shots were choreographed to fool even the most ardent observer.

We got so proficient at it that any two of us Crusaders could be fighting each other – rolling with the punches and moving our heads and bodies realistically from direct hits - and make it look like a truly real and vicious fight.

Paul looked over at Kenny, breathing heavily, and smiled. "That was some seriously good chase we just got."

"Yeah," Kenny replied. "And a good fake fight too."

"First time we've ever been chased by cops," Allan added.

"Un-fucking-believable," I said, looking around. "What'll we do now?"

The cop car raced by us to the next street and turned down it, lights flashing.

"Maybe we should hang out a bit and then go to In-N-Out?" Kim suggested.

"Good plan," we all agreed.

"Chased by cops," Kenny said, his head shaking. "That was too fucking cool."

"Epic, man," Kim said. "Swear to God."

Janet

Many months later, Janet and I ended up in the small playhouse in my backyard late one afternoon. It was planned by us both. Debby was somewhere else that afternoon, yet Janet told her parents (and her brother Allan) that she was going to see Debby. I was nervous as heck. And not sure what we were going to do.

Inside, we started kissing. Just the pressing of lips together. Nothing passionate. I wondered if this was all the big deal about making out. Didn't seem that exciting to me.

But it did get better.

There was no real sex involved, but we did explore each other and learned a lot about the differences between us. We would periodically meet in the playhouse over several months and continued along, each time going a little further, and yet stopping short of going all the way, which I was still unsure as to what that really meant.

We continued meeting until she moved to West Covina.

I guess she really did become my first *real* girlfriend.

And female friend.

I liked both.

Finally Caught

One of the most annoying - and endearing - things about Kim was that we never, ever were able to catch him in a swear to God.

If he swore to God about something, it was a fact. And he would explain to us exactly why he did not get caught. He wore that particular distinction as a badge of honor, almost defining himself as never having been relegated to being caught in a lie, which would be the same thing.

I would get caught all the time, many times on purpose, to allow Kim to bask in the light of having been the one to expose my transgression. Who really gave a shit, anyway?

Same with the other Crusaders. We were always getting called out by Kim and never were able to reciprocate.

It was a hot, sweltering summer day. The skies were blue, the humidity was high, and we were walking to the Dairy Delight to get something cold to drink. Paul, Kenny and Billy were there, besides Kim and me.

For some reason I looked up and thought I saw the moon. It was low on the horizon, midday. Barely visible, but nonetheless there.

"I swear to God, I can see the moon," I said.

"Swear to God you can't," Kim shot back almost unconsciously, as if it were self-evident I could only be wrong.

"John," Billy said. "Kim is right. You can't see the moon."

"Swear to God, I can," I said.

"Swear to God you can't," Kim again said, this time with more authority and particular emphasis on the word can't.

I turned and pointed. "It's right there."

Four heads stared into the sky for a few moments.

"Holy shit," Paul said. "You can see the moon."

It hit all of us at once. We turned our attention to Earth.

"Kim got caught in a swear to God," Paul shouted. Stanley and Billy joined in. "Caught in a swear to God."

"You can't really see the damn thing," Kim said.

"Bullshit, Kim," I said. "I swore to God I could see it, and I could. You finally got caught."

We could see the blood racing to his face. His eyes looked left, right, and then back up at the moon.

"Shit," he said in a whispered tone.

The taunts continued and escalated. "Kim got caught in a swear to God, Kim got caught in a swear to God." Kenny was the most boisterous.

"Fuck you guys," Kim finally spat out. "I didn't get caught. And I'm going home."

He stormed off, picking up speed as he furthered the distance between us. The vocals followed him until he turned the corner and was out of sight.

We laughed, shook our collective heads and continued to the Delight.

"Think he'll be okay?" Paul asked Stanley.

"Sure."

"It was fucking funny, that look on his face," I said.

"Yeah," we all agreed.

"Sure he'll be okay?" Paul again asked everyone..

We just shrugged.

You had to be able to take it as well as dish it. This was the first time Kim was given it. We'd have to wait and see.

Edgewood Incidents I

Valentine's Day was always fun - everyone at school would give everyone else a card, and at the end of the day you'd take them home to read. They were quite innocent. They only meant friendship at that age in junior high.

In class, Stanley made a bit of a commotion, drawing the teacher's attention. Mr. Smith could see a card in Stanley's hand, which he immediately tried to hide. Students were not allowed to exchange cards in the classroom.

"What have you got there, Mr. Anding?" Mr. Smith asked.

"Nothing."

"Looks like something to me." Mr. Smith walked down to Stanley's desk and held out his hand. "Will you hand it to me, now." It was a very authoritative request.

Stanley reluctantly handed it to him. A Valentine card.

"Let's just read this in class and see what the big secret is all about, shall we?"

Mr. Smith opened it up.

"Dear Stanley. Will you be my valentine. P..." He looked over to Stanley and then to Paul. "Signed... Paul?"

Stanley started laughing. Paul turned red. "You asshole, Stanley. I didn't send you that card," Paul shouted.

"Knock it off right now," Mr. Smith exclaimed. The class was snickering and laughing.

"That is so uncool," Paul screamed.

Stanly mouthed "gotcha" to Paul and winked.

"Both of you to the principal's office, now!"

Edgewood Junior High had a very extensive wood shop class in which you could make everything from wooden paddles (which they did for the principal to use on us students) to amplifier cases (which we made for our band).

Stanley was up to his tricks of passing around a slam book, where kids could write notes and sign them - much like a yearbook. The substitute teacher noticed, and asked Stanley what it was. He said "Nothing." He demanded Stanley bring it up and hand it to him. Stanley refused.

The teacher rushed up to him and asked who he thought he was talking to.

"Someone big and dumb?"

The teacher's face flushed red, his clenched knuckles turned white. He grabbed Stanley by the shirt and physically lifted him up four feet and onto the top of one of the cabinets that lined the walls of the shop room, setting him up there on his ass.

"You can just sit there until class is over, Mr. Smart Ass," the teacher said, pleased with himself.

Stanley quickly jumped up.

And then started soft-shoe dancing on the cabinet, singing to himself. "Mr. Big and Dumb, la la la la la la... Mr. Big and Dumb."

He jumped sideways to the next cabinet, kept dancing, using his arms for good measure, Fred Astaire style, leaped onto the next cabinet and then jumped down at the doorway and ran out, laughing.

It took a few moments for the class to realize what just happened.

What the fuck was that all about? Paul thought.

Then he got it. It was Stanley.

Vase Face

"What the heck did you just do?" Paul screamed at me. "My mother is going to kill me."

I just stared at him and the mess on the table, unable to speak, gape-jawed.

* * * * *

When Paul's parents left their house for any period of time, we'd rush over to hang out. First of all, it was a really cool house. Everything was from Sears - the furniture, the carpet, the drapes - it looked like a page out of a Sears early-American maple-style furniture catalogue. Reminded me of my grandmother's house in LA. Knick-knacks everywhere.

The real attraction was the pool. Kidney shaped, it took up most of the backyard. We would swim in it every chance we could, which was not often, since Paul's parents usually wouldn't let us so we had to wait until they were gone.

Speaking of pools, there was also a backyard pool on my block about halfway down the street. Michelle F's house. Her mother would take off for work, and after school we would hang out with her. It was painful. She was a spoiled, narcissistic brat who relished our attention, which was begrudgingly given for only one purpose: when her mother came home she would ask Michelle who she wanted to swim in their pool, and she'd choose those who had kissed her ass the most the previous couple of hours. We laid it on thick. Brought her flowers (picked from the neighbor's yard), candy, whatever it would take for her to say we were her favorites and could come and swim.

When we couldn't take it anymore, we'd blow her off, not visit for a couple of weeks, and she would pout and scream saying we would never swim in her pool again. Then, when the summer heat started to roar down on us, we would re-start the seduction. Kenny or Stanley would knock on her door, tell her we were sorry, and plead to be forgiven for our transgressions. It usually took two or three days, but she'd give in. Always did. They moved by the time we were in high school, and we never heard from her again.

However, once, when she was in one of her good moods after we had been extremely disingenuous and flirtatious, we had access to the pool without her mom there and then we came up with an idea. *Sea Hunt* was a popular TV show then, Lloyd Bridges being the cool role model, and we thought: *What if we could go under water and dive like him?*

After planning our scheme, I was chosen to be the first to try it. We found some big rocks and brought them surreptitiously to the pool area during the day without Michelle being aware of it. I grabbed a hose from my parents' backyard, cut off one of the ends and brought it over to her house, stashing it out of sight in her backyard.

I donned my surf trunks, put the rocks into my pockets, grabbed the end of the hose and jumped into the deep end. Slowly sinking to the bottom of the eight feet of crystal clear water, my butt finally reached the bottom with a slight thud.

I took the hose, lifted my thumb off the end to keep the water out, wrapped my lips around the end and took a breath. First breath okay. I could see my rippling Crusaders looking down at me through the water, waving. I put the hose to my lips again. After taking that second breath I started feeling a little dizzy. I was in pretty good shape, surfing and swimming all the time, yet something didn't feel right. My head started to swim in a dizzy symphony of vague thoughts, and I started feeling a bit giddy.

What the heck is going on? I thought. Suddenly I went into a panic. *How long had I been down here?* Then I remembered the rocks in my pockets. A sickening realization started to course through my body. *I was lying at the bottom of the pool, almost out of air, weighed down by a lot of rocks.* I started to unload them as I pushed off the bottom.

It took all of my strength, and I was still on the bottom, only standing. Terror started to envelop me. *What had I gotten myself into?* My throat burned, aching for air. The hose was floating next to me, taunting. I grabbed for more rocks to release as I bent my knees and pushed up with all of my inner resources. Slowly, I started rising toward the surface. It seemed too slow. *Would I make it?* My arms whipped frantically to help my assent.

Finally, I broke the water's surface and gasped for air, coughing and choking. Stanley and Billy stared at me, wondering what was going on. I thrashed to the edge and held on.

Billy looked concerned. "What happened?"

I couldn't answer. I kept gulping for air, hanging on the side with my arms up over the cement edge. Finally I was able to speak, still gasping for breath.

"Fuck *Sea Hunt*," I sputtered.

They started laughing, and I finally did too.

* * * * *

Simply put, I'd screwed up. When I shrieked "Oh no," Stanley, Billy and Kenny looked over at the table where I'd picked up a beautiful cloisonné vase to examine, having never seen one up close before. When it slipped out of my hands, I watched in horror as it descended in slow motion toward the Maplewood end table it had been sitting upon.

The noise seemed to fill the entire front room, shards flying everywhere. Paul turned around and stared as if he wasn't actually seeing what was happening. Disbelief engulfed his piercing hazel eyes, white surrounded their outer circumference.

After shouting at me, he scrunched his forehead and eyebrows, wrinkled his nose and started to laugh, in spite of himself.

"You have such a 'vase face' I can't believe it," he spit out, laughing out loud. Stanley and Billy started laughing as I continued staring at them gape-jawed, eyebrows raised and ghost-white, feeling like shit.

"Vase face," Stanley shouted.

"I am so sorry, Paul," I finally stammered out.

Paul was laughing so hard, he was literally unable to talk. Catching his breath, he continued.

"You are in so much trouble, dude. That was my mom's favorite vase."

"Paul, I don't know what to say. It was an accident."

"She told me that no matter what, I was never to touch that vase." He looked at Stanley, Billy and Kenny. "It was a family heirloom from my great grandmother, for Christ sakes."

If I felt bad before, it was in spades by then. What could I do or say? I messed up and knew it.

"Come on, vase face, I'm goofing on you," Paul started laughing again. "Who the heck knows where they got the vase."

"Vase face," Stanley said, "That's funny. You should have seen the look on your face, John."

"You guys better leave," Paul suggested. "My parents will be getting home soon."

"Paul, I'm really sorry."

"Yeah, vase face, you should be." He winked as we left, still chuckling to himself. Me, I still felt bad, but it must have been pretty funny to watch. We Crusaders used the term "vase face" from that time forward, whenever we did something and got caught for it. "You've got such a vase face!"

One more thing.

After the pool incident, I returned the hose to my parents' backyard as if nothing had happened. The next day my dad went out to water the yard and started swearing.

"Johnny!"

Running through the house toward the backyard, I stopped at the patio door, meekly sticking my head out.

"Yeah, Dad?"

"What the heck happened to my hose?" he shouted tersely. He always used heck instead of hell, except when he was really pissed, which only happened once or twice that I can remember.

"Sorry Dad. I thought..."

"What the heck were you thinking? I can't screw on the water sprayer now."

I knew it was too long a story to tell him, so I apologized about doing it and promised to save up and buy a new hose. Naturally, I was also put on restriction for the weekend.

Damn that *Sea Hunt*.

Jack the Ice Cream Man

1963

"What's that?" I asked.

My little brother Patrick cocked his head and listened. "I'm not sure. Sounds sort of like circus music."

We strained our ears and listened as it got louder and closer. Rushing out the front door of our house, we made our way around the hedge and into the street. Down the block, a truck slowly approached, a bullhorn strapped atop the cab. Neighbor kids ran into the street and waved their arms for the truck to stop. We watched as a man dressed all in white with a white cap came out the driver's door and headed round toward the rear of the truck. We followed him.

Ice cream stickers plastered the sides of the truck: pictures of Creamsicles, popsicles, chocolate covered bananas, Fudgesicles, Drumsticks, Nutty Buddies, orange and raspberry pushups, ice cream sandwiches, and frozen Mars bars. We observed the man taking money from the kids and handing out ice cream delicacies as if he were Santa Claus on Christmas day.

"Who are you?" I asked.

"Jack, the ice cream man."

He spoke with a definite accent, but what kind of accent I didn't know.

I ran my tongue across my top lip. "How much?"

"What kind did you want?"

I looked to Patrick who shrugged. "We're not sure." Checking my pockets, I fished out a quarter and displayed it. "What can I get for this?"

He eyed my little brother and me and smiled. "You just moved here, yah?"

We nodded.

"How about a Dreamsicle and a chocolate covered vanilla bar?"

"Sure," we replied.

He whipped them out, frost rising from them like a misty morning, and handed them to us. He returned a nickel from the quarter. "Welcome to La Puente," he said as he slammed the small rear door shut and hopped back into the ice cream truck. We tore open the paper wrappings and slurped away. They were delicious.

Imagine. An ice cream man who came by your house every day. Was this heaven or what?

It soon became a tradition in our family. After school, late afternoons, Jack the ice cream man came down our street and we would get some ice cream or, if we were short on funds, a little candy, which he kept a lot of on the front passenger seat. We could his music four or five blocks away, and like Pavlovian dogs we would salivate the closer he came, until we spotted him at the head of the street. By then, we were ready to buy as much as funds would permit.

Jack had a great gig. The neighborhood was full of kids for miles, and he had figured out the best times to drive around and "chum the ice cream waters." We found out later he lived two blocks away.

He wasn't the only traveling food merchant in the neighborhood. Twice a week we would hear a sort of train whistle -- toot toot - and that meant only one thing. The Helms man was making the rounds. He had a really cool butter yellow panel truck. After he stopped he opened the rear doors and beautiful wooden shelves slid out stuffed to the gills with donuts, bread, hamburger buns, and all sorts of baked goods that gave off a succulent odor long before they appeared. I specifically remember the cinnamon smell. Yum.

Moms would come out and buy bread and buns, while we kids vied for the position of first in line to purchase donuts.

I also noticed that a couple of times a week milk and butter would show up on the front porch. Alta Dena Dairy was printed on the sides of the half-gallon glass bottles. And boy did we drink a lot of that milk with our morning cereal.

Being Catholic, we of course ate fish on Friday. It was an edict from the Pope. I learned in school that he made it because at one time a bunch of friends of his, fishermen, were complaining about not selling enough of the little guys, so he solved their problem by making it mandatory that you had to, without fail, eat fish once a week. How it became a mortal sin to eat meat on that day was a mystery to me, but I was not one to make an issue of it. Not yet, anyway.

So another tradition was born: Friday night fish sticks for dinner. Fish sticks, by the way, are fish in name only. I am not sure, even to this day, that those golden morsels had ever actually been part of a fish. Covered in breading, there was a sticky white something inside them. Tartar sauce and catsup seemed to make them taste good, and, between the seven of us, we must have eaten fifty of them every Friday.

Years later, when the edict to eat fish was lifted by His Most Holiness, I was truly grateful, and I've not eaten fish sticks, in any form, since that day.

After the reprieve from fish sticks, my dad came up with a new tradition - Gigi burgers on Friday nights. There was a little hamburger stand on Amar Road called Gigi's, and they had only four or five items on the menu, the most popular being the Gigi burger for fifteen cents. It had a really enticing sauce on it - I think it was a mixture of mustard, ketchup and relish. It wasn't as good as an In-N-Out burger, but it cost a dime less at the time.

About 4:30 Friday afternoon we'd stand outside and wait for the blue Lancer station wagon to drive up, and meet our Dad who was carrying three bags filled to the brim with Gigi burgers, french fries and drinks. I usually got three or four, Debby and Kathy the same, and then lesser amounts for Patrick and Maureen. We piled french fries high on a plate in the middle of the table, that had about a quarter of an inch of oil covering it by the time we were through.

Burps and distended tummies followed our Friday feast, but no one complained. It was better than those darn fish sticks.

I've mentioned that my dad loved spaghetti. I'm not sure why. He wasn't Italian.

He did share with us how he grew up on Staten Island, where he had seven brothers and one sister. His mother left when they were young and my dad and Uncle Jim became the patriarchs of the family. Growing up they were so poor that they used to skim the cream that expanded in the cold from the top of milk bottles on neighbors porches, and siphon gas from cars to get around.

Years later, while at my parents' home in Reno, there was a mobster killed in front of a restaurant in New York. It was in all the news.

Dad looked up at me with a smirk. "You know what, Johnny? I grew up with that guy on Staten Island." Then he laughed. "He was shakin' down fifth graders a nickel a week for protection from the bullies, who were his buddies. Later he started running numbers. Yeah, I remember him well. Went over to his house a couple of times for spaghetti dinners with the family."

I never questioned him further about it.

Since Dad loved spaghetti, it became another ritual at our household. Saturday morning he would get up early and start peeling tomatoes for the sauce. Then he would stew them, put in his "secret" blend of herbs, brown some hamburger meat, and slow-cook the concoction for the entire day. The smell blended into and through the house until by dinner time, we couldn't stand it any longer. Two pots of noodles were cooked on the stove and the feast would begin. Dad dished out a plate for each of us.

The rule was, you had to twirl the noodles onto a fork to eat them. There was an art and science to the twirl. I practiced until I could get a full two-inch noodle circle on my fork without any of it falling off. Once Maureen said she wanted to cut up the spaghetti and eat it. Dad's face flushed. His fingers started tapping the table in a staccato rhythm.

"You do not cut up spaghetti, Maggie. Period."

She learned to twirl pretty quickly.

1966

Jack, the ice cream man, became Jack the Gypper and then Jack the Jew.

I'm not sure why, but that's what a lot of the kids called him. The Crusaders would refer to him that way once in a while, but to be honest, at the time, we weren't even sure what it meant and why it was a big deal. Allan and Janet were Jewish, and they would refer to him that way too.

One day, we were talking about ice cream and Jack. As usual, we had no money and thought ice cream on that sweltering July afternoon would taste mighty fine. What to do?

Stanley flicked his cigarette butt into the street. "I've got an idea, but it will take some balls."

"What?" we asked.

He ran his fingers through his light brown hair and smirked. "We use a Stingray. One of us sits up on the handlebars. We follow behind Jack, ride up, and while he is driving, we open the rear door and..." He motioned with his arm as if tossing something to us.

"I don't know," Kenny said.

"I think it is a cool idea," Paul interjected. "I'll ride the handlebars."

Resigned, Kenny stood up. "Then I'll pedal the bike. Stanley, you and John pedal next to us to catch the ice cream."

We listened for Jack's familiar sing-song music as the truck came closer. We chose Mayland Avenue because it was a longer street and would give us a chance to pull it off. In position, we waited for him to pass us, and Kenny started pedaling. Paul precariously sat on the handlebars, and the bike was zig-zagging back and forth. Once speed picked up, it started going straighter.

Stanley and I were riding far to the sides as Kenny moved up toward the rear of the truck. Paul reached out. Still too far. Kenny picked it up a bit, and Paul reached out again. This time he grabbed the handle and pulled it open. I could taste the ice cream in my mouth. Paul beamed. Just as he started to reach inside, two little kids ran to the driveway and motioned Jack to stop. The truck braked to a stop. Paul and Kenny slammed into the rear of it.

Paul, somewhat dazed, started to limp away while Kenny picked up the bike and ran away from the ice cream truck. The rear door was still open as we all took off. Jack jumped out to see what hit his truck. We didn't look back.

Next time we saw Jack, his rear door had a lock on it.

For some reason, forgotten by me now, we took a dislike to Jack. It could have been that there was newer competition from Don the ice cream guy who had a large van full of ice cream. The Good Humor guy. Same prices. I'm not sure. But when he came around we would yell:

"Jack the Jew! Jack the gypper!" And then we'd run.

He never chased us, so it didn't really matter.

One day, however, we were especially loud and repetitive. "Jack the Jew. Jack the Jew!" Jack slammed on the brakes and the truck skidded to a stop. Standing in my driveway, we were unprepared for this reaction. We dashed hurriedly into my house while Jack started running toward us. Once inside the house, we slammed the door and locked it.

"You bastards had better stop that, you hear me? You shut up with that talk." He was spitting it out, face scarlet red and slamming his hand against the door. I could see him clearly through the door window. Then I saw it.

On his right arm were numbers - tattooed onto it.

My heart sank. I could feel the color leaving my face. The guys were laughing, but I didn't have the heart or enthusiasm to join them. After he started the truck and left, the guys went home, and I sat in the front room alone. Thinking. I knew what the numbers meant. He had been in a concentration camp in World War II. I remembered reading about how soldiers rounded them up and put them into camps, tattooing numbers onto their arms to keep track of them.

I felt like a heel. Lower than a caterpillar's belly. *Why did we tease him like that? What were we doing? Why did we push him to the brink? For fun? For a laugh? What about his feelings? What had he been through?*

We never called him Jack the Jew again.

It took a long time before Jack the ice cream man came down our street again.

Luckily for us, he did.

Beatles and Dad

The 1963 light-blue Lancer station wagon pulled into our driveway. I always liked meeting my dad when he got home, and I had timed it just right. He turned off the engine, pushed on the emergency brake, and opened the door. He smiled at me as he exited the car.

"Hey Johnny."

I leaned in and kissed him on the cheek. "Hi, Dad. How was work?"

"Great." He fumbled with some papers he was carrying. "By the way, I heard a great song on the way home. It had something to do with an octopus."

"*Octopus's Garden?*"

He thought for a moment. "Yeah, that was it." His eyes searched for the words as he bit his lower lip. "I want to be, under the-"

"-sea, in an octopus's garden, in the shade."

"How'd you know the words?" Dad asked.

"Dad, The Beatles wrote that."

He grimaced and dismissed the thought of it with his arm. "You're kidding?"

I shook my head. "Ringo Starr is singing."

He immediately tightened his lips into a grumpy smile and shook his head as he walked up the entryway sidewalk toward the house. "You had to ruin it for me."

I smiled.

Dad was starting to come around.

Barely.

Surfing

As I mentioned earlier, we Crusaders were surfers before we actually surfed.

There was really no choice in the matter. It was settled before we were even conscious of the two main social groups: surfers and beaners.

In fifth and sixth grade, we were an agnostic group of kids - no boundaries or distinctions. Everyone played tetherball, flag football, caroms, and marbles. We were kids having fun and enjoying each other.

When we reached seventh grade, which was technically pre-high school, small changes started to occur. Subtle but significant.

In addition to car and rock magazines, we read surf magazines and started to build skateboards. Our hair grew a little longer and our mode of after-school dress started to morph. Penney's all-cotton high-neck t-shirts, surf shorts, huarache sandals or Vans tennis shoes, and Saint Christopher medals became the dress of choice. Not to make a specific statement. Rather, just because we thought it looked really cool. Like surfers.

Beaners took the same approach. Their role models, the older vato beaner guys, dressed in a certain way: tan baggy pants, white t-shirt, Pendleton long-sleeve shirt over it, pants riding high on the waist, black shoes, hair slicked back. Mustaches, if you could grow one.

The exceptions were the nerdy kids who didn't lean one way or the other. They became invisible for the most part.

Each year the two styles morphed further and further apart. In our case, we also had rock-n-roll to deal with, which means we created a blending of the surf look with the rock look. This in turn gradually became the newly defined hippie look, which was suspiciously close to a cross between early surf and rock. Tie-dyed t-shirts, scrappy pants, sandals, and the requisite long hair. Mustaches, and side burns, if you could grow them.

In the seventh grade we were well into our surfer phase. That's how we defined ourselves, and how we were defined by our peers. Problem was, we had no idea how to surf. Nor did any of us Crusaders have a surfboard.

Stanley's brother Paul had a surfboard. He took us to the beach and let us try it. I almost drowned; Stanley and Paul didn't get anywhere on it either. Seemed like a big setback.

It was only temporary.

We did make skim boards out of plywood, and became pretty proficient with them. As the waves were pulling back after breaking, you threw the round piece of plywood onto the water, ran, and jumped on it, propelling it toward the next set of waves. We experienced way more wipe-outs than rides, but it helped us learn some balance and coordination.

My cousin-in-law from Hawaii, Ron Li, was a surf champion. He was married to my cousin Patty from Washington. He came over to visit when I was in seventh grade and, with my parents' financial help, found a used board for me - a Jacobs 9'6" with three stringers (pieces of wood going down the middle). There were only single skegs available back then. Stanley ended up with a board. I think Paul bought a used one shortly thereafter.

From then on, we were officially surfers.

And, we had the boards to prove it.

We only had to learn to surf to seal the deal.

No problemo.

We were close to thirty miles from the ocean --
Huntington Beach being the nearest place we could surf. Our
plan?

Thumbing our way there. With our boards.

It was no big deal. Didn't angst about it or even give it a
second thought. We broke off into teams of two and hit the
road.

We would arrive at the beach, spend the day, and then
hitchhike back again.

Looking back at it now, one would look at it through a
different filter. At the time, no one gave us a hard time.

It was fun.

Earlier that summer, Guy got his 1951 Woody. After
months of working on it, the wagon was ready to go on its
maiden voyage to the beach.

By the way, Guy was an honorary Crusader. He was a
surfer too, but was seldom around because he went to Bishop
Amat High School and lived about a mile away from us. Billy
went to Bishop Amat too but lived behind Stanley and was a
founding member.

When Guy could, he hung around.

But mostly he worked after school - either at his dad's
hardware store or later in a gas station on the corner of
Francisquito and Willow.

Very industrious fellow.

Beach Safari

"You bet I'm ready," I said, straightening out my hastily donned t-shirt. I'd barely been able to sleep the night before, waking up every couple of hours checking the clock and restlessly nodding off again. By the time 6:30 rolled around, I was exhausted. I dragged myself out of bed.

Dressing quickly, except for taking the time to make sure every hair of mine was methodically combed into the perfect surfer do, I raced over to Paul's house. Stanley and Paul were already there, every hair on their heads also meticulously combed. Kenny soon joined us.

We hustled over to Guy's house, about a mile away on Willow Street, and found him in the garage, where he kept his 1951 Woody, the fixation of all of our restlessness.

We were going to the beach in it.

Having planned our first trip to Huntington Beach for weeks, we were soon to embark on our journey. Guy was still fifteen, so Paul would drive us there in the beautiful machine. We put a couple of boards on the surf rack on top and piled into it. Paul and Guy in front: Kenny, Stanley and I in the back. Paul fired it up.

Glass packs rumbled the garage walls as he revved it up, put it in reverse and rolled back into the street. So far, so good. Aiming it toward Amar Road, he shifted it into gear, hit the gas, and we lunged forward.

Success!

Guy had worked on it for months, and it was tricked out: straight front axle, big Ford engine, dual carburetors, headers, slicks in the back, chrome rims.

Heading down Hacienda Boulevard in this bitchin' Woody with surfboards on the roof, we were thrilled beyond belief. The windows were down, a cool breeze blew through our hair (messing up the perfect do's we'd all struggled so hard to create earlier), we all had smokes and the stereo was playing *Pipeline* by the Safaris. It seemed nothing could be wrong in the world.

We did notice the Woody shimmied a bit, especially when Paul hit the brakes or we sped over forty. Paul decided to go a little slower through Hacienda Heights, where the roads wound lazily up and through the hills.

Heads turned from every car we passed, most usually followed by a thumbs-up or an okay given with the thumb and forefinger touching and accentuated by three other fingers in a rooster tail. Once in a great while, a cholo would flip us off. Didn't matter. Nothing could upset our Zen/surf lifestyle moment.

We stopped for gas near Whittier Boulevard, and after filling up we took off south on Beach Boulevard.

About ten minutes later we were approaching Imperial Boulevard. Paul was booking along at a good rate of speed, but we could see the light flash to yellow, and I mentally calculated that we would not make it. Paul came to the same conclusion. I heard him hit the brake pedal and then a clunking sound. Nothing happened.

"Holy shit!" Paul yelled.

"What?" we collectively answered.

His leg was pushing on the pedal, but it was down to the floorboard and wasn't going any further.

"No frickin' brakes," he screamed as the light turned crimson and we were heading right for the intersection. Cross traffic had started to move into our path.

I might point out that this car did not have seat belts, nor would we have worn them if it had. It would have been un-cool, and seatbelts were not even a requirement of new cars back then.

Paul bore down on the horn, which thankfully worked, and entered the intersection. Cars skidded and swerved on both sides of the street. We barreled around two cars and then squealed to the left, missing a couple of other cars that hadn't heard the horn. We flew out of the intersection as quickly as we entered, not having hit anything, and glided to a stop about a half mile past the intersection. Paul put it in park and turned off the engine.

It sounded like a big vacuum cleaner as we all finally took a collective breath at once.

"Gee, guys," Guy finally said. "I thought I'd fixed that problem."

"Ya think?" Paul stated, laughing. "That was pretty frickin' close, man."

"It's the brake cylinder. We need to get to a gas station and tighten it up."

Paul tested the emergency brake, and it worked since it was cable operated.

"We'll use this," he said, showing us, "until we can get it fixed."

Sounded good to us. "No problem."

Paul started the car, took off and about two miles down Beach Boulevard, we found a repair shop. Ten minutes later, they'd tightened the connection to the brake line and topped it off with fluid. Back in business.

We arrived at the beach about forty-five minutes later. We were greeted by a beautiful summer day with an aqua blue ocean, puffy white clouds floating wispily in the sky, and a warm, inviting breeze gently blowing. The off-white sand was almost too warm to walk on beneath our feet.

We'd made it.

We spent the day surfing, lying in the sun, slapping oil on our bodies, staring at girls, eating junk food, fake fighting, body surfing, and generally having fun. It was more than that. It was a feeling of belonging. To a group. To a lifestyle. To some inner club.

That magical day changed our lives.

We spent the entire summer and all of our attention on getting to the beach - whether with the Woody, hitchhiking, or cajoling friends and neighbors into taking us.

Beaners

I think Stanley was the most sensitive of the group. Or maybe Billy. Mostly because of their mothers. I noticed a completely different family culture in Hispanic families: very maternal upbringings. Billy was a full Hispanic; Stanley's mom was Hispanic. By the way, I use Hispanic because that is the preferred way to refer to Mexicans today. But back then, Mexican was not a pejorative term. Beaners was, though, and freely used by us.

However, Billy and Stanley were never called beaners.

Ever.

Billy's mom was totally over the top. Every time he left or arrived at his home, he was always greeted the same.

"Oh, my little mijo, how are you?" she would ask. Or

"Goodbye my little mijo. I love you."

He pretended he hated it and always said something to that effect to us, but I suspect he was hiding the fact that he appreciated and cherished his mother's love, and her endearing and natural way of expressing it. Same with Stanley's mom - only she was not so over the top.

In fact, it seemed to me the whole nature of the machismo Spanish male stereotype might be predicated on overcoming that maternal influence growing up.

At it definitely explained the macho overcompensation in many respects.

Lovers' Island

"Let's hitch to the beach and go body surfing," Stanley suggested as Paul, Kenny, and I walked down Nolandale, smoking away.

Paul took a long drag, scanned the bright piercing blue sky and thoughtfully blew the smoke out. "Nah, it's too hot for that, man."

Kenny stopped and faced us. "Then let's go to In-N-Out."

Stanley pointed with his hand, a cigarette between his fingers like a bandleader's wand. "You're always hungry, Kenny."

"So what if I am?"

"So ... we've got no bread anyway," I reminded them.

Paul chuckled. "I saw a garage full of pop bottles on Barrydale just waiting to be liberated. We can cash them in."

"You didn't see any bottles," Stanley said.

"Swear to God I did ... on the way over here."

"Knock it off you guys." Kenny'd had enough.

"Yes I did." Paul gave Stanley the lowered eyebrow evil eye.

Stanley returned a slight grin and shook his head, flipping his cigarette butt into the air, watching it land against a curb.

"Hey, let's go to the mall and get some chase," I suggested.

That elicited unanimous affirmation. We were almost to the end of my street where we usually cut through the fence to Puente Avenue, when Kenny eyed something on the chain link fence next to his house. He strode toward it.

"What's up, Kenny?" Paul asked.

"I've got an idea." He reached the rose bush and picked off one of the large, hardened buds. Looking at us, he winked, wound up like a pitcher, raised his right leg and threw it squarely at a car driving past us.

"Waddaya doing?" Stanley asked, incredulous.

Thump.

It bounced off the car's door.

"Jeez, Kenny," I said.

Paul shook his head and laughed. I couldn't help myself. I joined him.

"You're crazy, Kenny, ya know that?" Paul said.

"Not really, man. Think about it. We can hit cars, leave no dents and who's the worse off for it?" He searched around for more buds. "Besides, we might get chased."

"Come on dudes, let's get going." Stanley motioned with his arm.

Kenny held out his hand like a stop sign. "Wait, Stanley. Just one more."

Groans erupted.

I peered over the chain link fence. A low-rider car was bouncing jerkily and squeaking its way toward us. Kenny wiggled his eyebrows up and down, widened his eyes and smiled deviously as he picked a nice fat bud from the bush and stood dead still.

"Don't do it to this car, Kenny," I said. "Swear to God."

The car drove closer - a powder blue 1952 Chevy coupe, lowered almost to the ground. Brown arms hung out the windows. "Lovers Island" painted in light blue graced the rear side window. Kenny wound up and looked back, left, and right, Sandy Koufax style. As they neared, we could see tattoos covering their forearms.

"Hey, Kenny... come on man, don't do it," Paul implored.

Too late.

Kenny threw the bud in one fluid motion, releasing it while he yelled "Hey, you!"

Three pairs of wide-eyes followed the rose bud as it flew directly toward the passenger window. The guy in the front seat, a "beaner" about forty years old with a bandana wrapped high on his head, quickly turned around at the taunt, sneering.

We watched it splatter hard against his right cheekbone.

Direct hit.

A horrible shout erupted from the car. "Shit! Pendejos."

Screeching brakes were followed by louder swearing in Spanish. The car's door flew open as the enraged passenger jumped from the car and stared directly at us. His face was pock marked, with thin lips and beady eyes. He wore typical "vato" clothing: black shoes, khaki pants three sizes too long in length, and a Pendleton long-sleeve shirt over a white t-shirt. Only the wounded passenger had one thing not typical - a six-inch Bowie knife in a dirty brown leather case strapped to his right leg.

I glanced at Kenny. Disbelief flooded his face at the realization of what he had just done.

"H-o-l-y -s-h-i-t!" he whispered aloud.

Stanley raced toward my backyard and yelled, "Chase!"

Paul and Kenny followed immediately.

My heart's pounding almost drowned out Stanley's rallying cry. I knew we could outrun them. However, my legs hesitated for a moment, the scene being so incredibly stupid. *What the heck got into Kenny? Why did he pick that car to hit? Did he even think about us being near our houses? What if we don't get away? Wait. What if ... Holy crap! I need to get outta here.*

I sprinted across Kenny's lawn to my side yard, leaped up on the block wall, down into my yard, across and around the playhouse toward the rear wall. Jumping and pulling myself up and over it, I reached the other guys. All of us raced out through the wooden gate to the next street, ran across the asphalt to the other side and rested to catch our breath. No one spoke a word.

The car's tires screeched as it careened around the corner and headed directly toward us.

Kenny motioned with his arm like a traffic cop. "Come on guys, this way."

We sprinted through the side yard of the house. *Damn it.* They had a couple of golden retrievers that started barking and nipping at our legs. We reached their cement block wall, went over it and into the next yard, scraping our arms and legs. We could hear the screech of rubber around the corner of the exact street we were just on.

Shit.

They chased us for another ten minutes going up and down streets. We ran five blocks away, jumping walls, tearing through neighbors' yards, barely avoiding them. We finally stopped, did an about-face and started making our way back toward my house.

Two blocks away we dashed across the street into another neighbor's yard, where more dogs barked. We reached a six-foot block wall. Paul pulled himself up and straddled it. Kenny dove completely over it. Out of breath and muscles aching, I struggled to pull myself up. I was a short sprinter. This was taking too long.

I lifted my arm. "Paul, give me a hand up, dude."

Paul reached down and pulled me up and over the wall. He yanked Stanley over next. The screeches and roaring engine were getting closer. We ran to the next wall where they must have added another row of cement blocks, because it seemed a lot higher. Paul cupped his hands.

The Crusaders

"Come on, John, jump over."

I stuck a shoe in his cupped hands, reached the top and pulled myself up and over. Kenny followed and then Stanley, who straddled the wall. Paul realized that he needed to get over and looked up at Stanley, panic in his eyes. We could hear tires skidding and car doors flying open on the street next to the wall.

"They're over here," one of the vatos yelled.

Stanley reached down and whispered, "Grab my hand, man."

Paul clasped it while Stanley, being the smallest of the group, leaned back to leverage him up. Paul struggled before he looped his leg over the wall and fell to the other side. Stanley plopped on the grass next to him.

I was already across the street between two houses, shouting and motioning for them to follow. "Come on."

Stanley, Paul and Kenny darted across the street and then, hopping two more block walls and eluding one irritated Doberman Pinscher, we finally ended up in my backyard. Bent over with hands grasping our legs, gasping for breath, exhausted, and scared shitless, we wondered collectively if we would ever get away from those guys. They were relentless.

We faintly heard their car as it slowly cruised down a street two blocks away, circled back to Barrydale, and then headed to the next closer street. Stalking us. Daring us to try and run away from them so *they* could see where we were. Glancing at each other, we intuitively knew what the game had become. We were the hunted. It was no longer a fun game of chase. Those vatos were determined to beat the crap out of us.

Or worse.

After I'd caught my breath, I had an idea. A large-leafed maple tree grew next to my house. It partially covered the roof. If we stealthily crawled up to the roof's pinnacle and peered over, while obscured beneath the leaves, we could see them, hopefully without them seeing us. At the same time, we could stop running and rest up. The Crusaders agreed.

The jump from the playhouse to the roof was an easy one, and presented no problem. We crab-crawled our way up and cautiously peeked over the top. The low-rider Chevy was inching its way down the street, the beaners in it looking left and right. Surreal. Like a predator stalking and searching its prey. It came almost to the end of the cul-de-sac and stopped.

The victim of Kenny's bud stepped out and looked around. His compadres exited and stood by the car, searching between houses with venomous eyes. A friendly Mexican neighbor of ours, Mr. Fierro, walked out to speak with them. They spoke in hushed tones. The one with the bright red lump on his cheek waved his arms wildly.

Mr. Fierro finally cut him off. "Come on, man, they're just stupid kids."

"Stupid kids, my ass."

The dark-skinned vato bared his clenched teeth, stretched his lips and pointed his arm with an outstretched finger, as if he *knew* we could see him. The sunlight made his beady eyes look even more sinister. He spoke as he turned in a half-circle. "I'm gonna get you, you little rat bastards."

He slammed his fist onto the roof of the car before he and his buddies got back in. Four doors slammed shut. Tires squealed as they put it in gear, made the turn around the cul-de-sac and tore off toward the end of the street and out of sight. Spanish swear words and squealing tires echoed into the distance.

Paul looked over Stanley's shoulder toward Kenny, who was lying next to me, and swung at him with his fisted right hand. "You fucking idiot! You almost got us killed." He continued hitting Kenny until Stanley pushed him off and kneeled upright.

"What are you doing, Paul?"

He stopped his punching and kneeled back on his legs. Kenny rubbed his shoulder and feigned as if he were hurt. "Paul, that was uncool."

"I'll tell you what was uncool, Kenny," Paul hooked his thumb toward the street. "Fucking with those assholes."

Kenny started smirking, shoulders shaking. Stanley caught it and started smiling too.

"What?" Paul questioned, looking around.

Kenny and Stanley broke out laughing. I quickly followed. Couldn't help myself. It was infectious. Paul couldn't resist either and finally joined in, the nervous laughter quickly growing in loudness until it hit a crescendo.

We all turned onto our backs and laid there, still chuckling. Stanley pulled out a smoke and lit up, slowly blowing the smoke out. "How long do you think we'll have to hide before we can go anywhere?"

"We should probably lay low for at least a couple of days," Paul said, putting his hands behind his head. "Those guys seemed pretty pissed off."

I leaned up on my elbows. "*Seemed* pissed off? I'd say that ship sailed, dudes. They were way past that."

"Johnny! Johnny?"

My mom was calling from down on the front porch. I sat up and yelled back.

"Hey Mom, I'm up on the roof."

"You better get down before your father gets home or you'll be in trouble, you hear?"

"Yeah Mom, I'm coming down now."

Paul sat up, leaned over toward me and sang out in singsong: "Johnny's in trouble. Johnny's in trouble."

I gave him the "turbo" evil eye. It didn't faze him. Kenny started laughing, and then the dams burst. Tears ran down our cheeks as we joined in. We scooted our way to the edge of the roof and jumped down near the playhouse.

My hands started shaking as we sat down.

"Dudes, that was some seriously scary chase," I said.

Paul stretched out his legs one at a time, trying to stop the cramping. "That may be the best chase ever, dudes."

Kenny beamed. "See, I got us the best chase ever."

"Almost got us killed," Stanley said.

"But it didn't," I said, shrugging. "Luckily." My hands continued to shake. I rubbed them together.

We sat in front of the playhouse silently, each of us lost in his own thoughts. Mine were replaying the events of the past half-hour - of jumping fences, my heart pounding in my chest, observing my scraped and bloody arms from scaling and climbing over cement block walls, and how terrified I was. I assumed the rest were in the same frame of reflection.

"Let's get something from Dairy Delight," Kenny finally said. He looked to Stanley. "I know, I'm always hungry."

Paul examined his bloodied arms and the ripped pocket on his shirt. "Yeah, sounds good."

I pulled off some of the cement chips stuck on my arms and reminded him, "We don't have any money."

"Let's walk by that garage I was telling you about and pick up some bottles," Paul said as he stood up. He gazed at Stanley. "I wasn't bullshitting, taxi cab."

Stanley flipped him off and rose. "Think it's okay to go out there?" he asked, pointing with a freshly lit cigarette. "I don't know how much more chase I can take for one day."

Paul brushed himself off with both hands. "Let's all go home and change our clothes and meet at the field. They won't be able to recognize us anyway."

"Maybe not you, Paul, but that vato looked me directly in the eyes," Kenny said as he shuddered. "Damn evil looking."

I lit a cigarette and slapped the lighter shut. "Fuck 'em. Let's get changed and chow down at Dairy Delight." I exhaled the bluish smoke and stared at Kenny, shaking my head. "That may have been the dumbest thing you ever did."

"But it was some bitchin' chase, man," Kenny replied, winking.

I couldn't hold back my smile. "Yeah, it was," I agreed. "It surely was."

Thankfully, we never saw "Lovers Island" or those beaners again.

And we never played our favorite game of chase again, either.

Didn't seem as much fun anymore.

Living Color

Kenny and I were at a party near Edgewood. Music, dancing, and no beer, since their parents were home.

After saying our hellos to everyone, we walked into the den and were stopped in our tracks. The television they were watching was in color. It was rounded at the edges like our black and white TVs at home, but still.

Color?

We stood transfixed by the picture. Illya Kuryakin and Napoleon Solo - the men from U.N.C.L.E. - were running across the screen. Buildings blew up. Locations were exotic. It was really - colorful - almost over-saturated. But it still looked great. We watched the entire show and then left the party.

I mentioned the incident to my dad, who appeared to be disinterested. I was wrong.

A few months later, we got a brand-new RCA color television. Wood cabinet.

Most of the shows we watched were still in black and white. But some were not. My dad's favorite was *Bonanza*.

Watching television became an event for the entire family. Like when we went to drive-in movies in the station wagon and watched classics like *Flubber* with Fred MacMurray on the big screen.

Television series quickly adopted the new technology, and soon we were watching *Batman, Gilligan's Island* (with Ginger *and* Mary Ann), and dozens of others.

Mary Ann in color. Wow!

Edgewood Incidents II

Eighth grade at Edgewood Junior High was a great year on the whole, but there were incidents that further opened my eyes and heart and caused me to start questioning some of my actions.

It was the second year of having multiple instructors and a home room class. It had been a tough transition the year before, going from one teacher to six. But once I got used to it, I really enjoyed the diversity of the teaching styles and the little bit of freedom it afforded between classes and lunch.

Book lockers were four high and in rows of twelve to fifteen located throughout the red-brick school buildings. Locks were rotational with a right, left, and right number to open them. I was fooling around with mine when Howard Feingold came up next to me to open his.

"Man, did you see Debbie A's hair today?" I asked him, just shooting the breeze with no particular agenda.

He cocked his head slightly. "Why?"

"Well, it looks like she dyed it or something.... looks like straw."

He thinned his lips. "Naw, didn't notice."

I slammed my locker shut. "Check it out, man."

Two class periods passed. One more left before lunch. I was walking down the hall when Howard came up from the opposite direction and pushed me with both hands back about a foot.

"Take back what you said about my girlfriend," he shouted.

"What the fuck are you talking about, Howard?"

He went into a fighting stance and threw a quick jab at me. Missed by a mile. I looked around and saw a crowd gathering. Funny how that happens at school. No one tries to stop it. They just huddle around in a large circle like lemmings and watch.

The initial crowd draws a bigger one, and pretty soon you've got a large audience like a fight ring on your hands. I was trying to think on my feet. *Was Debbie Howard's girlfriend? I didn't know that. I actually thought she couldn't date yet. And what's up with Howard. We're friends, for chrisakes. At least I thought we were.*

"I'm gonna kick your ass." He jabbed a couple of more times, obviously missing me.

"After school," I blurted out, trying to buy some time.

He stood up from his fighter's pose. "Alright then, after school. I'll be waiting."

My feelings were hurt more than anything else. I didn't intend or mean to get Howard mad at me. It was simply a passing comment between two supposed buddies. But let a woman get in the way, especially one with the biggest tits in school, and trouble wasn't far behind.

Stanley and Paul came up to me at lunch and asked what happened.

"That asshole Howard told his..." I made parenthetical marks with my fingers, "'girlfriend,' that I said her hair looked like straw. Next thing I know he wants to fight with me."

Paul shook his head. "It does look like straw."

"No shit. But apparently he's going out with her. I had no idea."

"What are you gonna do?" Stanley asked.

"Well, I'm not going to get in a fight with him, so I guess I'll just go home early."

"Want us to go with you?" Paul asked.

"Naw... he'll probably get over it by tomorrow anyway. He made his play today so she could see it."

"Pussy, man," Paul commented. "We're all chasing it and we don't even know what to do with it once we get it."

Stanley fake punched at Paul. "Speak for yourself, asshole."

"Okay, Casanova," I cut in, laughing "Let's get some lunch."

Lunch at school was the equivalent of a Clifton's cafeteria. You would wait in line, grab a tray, and walk through the kitchen area, sliding your tray on a stainless steel counter shelf, and then point to what you wanted that day. Hamburgers, fries and hotdogs were staples. Each day of the week would feature something special - meat loaf, lasagna, chipped beef, and an assortment of vegetables and potatoes. And finally, dessert.

Everyone always got a small carton of milk. And this lead to a lunch ritual that, although short-lived, was very fun.

Tables and benches were folded down from the wall in the gymnasium so we could eat inside. We usually ate outside, unless it was raining, which was not very often in La Puente. One rainy day Allan Weiss, Stanley, Paul, and I were eating at a table when, on the other side, this big black girl and her friends sat down. I am not sure how or when it happened, but Allan started calling her Magoo. She didn't wear glasses, was not short, and was not old. But it stuck. And when she was called that, she went nuts and started yelling at the perpetrator.

From our lunch bench Allan would yell out "Magoo" and pretend he had nothing to do with it. She'd jump up and start going off, hands on her hips.

"Who said dat?"

Silence.

"You best watch your mouths over there before I cum ova and kicks yer asses." She sat back down and continued stuffing her face.

This went on for days. We'd laugh under our breaths and elbow each other.

One day Allan came out from the lunch line with two milk cartons. I knew he didn't even like milk, and asked what was up.

He raised his eyebrows a couple of times. "I have an idea."

He took one of the cartons and pushed the spout out but not opened. Then, he sighted where Magoo was sitting, and with one huge swing of his arm tossed it up and toward her. It was so unexpected that we all sat slack-jawed and watched as it sailed through the air and landed flat on her table, exploding into a white cloud of foam that covered her and her friends.

Dead silence. We were laughing with no sounds coming out, trying as hard as we could to be quiet.

She jumped up and screamed. "Who did dat?" She started shaking her arms and body. "Who threw dat milk?"

Finally, we could hold ourselves back no longer, and Stanley let out a yelp and started laughing hysterically.

"Did you throw dat, you little asshole?" she screamed across the gymnasium's wooden floor.

She picked up her milk carton and slung it toward our table. It missed and slammed into the wall. Allan took his other milk carton, stood up and threw it directly at Magoo. She ducked, and it hit her wall. The next thing I knew, food was being tossed -- by everybody. It was meatloaf day.

"Food fight!" was shouted by various kids as they stood up and entered the fray.

Teachers ran into the gym and started yelling to stop. Didn't register. Food kept flying. Then trays. It seemed like one or two minutes passed before everyone ran out of food, and more teachers arrived to try and stop us. By this time, Paul, Allan, Stanley and I were laughing so hard we had a difficult time staying on the benches.

Finally Mr. Purdy, dead eye Purdy himself, entered the gym and started yelling for everyone to stop it immediately. Since he was the only who had the power to use the infamous paddle and delegate swats, his word was golden. The food fight stopped, and everyone was ordered to leave the gym.

It was a mess. Food everywhere. I tried to walk by him without catching his eye.

"You have anything to do with this Mr. D.?" he asked.

I held back my laughter and blurted out. "No sir."

He held his one real eye on me and finally dismissed me with a turn of his head as he walked further into the gym to survey the damage.

Once we were outside in the courtyard of the school, Magoo came toward Allan.

"Did chew throw dat milk at me?" Her manner was more than threatening.

Allan put on his most innocent look. Eyebrows raised, lips taut, eyes looking up as if he were praying. "Of course not. Why would you think that?"

She stared at him menacingly. "It better not have been you, dats all I gots to say." She stormed off and down the hall.

Allan cupped his hands and shouted, "Magoo!" It echoed through the hallways a dozen times. We all started laughing.

The reason the principal asked me if I had anything to do with it was due to an incident that happened in the seventh grade. Billy had access to fireworks because his parents had a store on Olvera Street in Los Angeles. For some reason, unknown to us, he was able to get all the illegal fireworks we wanted. We had cat tails, cherry bombs, even M-80's.

We were sitting around Stanley's garage and the subject of cherry bombs and toilets came up - in the context of what would happen if you flushed one down when the fuse was lit. I didn't think the fuse would work under water, but Billy and Stanley were convinced it would. We decided that I would try it at Edgewood the next day.

I planned the whole thing out: getting out of class a little before lunch, timing how long it would take to get to the bathroom. The works. When the time came, I slipped out the back door of the room, raced to the bathroom and used my lighter to flame the fuse. Dropped it in the toilet and flushed. However, before I was able to leave the bathroom a huge boom exploded and the toilet flew up and landed sideways in the stall. Water started gushing everywhere.

I hauled ass out of the bathroom, skidded on the cement and met everyone in the field. In the background I could hear teachers yelling for me to stop. I didn't of course. I figured on blending in with everyone hoping they wouldn't know who did it. That was the major part of my escape plan.

We were laughing about it when Paul's eyes widened as he looked past me at something. "Holy shit," I heard him whisper. Suddenly, I felt a hand on my shoulder and was forcibly spun around. Mr. Purdy, with two other teachers, was standing there shooting daggers of anger directly into me.

"Follow me," Mr. Purdy ordered.

The Crusaders

How'd they know it was me? I wondered as I was paraded past students toward the principal's office. We walked past the bathroom where the janitor was busy trying to stem the water that was gushing from the broken water line. I went over everything in my mind. *What had I forgotten? What went wrong?*

Once we were in the office, they sat me down and called my parents. After a short conversation with my mother to come down to the school, he hung up the phone and looked directly at me and asked why I did it.

"Did what?"

"We saw you running out of the bathroom."

I sat up straighter in the chair. "You couldn't tell it was me."

"Really?" Mr. Purdy said sarcastically as he slowly rounded his desk and sat on the edge. "Tell me, how could we possibly miss that Hawaiian shirt of yours?"

Holy shit.

My cousin from Hawaii had given me a dark blue Hawaiian shirt with white flowers on it for Christmas, and I loved it. And I wore it that day. I even had a couple of pictures of me with Allan taken for the yearbook in the schoolyard wearing that shirt.

I slumped down in the chair, head down, resigned to fess up and take my lumps.

The one thing I had forgotten. That damn Hawaiian shirt.

I had gotten into the habit of cutting into line at lunchtime, while the students were waiting to go through the cafeteria. It wasn't malicious. It was just that I was a surfer and Crusader, and they were... well... students. It wasn't often, but when I got out late from class, I would pick a nerd that I knew and just cut in front of him.

Walking to the row of students one day, I eyed Mark Mann, a short, pudgy kid with close-cropped blond hair, pimples and Clark Kent glasses. I'd cut in front of him a few times before, and did it almost subconsciously. Then I heard a loud voice shout behind me:

"No more!"

I turned and Mark kicked me right on the shinbone, turning red in the face at the effort he had exerted doing it. I grabbed my leg and screamed.

"What the fuck are you doing, asshole?" I reached out and managed to push him back. He hit the brick wall and reached into his pocket. Next thing, I saw a big folded Scout's knife in his hand and him fumbling to open it. *Holy shit.* I was almost on the ground in pain. From my side rushed Howard Feingold, who grabbed his hand and wrestled him to the ground. The two grappled for a few moments while Howard tried to wrench the knife away from him. I fell down on my knees, reached over and grabbed his knife hand and pinned it down.

Kids were screaming. A surreal scene. Teachers arrived and the coach grabbed Mark, yanked the knife out of his hand and pinned him on the ground. He was red with anger, veins popping, spitting, screaming "not again," and writhing under the coach. Howard got up and reached down a hand to help me stand, but the pain in my shin was too much. Shit, it hurt. More teachers arrived, and when the story came out Howard, Mark and I were ushered to the principal's office.

They let Howard go right away. They placed Mark and me into separate offices and got each of our stories. After a half-hour, our parents arrived, and I went through the story again. The principal and coach were in the room with my mother and listened. At the end they looked at each other, nodded, and Mr. Purdy cleared his throat and spoke:

"You probably did not know this, but yesterday there was an incident in the gym locker that I just found out about myself. It seems a group of your friends waited until Mark was alone in the gym. They went inside, stripped him naked and threw him out in front of the home economics class."

He cleared his throat and looked to the coach.

"I had no idea what happened until he," motioning with his head, "just now told us. Apparently, he ran back in, dressed and went home. You can imagine how he felt. Anyway, he told us he would never let that happen again and brought the knife to school to protect himself. And you happened to be the first one he perceived was attacking him again."

"But I had no idea that happened," I said. "And who are these supposed friends of mine who did it? No one I know would do that."

The coach looked up after reading his clipboard. "We're following up on that now. He gave us their names."

"In the meantime," Purdy continued, "we're going to suspend you for a week."

I looked to my mom and then to Mr. Purdy. "What? He pulled a frickin' knife on me. I did nothing wrong."

The coach held up his hand. "Stop it right there. You cut in line, which is against school policy."

"And pulling a knife on a fellow student is not?"

My mom shook her head. "Stop it right now, Johnny. You pushed the young man into attacking you."

"Mom, this is crazy."

"I said stop it. We'll talk about it with your father tonight." She turned to Mr. Purdy. "Will he be able to get his homework for the next week?"

"Of course."

My homework? That was all she was concerned about? We left and went home, me without saying another word until we pulled in the driveway.

"Thanks a lot for sticking up for me, Mom. You know, I could have been killed."

She turned and looked at me. "You weren't. And I must say, the way you treated that boy was terrible."

With disappointment written on every feature in her face, she exited the car and went into the house, calling me to follow her. I got out and stormed into my room, slamming the door. This was so unfair. I slugged my pillow until I was out of strength, then laid down, and recalled the day's events.

Then I remembered the incident I had experienced in seventh grade with the two bullies. I recalled how I went home after the incident, sulked and, *in my mind*, brought a gun to school and shot the two of them. I remembered how helpless and hopeless I felt. That no one cared what happened to me. That they were a couple of bullies who needed to get their asses shot.

I thought of Mark Mann again. Of his being in the locker room and the assholes who came in and surrounded him. I pictured them pulling off his clothes while he screamed and was powerless to stop them, and then being thrown out the door where all the girls from Home Ec could see him. I could almost feel the fear and embarrassment he must have felt running back into the locker room.

I wondered what he thought all the way home and last night as he laid in his bed replaying the incident. The anger and hurt that must have overwhelmed him, and the resolve he took to do something about it. It must have taken courage to actually bring a knife to school and have the determination to use it to stop the bullying befalling him.

My attitude about the whole incident changed. I no longer felt that my punishment was unfair. It was just my dumb luck to be the one who bore the brunt of his anger; but after thinking about it, I felt it was better it ended up being me rather than someone else where he might have hurt them.

I found myself empathizing with Mark Mann. It could have been me. And I realized that I would need to be really careful with other people.

Mark Mann was not suspended from school.

I made it a point not to cut in line anymore, and after a few months started acknowledging him with a hello.

He didn't acknowledge me, or trust me, I suppose. Who could blame him. But it didn't matter. I knew how he felt, and like him, I deplored and despised bullies.

He exposed me as one, and I was grateful for that.

And sad that I had become one myself.

Then I thought about Magoo and how she must have felt.

Maybe I'd say something to Allan.

Hitchhiking II

We were hitching to the beach but not getting any rides. Kenny and I decided to do the split trick: he would go a block ahead of me. If I were picked up, I would beg the person to pick up my friend and we would both have a ride. Worked all the time (except once in a while with Paul who would just blast past us as a goof). Very uncool.

Once in position, a light-blue Cadillac pulled over and offered me a ride. It was the perfect situation. A single man, about fifty, driving alone. I jumped in the front.

"Hey there," he said.

"Hi," I replied.

"Where are you going?"

"To the beach"

"Okay then." He swung the column shifter into drive and we took off.

"Oh, hey, stop, please," I shouted, pointing. "That's my friend Kenny on the side of the road."

"Uh... my back doors aren't... working. So... I can't stop," he stuttered."

"What?"

"How far do you want me to take you?" he asked.

"I said the beach."

"Right."

He continued driving. I was thinking how weird it was that the back doors wouldn't work. After a few moments, he reached his arm over and put it on my leg and started rubbing it. I looked toward him, startled. Not scared. Just taken aback.

"Do you like that?" he asked.

"Do I like that?" I asked back in mock tone. "Fuck no. What are you, some kinda queer?" I picked his hand up off my leg and threw it back.

"Stop the fucking car," I yelled.

"Now, now, don't get all upset," he said. The car was not slowing down. All of a sudden I realized what a vulnerable position I was in, and my stomach started tightening.

"I said stop the damn car, now!" I shouted. It was a bluff, but I knew how to play one. "Or I'll kick your fucking ass, hear me?"

I grabbed the steering wheel and turned it a little toward traffic and let it go. He overcorrected and swerved to the side of the road and began to stop. Before the car completely stopped, I pulled the door handle and jumped out. He floored the car with the door open and took off, leaning over to try and close it.

"Fucking faggot!" I yelled, flipping him off.

My hand started shaking, my heart was pumping, and my stomach grew tighter into little knots. *What was that all about?* I'd thought I knew, since we had heard of men who wanted to play around with younger boys. But I had actually just seen and experienced it firsthand.

I was at least a mile away from Kenny. He came toward me about ten minutes later, had the car stop and picked me up.

Once in the back seat, which was driven by a nice middle-aged woman, Kenny asked.

"What happened, John? Why didn't you stop?"

"You won't believe it, Kenny." I motioned for him to drop it.

By the time we reached the beach, my body had calmed down. I told Kenny, Paul, and Stanley what had happened. Paul said he thought the same guy picked him up a few weeks earlier. He also felt weird in the car, but the guy didn't try anything.

"You still have your knife, Kenny?" I asked.

"Yeah." He pulled it out and displayed it.

"Just make sure you don't give it to the guy to look at," Paul teased.

Kenny acknowledged Paul with the bird.

"Well," Stanley said. "We'll put the word out to everyone on this guy. And if he tries to pick up any of us again, we'll do something to his car."

"Like what?" I asked.

"Don't know," Stanley replied. "Maybe pick up a rock and break the window."

"Sounds good to me," Kenny said. "Don't really want to stab anyone."

I guess there were bad people even back then. We weren't worried about them. We just watched out for each other.

The guy never picked any of us up again.

It was lucky that it turned out the way it did.

Pot-Heads

"It's no big deal, really guys," Kenny's big brother Dave told us in whispered tones, looking around as if someone might hear us. We were in the front yard of his and Kenny's house. "I do it all the time. You can buy a lid for just ten bucks." He showed us a baggie in his hand.

"We don't have ten bucks," Kenny said, looking at me for confirmation. I nodded.

Dave winked and moved closer. "Well then, I'll cut it in half and sell it to you for five. It's a good deal man. Stems and seeds are the essence of the plant. You'll get really high."

We were almost fifteen at the time, in ninth grade. It was late 1966. The album *Rubber Soul,* by The Beatles, had been released in 1965, and we were introduced to sitar music and a strange sort of cosmic consciousness; the faint beginnings of psychedelic music. With the release of the album *Revolver* in 1966, there could be no doubt something new was afoot. We didn't know what, but a sort of instinctual knowing gnawed within all of us.

Long hair was coming into fashion, which The Crusaders as surfers readily embraced, much to our parents' chagrin. "Innocent fun," they would say, along with "How can you listen to that junkie music?" That was mostly from my dad, who brought us up on single-sided 78's with the likes of Cole Porter, Jimmy Dorsey, Glenn Miller, and all the big bands of the era.

I had a small suitcase box-type turntable in my room. It was made for 78's, but if you put a plastic insert into the center-hole, it would play single 45's. In addition to my surf singles, I played The Beatles albums over and over, listening for... I didn't know what. There were rumors in the magazines about hidden messages. But what did I know?

The Rolling Stones were still the coolest, at least in my book. *The Rolling Stones Now* and their *Out of our Heads* albums were released in 1965, and contained the songs *The Last Time* and, of course, *Satisfaction*. There were so many cool songs from these vinyl discs that it was hard to imagine. Cool? Of course -- mainly because we could play almost every one of them. Besides *Satisfaction,* we played *Get Off of My Cloud, Lady Jane,* and others. They weren't exactly dance numbers, but they were bitchin'.

The Beatles were definitely more sophisticated musically, and truth be told, I just couldn't at that time figure out a lot of their tunes. *In My Life* by Lennon/McCartney was perhaps the most intricate meshing of music and lyrics I'd heard, and I played it over and over again. But we couldn't translate it to work the band.

But back to the main point.

A sort of psychedelic movement was emerging in late 1965 and throughout 1966, and The Crusaders were growing up right in the middle of it.

Along with the music, the books, the fashion, the radical philosophy and the sexual politics, there were the drugs we had heard about. Pot mostly. We had already tried beer and liquor, not really being drugs in the true sense, and found them to be no big deal. If you drank too much, you upchucked holding the porcelain goddess and got over it. But pot was different. It was illegal – although so was drinking under age... but the authorities often seemed to overlook that particular transgression. Pot, on the other hand, was considered hand-in-hand with hard drug addicts. That was hammered home by the screening of the film *Reefer Madness* in the junior high school's cafeteria one day. It was horrible. Skinny drug addicts were shooting up heroin. Kids in catatonic states from smoking the "evil weed" were shown getting in accidents, screwing up their lives, and finally getting arrested.

The movie scared the crap out of me. It painted the picture of dope-heads as shiftless, clueless idiots, or the equivalent of trailer trash gone bad. I wanted no part of it.

And yet.

Here was Dave telling us it was no big deal. Everyone was doing it. Completely harmless.

Kenny and I looked at each other, and really more for the fear of looking like pussies in front of Kenny's older brother rather than a keen desire to actually try the stuff, we bought a half lid of pot. We hid it in the little playhouse behind my house.

"Guess what we have?" Kenny said to Stanley, smoking in the field next to the convalescent hospital.

"Who the fuck knows?" he replied.

"Pot. We bought it from my brother."

"No shit," Paul said. "That's pretty heavy."

Stanley blew some smoke rings "We gonna try it?"

"It's in the playhouse," I said.

"We'll need some papers," Paul said. Off my look. "To roll a joint in, man."

So we beat it up to the music store, which carried Zig-Zag papers below the counter in the glass case, and bought a premium black package. We didn't really discuss whether we were going to try it, or what the consequences might be, or if it was addictive, or whether or not it would lead to us losing our minds. Those weren't even issues, and we didn't really care.

We were focused on getting the papers, figuring out how to roll it, and then just trying it.

We returned to the playhouse in my backyard and pulled out the half lid. My parents weren't home, and my brother and sisters were out playing somewhere. When I unrolled the baggie and looked at it, Paul commented.

"Dude, that looks mighty skimpy to me."

I looked at it and frowned. "I don't know. Dave said it was the good stuff."

"Looks like stems and seeds to me," Stanley said.

"Supposed to be the best part of the plant," Kenny interjected. "Dave said that's where everything sort of... concentrates."

Paul laughed. "No shit?"

"Let's get on with it," I suggested.

We pulled out the packet and extracted two papers, turning one around, licking it, and then attaching the two together. This much we had seen Dave do many times in his backyard. The bottom half of the baggie was half an inch thick with seeds. The twisted vines that resembled grape stems when they were all plucked took up most of the room. We 'v' shaped the paper and poured in the seeds, and added a flat part of the stem.

Careful manipulation of the paper finally resulted in a joint. Stanley licked the paper and sealed it. *Cool, our first joint.* Paul pulled out some matches. Kenny wanted to be the first, since it was his brother who had sold it to us. Not sure why that gave him priority, but he thought it did. We acquiesced.

He put the joint between his smiling lips. Paul lit the match and held it in front. Kenny took two large inhales and then BOOM -- a huge explosion. Burning seeds flew everywhere. We were jumping out of the way, slapping at them and trying to get the little red projectiles off our clothes, swearing at the same time.

"What the fuck happened?" I screamed. Looking around I saw wisps of smoke everywhere, including over all of my sister's Barbie dolls.

"I don't know," Kenny said. "Maybe we did something wrong?"

Paul was shaking his head. "How could we do something wrong? All we did was light the damn thing."

"Maybe you inhaled too hard, Kenny," I suggested. "Maybe we have to have it lit a little while before we really take a hit."

Kenny let out a big exhale and grimaced. "Okay, let's try again. But I tell you what, that hit sure burned my throat."

We went through the same machinations as before. Papers licked together. Seeds poured into them. A little branch laid carefully on top. Rolling it all up and licking it closed. Paul said he knew what we were supposed to do, so he elected himself to try and get it right in round two.

He handed the matches to me. Striking one, I held it in front of the joint, although this time I leaned back. Paul carefully took only shallow breaths to get it going.

Boom!

Seeds flew everywhere, smoking like fireworks after they flashed and started falling. They landed all over us.

"Shit," Stanley yelled. "You guys got burned, man. This isn't pot."

"Dave told us it was," I said.

"He must have been screwin' with you," Paul said, slapping at and extinguishing little smoke fires around him.

A collective sigh went out. "Now what do we do?"

Back to the dealer.

Dave was laughing. "You guys got burned."

"What the fuck does that mean, we got burned?" Paul asked.

"Stupid fucks. You deserve it. You don't buy stems and seeds. What kind of idiots are you?"

"But you told us it was the best part," I said.

"That's because you dick-heads don't know shit. You should have known you were being burned and not bought it."

"How would we know, Dave?," I said. "We want our money back."

Kenny was there, but he didn't say anything. He probably would have got his ass kicked later in the house if he spoke up.

Dave chuckled, licking his upper lip. "There's no refund on pot, man. What do you think this is, Woolworth's or something? You bought the shit. You got burned. You move the fuck on."

We didn't like it. But it was Kenny's brother, and he was a lot bigger than us, and in the end he was right. We didn't know what we were doing, or even what pot was *supposed* to look like. So now that we were committed to smoking it, we had to find some. It took a week. Finally George C from Torch Junior High sold us a three-finger lid, and we all proceeded to smoke it and get high.

There was no outward conscious realization of it. No discussions ensued about it. No debates. No resolves. But the fact was, we had crossed a line. An imaginary line put in place by those in power and wanting to keep us -- us being the future hippies and questioners of authority -- from crossing that line. But a line, nonetheless. Why didn't they want us smoking pot? We had no idea. Our first experiences getting high were fun. Hilarious, actually. But they did want to keep us away from it.

Alcohol? That was perfectly okay.

But alcohol really didn't suit us. We had to stand near the front door of the liquor store on Amar Road, and ask people to score it for us. That usually wasn't a problem, but it was a pain in the ass, and many were the times we were refused by some do-gooder who lectured us on the evils of drinking. Surprisingly, they were usually buying alcohol.

One time, when we asked this woman to buy it for us, she asked if Kenny was Kenny R.? Why? Because she worked with his mom at Mattel, she told us. *Holy shit, Kenny was in trouble now*. She told us to scoot and she wouldn't tell. We obliged.

With pot, all we had to do was buy a lid (three fingers or more of leaves and buds only, no seeds, we finally learned), and then smoke it when we liked. Clean, easy, no problems. We didn't smoke it all the time. Usually in the evenings, and usually just before we went to Dairy Delight or In-N-Out for some food. It seemed to make things taste better.

Everything seemed lighter and funnier.

That week we entered into the world of pot.

Not drugs.

Just pot.

We justified it that way, and in the process proved to ourselves that the *Reefer Madness* movie was just some fiction put out by "the man," whoever the fuck he was.

A lot more changed that week.

Suddenly, going to band practice and playing surf songs didn't seem so cool anymore. Actually, being "just" a surfer began to pale. The innocence of stealing Coke bottles, getting chased by bigger guys, riding Stingray bikes and eating at In-N-Out, skateboarding to each other's houses, and a myriad of other formerly fun things to do was eclipsed; by a constantly growing awareness in the background of news of the world and the introduction of a crazy new psychedelic form of music. Of being hip instead of cool. Of being stoned instead of straight. Of listening to groups like Led Zeppelin, David Bowie, and Pink Floyd. Our consciousness started expanding to include, and then start arguing about ideas that we'd never entertained before. Weird shit.

What was this hippie thing all about? What did this new music mean? Who was President Johnson, and what was this talk of a war somewhere? What are they talking about with this peace and love shit? What the hell was meditation?

We didn't change right away. But the die was cast, and there was no turning back. The Crusaders were now surfers, *potential* hippies, and potheads.

Seemed like nothing could really go wrong.

After all, it was only pot.

The Crusaders
Part Two

1967-1969

"All you need is love, love...
love is all you need."

Lake Gregory

1967

Lake Gregory is a quaint little village nestled high atop the Big Bear Mountains about fifty miles from La Puente. Every year my parents would take us there for the last three weeks of summer vacation, ending on Labor Day weekend. We would all pile in the station wagon at five a.m. and make the four-hour drive East on Interstate 10 and then up the mountain on Highway 18.

The first thing I'd notice when we arrived in Lake Gregory was the scent of pine sap that permeated the air. It was intoxicating and immediately let me know I'd left the 'burbs' and was on vacation.

Our wooden cabin was a small two bedroom tucked within a forest of towering pine trees. The size of the cabin also gave it a sort of intimacy; the family had to get along. We had no choice. However, it was never a problem - we all loved it there and made a special effort not to get in each other's face.

The lake itself seemed huge to me. There were beaches on both sides of the west end covered in sand. A couple of large platforms floated in the middle of the water. No motorized boats were allowed. If you wanted to fish, you had to row. The water was fresh, cool and clear.

The town was small and a one-street affair with businesses on both sides of the street. The main attractions for us as kids were the penny arcade and roller rink on one side, and the putt-

putt miniature golf on the other. Tourist shops, a couple of restaurants and real estate offices filled in the gaps.

Skee-ball became our game of choice in the arcade, and we played it for hours. Every time you'd get above a certain score, tickets would pop out of the machine. Get enough of them and you could exchange them for all sorts of prizes. It was addicting and loads of fun.

At the corner of our street on the way to the lake's entrance was an A&W root beer stand. Frosty mug root beer became a daily staple in our noontime diets, and every once in a while we were able to buy a hamburger and fries. A&W root beer burps taste different -- much better than regular burps, especially at 5000 feet above sea level. Patrick and I were constantly trying to see who could elicit the largest eruption.

The whole family went to the lake every day. We staked out a small area and laid our bamboo mats and towels down to mark it. Tanning oil would quickly follow and then it was a day of swimming, sunning, and seeing how much energy we could expend without passing out. In short, we were having a ball and loved every minute of it.

When I saw her strolling in the sand along the water's edge, my conversation with my dad stopped, mid-sentence.

And although hard to understand or even explain, I fell in love with her.

In the time it took to catch a breath, experience a heartbeat, entertain a thought; I was captivated. Long, straight, dark-auburn hair a little past her shoulders. Slightly tanned skin. Deep green eyes, framed by light brown eyebrows. And full red lips, slightly parted into a smile. She was thin, wearing a light-blue bikini, which left nothing to my imagination. She looked over in my direction and her eyes seemed to lock onto mine for a split second, and then the stare was gone. My dad finally broke my concentration and brought me back to my normal senses.

Although I continued speaking with him, my attention was still on her as she walked all the way around the end of the lake to the beach on the other side, and sat down with people, I assumed, were her family. She was without a doubt the most beautiful girl I had ever seen, even forgetting about the bikini.

And she had looked at me.

The next day I rushed to the lake when it opened, and sat there all day, hoping to see her again. Even the lure of an A&W root beer float offered by my parents at lunch couldn't budge me. She didn't show.

That evening, Wednesday, was dance night at the skating rink. You'd rent roller skates, and then skate around in a large circle while music played. Debby, Kathy, Patrick, and I always went to the rink on those nights. Cost about twenty-five cents for the evening.

Satisfaction by the Rolling Stones came out of the speakers. Everyone pushed off and started the trek around the track. For some reason we all went right. Maybe it was a rule?

As I was skating I saw her arrive, and promptly fell over and hit the cement floor. Skaters veered left and right around me. Awkwardly, I got up and moved to the side rail. She went to the window and rented a pair of skates. A tank top and tight-fitting jeans complemented her dark-auburn hair. While she put on the skates the next song started and she merged into the hordes of people skating. I waited until she zoomed past me and pulled in behind her. I wanted to get next to her, but I was scared. Why? I have no idea. I would get close, start to close in and pull back. Maybe it was a fear of being rejected? Maybe I could live on a fantasy from just that one look at me on the beach? Maybe it was some attraction to unrequited love?

I was absorbed in these daydreams of mine when I suddenly noticed I *was* next to her. She looked over and smiled. *Oh my God. She smiled at me.* I managed to smile back and made it a point to skate next to her. After the song was over she pulled over to the side rail and rested. I continued going around and then stopped next to her.

My heart was beating so loud I was sure she could hear it. I started to speak and then stopped. Finally, unable to stand it anymore, I spoke: "Hi there." That was it. All I could say.

"Hi," she replied.

Now what?

"My name's... John."

"Pleased to meet you, John." She held out her hand to shake. "My name is Mary."

I returned the shake

"Would you like to skate together?"

"I think that would be fine," she said.

Wow. We entered the crowd circling the rink and started skating around. I found myself chit-chatting about everything and anything over the music. Mary chit-chatted back. What we spoke about I have no idea. Before I knew it, the skating was over, and it was time to go home.

I said goodbye to Mary, and mentioned that maybe I would see her at the lake. My brother and sisters were anxious to get home, so we left. All I thought about was Mary during the walk home, and the couple of hours it took me tossing and turning to fall asleep. What would happen at the lake? Would she still want to speak with me? What if I don't see her?

Sitting on the beach in my swimsuit, I was constantly scanning for any sign of Mary. I had already rubbed my daily dose of Coppertone all over my body. The tan was burning in nicely. Combed my hair a dozen times and rubbed in an extra dose of Brylcreem. In a word, I was ready.

Two hours later I saw Mary and her family walking onto the beach on the other side of the lake. I jumped up, ran to the water's edge, and started walking around the end of the lake toward her. By the time I got in front of her, they were settled and rubbing on tanning oil. Mary noticed me and waved me over. She introduced me to her parents, who were nice as could be. I asked if she wanted to go swimming, and she stood up and raced me to the water.

We swam for an hour or so; to the floating docks, back again to the beach, and then to the other side of the lake. Getting out we sat on the sand to let the warmth of the sun help dry us. Chatting away. I kept her laughing with my stories, and she told me about her family, where they lived in San Bernardino, and that they came up to Lake Gregory every year. I suggested we walk back to her side of the lake. And then it happened.

Walking side by side, she reached over and grabbed my hand. *Did she really do that? Oh my God. Am I grabbing her hand too hard?* I looked over at her. She smiled. I stared into her deep green eyes, and I swear I was more in love than I could imagine. We continued walking along the water, hand in hand, and I kept wishing the shoreline was longer. Once we got to where her little brother was, she sat down and motioned for me to join her, which I gladly did.

Engaged in conversation with her parents and Mary, I barely noticed that it was almost time for the lake to close. Her mom looked at Mary and said:

"John, are you going to the dance this weekend at the San Moritz Country Club?"

I looked at Mary and then down at the sand. "We're not members of the Country Club."

Mary tapped me on the arm. "Silly, you don't need to be a member to go to the dances."

"Really?"

She shook her head and laughed. "So are you going to meet me there?"

"Of course I will."

They rose and started packing their beach towels.

"Good," Mary said. "I'll be there around 6:30." She winked.

I winked back. "So will I."

We said our goodbyes, and walking back to the other side of the lake I reviewed the day. I couldn't believe how easy it was to be with her. How I never felt uncomfortable. How we finished each other's sentences. How she liked to play in the water. How every time I looked at her I felt so lucky. She was beautiful, smart, and fun.

And... just maybe, she was my girlfriend. A true girlfriend in every way. Whatever that meant.

She and the family didn't come back to the lake before the dance, and I had no way to get hold of her - forgot to ask for a phone number, although most of the cabins didn't have phones anyway.

My parents were excited about my going. They had been to a dance there a few years before and said the country club was beautiful, although their musical entertainment had been a large orchestra. They played my dad's favorite music - big band sounds like Glenn Miller, Jimmy Dorsey and Les Brown.

I had heard that the group playing was a local rock-n-roll band from San Bernardino.

The Crusaders

Getting ready for the dance I nervously combed and re-combed my hair for what seemed like an hour, although it was more like ten minutes. An eternity to me. I did not have my best jacket -- we were on vacation and I had no expectation of needing it -- but a nice light-blue shirt, khaki-colored pants. My dad loaned me a sports jacket. Polished brown shoes rounded out the look.

Dropped off at the San Moritz Country Club by my parents, I entered the lobby and was directed to the dance hall. It was about the size of half a basketball court with an elevated wooden stage at one end. The band was set up and tuning. I looked around. No Mary.

Got a Coke and walked out to look over the lake. It was near sunset, and the sun's rays were spiking through the trees, gently lighting up the deep blue water. I was nervous as hell.

"John?"

I turned around and stared. She wore a light-blue dress, just above her knees. The neckline was low, with a pearl necklace. Hair straightened and clean, deep green eyes that blinked rapidly, a slight smile baring her pearlescent teeth framed in red lipstick. She stood awkwardly; shoulders slightly slumped, staring at me as if waiting for a verdict, which I quickly spat out.

"You look beautiful."

Her smile widened, and she laughed. She stood up straight and walked toward me, hand extended. I took it and gave her a hug. I smelled her hair. It was fresh, with a slight scent of baby shampoo. A tasteful amount of perfume was mixed in for good measure.

We walked back into the main ballroom. The band started playing, and we danced. And danced. Looking into and away from each other's eyes. Furtive glances going back and forth.

Neither of us aware of the dozens of other kids who shared the dance floor with us.

The band played for an hour and then took a break. I suggested we walk outside near the lake. She agreed. We strolled over the bridge and to the lake's edge, under a gibbous moon that started to peek out above the pine trees. It was warm, and the smell of fresh mountain air mixed with pine was intoxicating.

Holding hands, we walked and talked about everything. And nothing. I simply wanted to hear her voice. Soft, entrancing, sexy. And, I was afraid of silence. Not sure why. Maybe the magic of the night would go away if we stopped speaking to each other. Maybe I was afraid of being alone with her, not knowing what to do.

We reached the end of the trail and turned back, and found ourselves facing each other. She grabbed my other hand and stared into my eyes.

"Do you like me, John?"

"Of course I do."

She smiled and continued to hold my gaze with hers. I found myself leaning closer, and she closed her eyes, lifting her lips toward mine. I gently touched them with mine and held them there. Butterflies flapping within my belly. Feelings erupting and racing through my body that I had never known. I kept my eyes open. A few moments later I pulled back, and she opened her eyes, a dreamy look glossing over them.

"Can we do that again?" I asked.

She nodded. I kissed her again and pulled her closer, her breasts pressing against my body. This time I closed my eyes. The butterflies calmed down. But the other feelings grew in intensity. We kissed for several minutes, and heard the band start up again. She pulled back slightly and leaned against my arms around her.

"I leave tomorrow. Back home."

"I'm staying through Labor Day," I smiled.

"My parents will be here at ten to pick me up. But I don't want to go."

My heart raced as she spoke the words. I didn't want her to go either.

"I'll write you every day," I blurted out.

She grinned and giggled, wrinkling her nose. "That will be a lot of writing."

"I mean it, Mary. I... I..."

I chickened out, is what I did. What I wanted to say was that I loved her. That I adored her. That she was the most important thing in my life. That my evening with her was the most romantic thing that had ever happened to me.

"I really like you Mary. I don't want the evening to end."

"Well then, Mister D.," she pulled away and bowed, sweeping her hand palm up. "Let's get back and dance away. Maybe it will never end."

I took her hand. We hurriedly made our way to the bridge. Almost over it, she stopped and swung me around.

"I think I love you, John.' Small tears formed around the outside of her eyes. "I don't want to leave tomorrow."

"Me either."

I leaned in and kissed her again. This time was different. We merged our bodies closely together. Our lips seemed as one. Moving in synchronistic circular motions that were effortless. My heart pounded in my head. I was afraid, and in love, at the same time. We danced for another hour and her parents arrived a little early. She took me over to where they stood, and we chit-chatted a little while longer. However, all the time I was thinking of our kisses and how beautiful Mary looked. And how I already missed her.

We walked out to the car. I said goodnight. She borrowed some paper from her mom and wrote down her address.

"You'll write me?" She handed me the paper.

"Of course I will."

"Promise?"

"Promise."

She leaned over and kissed me on the cheek, jumped into the car and waved goodbye as they pulled away and disappeared into the night. My parents were due in another ten minutes. I found a chair and sat down. I was in love. With a girl who lived forty miles from me. No way to see her unless my parents took me. I was barely fifteen. When would I see her again? What if I didn't see her again?

The thought terrified me. Of course, I would. I just knew it.

Little Brother Patrick arrived with my dad. I slid into the car's back seat and leaned into the tan vinyl naugahyde that covered it.

"How'd it go, Johnny?" Dad asked.

I shrugged. "It was okay."

"Did you get to see that girl friend of yours?"

"She left a little while ago."

Patrick turned around in the seat and sneered. "Did you kiss her?" it was more of a taunt than a question.

"None of your business, beaver."

"Yuck... you kissed her," he spat out.

I lightly slapped him on the side of his head. "Shut up."

"Knock it off you two," Dad ordered.

I leaned back into the seat.

I did kiss her, you little twerp. Closing my eyes, I tried to remember the feelings, the scents, the moon in the background, the softness of her hair. The taste of her lips. They were still fresh in my mind. I hoped they would not fade with time.

As we drove to the cabin, feelings of loss started to overwhelm my thoughts. I sat up straight in the seat and clenched my fists. A mild form of panic swept over me.

I got religion.

And prayed I would see her again.

Crusader 'mobile'

Fall, 1967

"What do you think of it?"

"I think it is one of the most beautiful cars I've ever seen, Paul," I said, studying its sleek lines.

"Where'd you get it?" Stanley asked.

"From my dad. He paid a hundred and twenty-five bucks for it."

"Really?"

"Yeah. We made a deal that if I got into Roland Heights High School he'd get me a car."

"What year is it?" I asked.

"It's a '55 Mercury," Kenny cut in. "Look at that bumper. It must weigh a couple hundred pounds all by itself."

It did look like it weighed a lot. Paul had driven over to Stanley's house in his new car – new for him, anyway. A light-blue dual-toned Mercury Monterey two-door hardtop, it seemed to be in pretty good shape. Beautiful lines of rust-free chrome graced the sides. We gawked and aahed over it while Paul beamed as if he held four aces in a high-stakes poker game, and I couldn't blame him. It was gorgeous.

Lifting the hood, Kenny looked in. "It's got a 292 V8 super-torque Y block engine, single carb – could be a Holly four-barrel. This really is a bitchin' car Paul." He slammed the hood. "Let's go for a ride."

We opened the doors, pushed the bench front seat down and piled in, front and rear -- Paul, Kenny, Stanley, and me. It was a beautiful fall day in the San Gabriel Valley. One of those crisp clear days where the cool air filled your lungs, and you could taste the orange blossoms in the background. Paul started the "Merc" up, put it in drive and peeled out, leaving black rubber tattoos on the ground. After the initial run-up of RPM's, the soft purr of the engine's horses kicked in.

With the windows rolled down, the breezes rushed through our hair. We landed on Puente Avenue, where Paul could open the engine up a little. Leaving some scratch as we merged, Paul pushed it to over sixty, and it was smooth... like gliding above the ground on air. The AM radio blasted out some Beach Boys and then *Wooly Bully* by Sam the Sham and the Pharaohs as we hauled ass down to Francisquito, slowed down and made a skidding right turn toward Hacienda Boulevard. An hour later we ended up back at Stanley's.

"So what will we call it?" I asked, lighting a smoke and clicking the lighter closed.

"What do you mean?" Stanley packed his Marlboros box solidly against his palm.

"The car."

Paul looked doubtful. "You mean name the car?"

"Yeah." I nodded for emphasis. "Don't people do that?"

"That is so queer," Stanley laughed. "Crusaders don't name their cars."

"Where is that rule written?" Kenny asked.

"On my fist," Stanley chuckled, shadowboxing with himself.

"Hey guys," Paul broke in. "We're not naming the car, okay?"

A collective okay followed. Then silence while we smoked and thought about what to do next.

Kenny finally pointed, "Look at how the front bumper is shaped like a B-movie bra."

I laughed. "Like Cadillac bumper tits."

"Yeah. I bet they could do some serious damage if we hit anything with it." Stanley added.

"Let's hope we don't." Paul said. "I'd probably lose the car for a month."

That '55 Merc changed our lives in a number of ways; some foreseen, others unintended. One of the first things was that everywhere we wanted to go, we drove. That cut down tremendously on our walking time, and the opportunities that being on the street presented us. The biggest casualty was the loss of income from pop bottles. But whenever we were together, we were in the Merc and cruising around, thinking we were the coolest dudes ever - the bee's knees.

We could go to concerts without our parents taking us, which had become a bummer because before we had to have them drop us off a block away from the venue lest anyone see them do it. Dating suddenly seemed like a real possibility. Drive-in movies. Getting somewhere like Bob's Big Boy in West Covina in a few minutes rather than the hour it took us to walk or skateboard there. Even scoring drugs would be easier.

A few days later we were at Kim's house on Donaldale, low on gas and hanging out in front of his garage because his dad wasn't there. Although we knew his mother was in the house, she never, ever came out. In fact, I'm not sure any of us saw her even once – even on Halloween when we went up to the door to get candy. Anyway, cigarettes in hand and too much time to kill birthed a new idea.

"Hey Paul," Kenny said, pointing, smoking a cigarette held between two fingers. "I was wondering... Don't you think this Merc would look really cool if we primered it?"

Incredulous, Paul answered, "What?"

"Yeah, you know, like those low riders the beaners are driving around. This light-blue and white color has pussy written all over it."

"That's a bitchin' idea," Stanley added. "We would look so cool in a primered car."

"Whoa," Paul raised his hand like a stop sign. "My dad would kill me if we did that."

"What are you talking about?" I asked. "It's your car, right?"

"Yeah, I guess."

"Then why would he get mad if we painted it?" Kenny asked.

Paul ran his tongue over his upper lip, brows furrowed. "I'm not sure... But knowing him I can pretty much guarantee he would."

"Well, if we primer it and it looks cool," Stanley said. "Then, he won't get mad... because... it will look . . ." he raised his hands and shoulders, "cool."

"But the paint is fine now."

I blew out some smoke rings. "That's not the point, Paul. The point is, if we primer it... then it will look like a *cooler* car, and when we cruise around, kids will say 'look at those dudes in that cool primered car.'"

"And so will the chicks," Stanley winked.

"We can go to Guy's dad's store and get the primer," Kim said.

"And some tape," Kenny added. "We want to tape off all the chrome."

"Can't you picture how bitchin' this car will look primered gray? Un-fuckin'-believable, dudes," I said.

"I don't know," Paul said, still not buying into the whole idea.

Stanley got up and motioned. "Come on, let's drive it to the hardware store and see what they have. I don't know if it should be light or dark gray."

"I like the dark color," I said, throwing down my smoke and toeing it out.

"I like light," Kenny said.

"I like light gray too," Paul finally admitted.

"Great," we replied, "let's go get the paint."

During the next few days we bought the paint (and stole a few cans too), found some masking tape in my parents' garage, and then planned the day it would be painted.

We started early one "bluebird" morning - you could see for miles, not a cloud in the sky. For a couple of hours we carefully taped the chrome off, and then started popping the light gray spray can tops and let them rip. We took turns painting, and by the time we finished the spraying, the car looked, well, bitchin'. I mean really bitchin'. We pulled the tape off (which took a while – there was a lot of chrome), and then stood back to observe. Even Paul was smiling at the result. A cool 1955 Mercury Montero with a new, light-gray primer paint job.

The Crusadermobile.

But it needed something else. We looked at each other simultaneously, deep in thought, scratching chins, perplexed. Then light bulbs went off. What the car needed was a really cool rake – the opposite of a lowering job the cholos did to their cars by heating and lowering the front and rear springs.

That presented a real challenge. Normally you would put spacers in between the rear springs so the car sat higher in the rear. But those cost money. And we were seriously short of funds after the paint job. We thought about it, discussed it and finally came up with an alternate plan.

Back to Guy's dad's hardware store.

That time we "purchased" two pieces of four-by-four-inch wood, and cut it by hand to about twelve inches. Then we put a slight "v" on the top of each wooden piece, so it would seat itself on top of the rear axle on one end and lay up flat against the frame on the other.

The next problem was how to get them in place. A car jack and lots of manual labor solved that. Paul started jacking, and when the frame was high enough in the rear above the axle, we set the piece of wood in place and lowered it -- one click at a time. Then we went to the other side and repeated the process. After lowering that side, we stood back and stared in awe. It was certainly on a rake then.

And, it was beyond cool. It was our first car. Like a first girlfriend you never forget. The smells of rich leather interior seats, the pungent odor of a slight oil leak, the visual lines of the sweeping hood, rounded fenders and gaudy reflective chrome bumpers. The almost sensual feeling of gently brushing your hand against the side chrome molding, front to rear. With the new rake and primer, it defined who we were – a group of self-absorbed, dopey guys who cherished having fun, getting drunk and loaded, surfing whenever we could, playing music in our garage band and generally goofing off while never really taking anything quite too seriously. Except our friendship.

And we finally had the perfect car to reflect those noble qualities.

However, when Paul drove the car home that evening, his dad went frickin' ballistic at our latest work of art. He grounded Paul, took the car away from him for a couple of weeks, and only let him use it to go back and forth to school.

Bummer.

Walking again.

At least for a while.

Sandy

"Who are we going to see?"

"I told you," Stanley said. "I met this girl named Sandy 'Wulf' something or other. She is really cool. Her mom is gone at work a lot, so we can hang out there."

Paul, Stanley, and I walked over to her house, across Puente Avenue about three blocks. She went to Torch Junior High. Stanley knocked on the door and she answered. Stanley was not lying. She was beautiful. Long blond hair, tall, brown eyes, full smile. *How in the heck did Stanley meet her, let alone become her boyfriend?*

Turned out "boyfriend" was a little exaggeration on Stanley's part. She did like him, and us, and soon we Crusaders occupied her house at least a couple of times per week.

We'd smoke pot, listen to records, and stare at her two older sisters who were drop-dead gorgeous and always wore very revealing clothes. But the main reason was Sandy. She was cool, hip, funny, and like a sister to us. She was a girl we could bounce questions off. Totally honest responses. A female version of a Crusader.

She quickly grew tired of Stanley. But it was too late. We had all adopted each other as friends, and over the years cemented the bond through concerts, smoking pot, going on adventures, and hanging out just being ourselves.

Her mom worked every day, but even after getting home she grew to love us too.

And, it was a democracy. Any one of us could take Sandy somewhere, even if the others were not going.

In essence, the Crusaders first girl.

I did notice, however, she seemed to eye Paul more than the rest of us.

Pot, Vietnam I, Caper II

"**I**'ve been drafted."

The response was non-emotional and monotone from Stanley's older brother Paul when we asked where he was going.

"I'm be sent to Vietnam after basic training."

"Where's that?" we asked.

"Some place full of gooks, you stupid assholes," he dismissively replied.

We'd heard about a war going on somewhere, but it really wasn't on our radar. The television news would mention it, and President Johnson was always quoted as pleading that the United States needed more troops over there - wherever "there" was.

We were too busy getting loaded all the time to focus on it. Our pot adventures morphed very quickly into other drugs - reds, which were small oblong red capsules that were considered downers, and whites, small round white pills with a cross etched into the top, which were Benzedrine and passed for speed or uppers.

Mixing and matching, we weren't very discerning. They were inexpensive and plentiful: one dollar for four reds, and one dollar for ten whites - both wrapped in foil. Not quite sure why the price discrepancy between the two. But economics dictated that we'd lean toward the uppers.

Turned out that pot mixed with whites was a very enjoyable high. The main problem with smoking weed at the time was that it ended up putting us to sleep. After, of course, we'd scarfed up anything we could find to eat. Combining weed with uppers solved both problems. You had the perfect high with the attendant goofiness while staying awake and not being very hungry.

Later that week Kenny's big brother Dave came up to us while we were hanging out at my house and said that he had a proposition, flagging us over to where we were alone and no one could hear - we were in the street at the time and no one could hear anyway.

He motioned us closer and whispered *I Spy* -like.

"I just came back from Cal Poly Pomona where I met some buddies of mine. They told me about a guy who was working on creating a sort of super pot plant. Don't know what the fuck he was doing, but it sounded interesting. So we went and met the guy in the dorms there. Neat guy. Long hair. Studying rocket science or some shit like that. But he loved pot and considered himself an expert in horticulture and cross-pollination of plants."

Stanley, Paul, Kenny, and I were listening intently as he continued to spin the tale.

"So he finally agrees to take us up to the secret spot where he is growing the thing, but first we had to promise not to reveal the location and to agree to wear blindfolds."

"No shit?" Paul said.

"I shit you not, assholes. Anyway, we get to the edge of the hill there, and he hands me and my friend a blindfold. We put them on, only I can see out the bottom of it if I lift my head up so, like this."

He demonstrated the ingenious technique he used, walking around like Frankenstein, arms out.

"So we walked up the hill at the back of the college, through these trails and then about ten minutes later he says we can take the blindfold off, and there it was. A six-foot-high pot plant. Fuck, it looked like a fucking Christmas tree or something. He explained how he grafted this and that, but I wasn't really listening. There had to be ten lids on the thing. Then he said he'd had problems with rabbits eating it, and had fashioned a wire fence around the bottom of it."

"So what does this have to do with us?" I asked.

He leaned in closer and looked around before continuing, licking his upper lip and slightly squinting his eyes.

"I know where it is, the pot plant, I mean. I wrote it down on a map. I want you guys to go up there and pull off a lid or two - from the bottom... so it looks like the rabbits got the leaves. I think this is some super shit, and we could sell it for five bucks a joint."

"A joint?" Stanley asked.

"We went back to his dorm room and smoked a joint. It was un-fucking-believable, dudes."

"Why don't you go back and get the leaves yourself?" Paul astutely asked, since anytime Dave suggested something it was usually to our detriment.

"He knows me, man. If he sees me anywhere near that campus he'll know. You guys are virgins." He started laughing.

"Fuck you, Dave," Stanley responded.

He continued laughing. "Seriously guys, you'll have no trouble finding it. The secret is to only take leaves from the bottom, and we'll have a continuous supply of this super pot."

He gave us the map and explained where it was relative to the campus. We'd never been to Cal Poly Pomona before, but it was right over the hill on the 10 freeway, so we said we'd do it and left for the caper early the next morning. Paul was still the only one of us who had a car, so we took the Crusadermobile, the '55 Merc, and drove the fifteen miles to Cal Poly's campus.

Weaving through the campus streets for about fifteen minutes, we finally found what we thought was the starting point for our adventure - the hill that backed up to the school to the west and probably connected with Forest Lawn mortuary, which was to the northwest of us and bordered the 10 freeway.

Parking the car out of sight, we started our trek up the scrub and weed covered hills. It took us a little over half an hour to find the trail Dave mentioned. We walked up. It weaved and turned, and although not being trackers, we could see where other people had been there smashing the weeds as they followed the trail. *Probably Dave,* I thought, *leaving signs on how to get there*.

The trail ended after ten minutes, and we searched around until we found the trampled weeds and continued to follow them. Ahead of us there were taller bushes, and we snaked through them, finally reaching a small clearing.

There, in the middle of the clearing, was the pot plant.

Dave's description didn't begin to convey how beautiful it was. The leaves ranged in color from dark Kelly to light forest green. They gently fluttered in the slight breeze. The plant was actually taller than my six-foot height, and the canopy of little jagged leaves spread out at the bottom to over three feet wide. And there, like Dave had mentioned, was the little wire mesh fence at the bottom to keep the rabbits away.

"Holy shit," Paul said. "Dave wasn't bullshitting."

"Let's hurry up and get some leaves," I said, feeling a little bit like we were in a bank at night and stealing some money.

We pulled out the baggies we'd brought and knelt down to start plucking leaves from the bottom. When we'd filled them up, we stood back and looked.

"I think we could get some more without anybody noticing," Stanley suggested. We all agreed and went back to picking. Before long we were more than halfway up and the bottom branches looked like a sheared rat - bare as a bone.

"Now he'll know," Paul said. "And we won't get to come back."

"No shit," Kenny agreed. "Maybe we'd better just take all the leaves and then we won't have to come back again."

"Dave isn't going to like this," Paul said.

"Fuck him. What's he going to do, report us?" Stanley said, laughing.

"We really don't have much choice," I said. "The guy'll know it wasn't the damn rabbits and move the plant, and we'd be fucked anyway. Let's just finish it off and get out of here."

Before we left, we observed the plant standing there without a leaf on it, swaying in the wind as if it were cold. It looked sad and pathetically bare. What the fuck. We had six or seven bags of leaves and would soon be on our way back to La Puente to dry them out and see just how good they were.

We went to Kenny's house, since his mom worked at Mattel during the day, and his dad wasn't home either. We weren't exactly sure how to dry the leaves, so we turned the oven on low and put about half of them in, just in case we fucked up and had to do it again. Checking them every ten minutes, we were rewarded with semi-dry leaves in about an hour.

However, they had shrunk tremendously, and we had only about a lid's worth. Four big bags of fresh leaves down to one bag of dry pot. Dave's calculations were a bit off.

While Kenny rolled a joint, I peeled the cellophane off a new album I had just bought by the Rolling Stones - *Between the Buttons.* Placing it on the Motorola turntable, I swung the arm on top of it and turned the knob to play. The turntable started spinning, the record dropped, and the arm automatically moved over and laid down the diamond-tipped needle in the record's groove.

Kenny came out of the kitchen with a huge joint.

"What is that?" Paul asked.

"Super joint for super pot," he replied, smiling. "I used four papers to make it."

We sat around in the front room in a circle. Kenny lit it up, took a big hit, and passed it to his right. Paul took a hit, started coughing and laughing, and took another. *Ruby Tuesday* was just starting on the stereo as Paul passed it to me. After my hit, I passed it to Stanley.

That's all I remember.

When I came to, I heard the record needle skipping at the end of the album, over and over again. Groggily, I sat up and saw the other guys lying down on their backs, drooling and snoring.

That was some serious shit we smoked that day.

Too bad we couldn't get any more of it.

B ack to Vietnam.

Stanley's brother Paul shipped out and that was the last of it to that point as far as touching our lives.

However, I remember coming home one day and the TV looked like it was broadcasting from within a war zone. But it wasn't some foreign country. It was from a college campus. My dad was glued to the tube, watching intently and slowly sipping on his beer.

Dad was a staunch, dyed-in-the-wool Democrat. Hell, I was named after Woodrow Wilson. And if Kennedy spoke it, he believed it -- and defended it. When he was assassinated, it was quite a blow to him. I was only in fifth grade, but even I knew something was really wrong. The news was broadcast over the intercom system at Tonopah Elementary School. Our president, killed. I ran home after school, and found my dad was already there, looking pretty somber. I think I even saw some moisture in his eyes. He just stared at the black and white television reporting on it, saying nothing.

My dad went back into the living room and sat down, reading the LA Times. I could tell he was not happy about something, but unsure as to what.

About that time the marches against the war were in full bloom. Buffalo Springfield had come out the previous year with *For What It's Worth*, and it quickly became the rallying cry for those anti-war marchers. Again, I wasn't too interested. Neither were the other Crusaders, really. Only Stanley's brother had been drafted, we were well under eighteen years old, so it didn't affect us in a direct way. But we all discussed it for one very troubling indirect reason. In the news on TV and in the press, they associated hippies -- people with long hair, baggie old Levi's and tie-dyed t-shirts -- with the anti-war movement.

And that association started to create problems for us, since those items were now part of our official outfit too.

People started looking at me - us - differently. Calling us hippies - which normally would not bother us or present a problem. But these slurs were delivered in a more vicious and pejorative way. It's funny how people start looking at you differently. One week we are seen as surfers, in traditional surf garb, and people are smiling and waving when we pass. The next week we are seen wearing hippie outfits, our hair a little longer, and the attitudes spin 180 degrees away from the warm and fuzzy feelings of yesterday.

I'd read a book called *Black Like Me* by John Howard Griffin. It was about a privileged white man who black-faced himself and went into the deep south. The way he described people treating him was horrifying, and to tell the truth, I didn't really believe it, being from Southern California and having no frame of reference. But the overt acts and attitudes against us Crusaders once we became, through no effort of our own, part of the "them" and "us" blame game, led me and the other guys to start realizing that the world was changing from the innocence of peace and love... to something else. Maybe it had always been like that and we never noticed.

Some inner rage, hidden by the illusion of a harmonious middle-class life -- the Saturday afternoon BBQ's, the trick or treat nights, the Christmas/Hanukkah holidays, the parties, the new cars every couple of years, the prosperity of slowly getting ahead -- all of this and more, was becoming overshadowed by the eruption of an anger that made its way through the veneer of civility, and we "dirty hippies and pot heads" were bearing the brunt of it.

It didn't feel good, and it also didn't feel right or just.

We soon found out how deeply this resentment of middle America toward people "they" didn't understand was anchored - especially by the police.

Fast Food

What started out as a goofy prank for us ended up being a pretty steady activity for the Crusaders. Mainly because of smoking pot.

Months earlier, while walking down the street, we passed a double garage that had its swing-up door open. Peering inside, we saw a top-loading freezer sitting next to a refrigerator against the rear wall. No Coke bottles to be seen. Cautiously we walked in and looked around. Paul opened the refrigerator -- nothing but milk and stuff like that. Stanley unlatched the freezer door and lifted it. Inside were berry, peach, and apple pies, steaks, chicken, chicken pot pies... a veritable list of frozen goodies.

We decided to take a berry pie and two chicken pot pies. The reasoning among us boiled down to this: would they really miss it? Probably not. In fact, realistically, not at all. Who keeps that close of tabs on their freezer contents? If we were right, we would be able to come back again and again, as long as we didn't take too much to cause them to wonder what was happening.

Hurrying to my house, we loaded our spoils into the oven and waited. Forty-five minutes later we chowed down.

Delicious.

One major side effect of smoking pot was the voracious appetite for munchies that followed. It didn't take us long to connect the dots. Days were spent scouting the surrounding neighborhoods, observing the various refrigerators and freezers within the garages, and scoping when and how to get in and take out what we wanted.

Pies, biscuits with honey, cereals, cupcakes, chocolate drinks, cakes, Hostess products, most anything you could think of we found, brought back to one of our houses and satiated our pot-induced hungers. It was a wonder we remained as skinny as we did. I think our other activities compensated for that.

One time we were loaded, hungry, and in my house. Nothing to eat. It was a Thursday, and Friday was my mom's shopping day for food. The cupboards were bare. We finally found some tuna cat food in one of those small cans. *It was tuna, after all. Looked like a Starkist can - how bad could it be?*

We opened it, mixed it with mayonnaise, toasted some bread, made up the sandwiches and triumphantly took a bite. And promptly spat it out, looking at each other and breaking into a big laugh.

How bad could it be?

Pretty darn awful.

We called Paul and ended up driving the Crusadermobile to In-N-Out to try and repair the damage to our palates.

Drive-in Movie

"**W**hat was that?"

"How would I know... it's pitch black in here."

"Holy crap, Stanley. Did you just float an air biscuit?"

"Hell, no."

"I swear to God, Stanley... Jezuz... A taco fart."

I pounded the inside of the trunk with my fist. "Paul, let us out, quick."

"Shut up in there," his muted shout came back. "We're almost at the gate."

"Oh crap. I can't take it anymore."

"If you smelt it, you dealt it."

"I'll deal you a fat lip." We heard a loud sound. "Oh my God, another one."

"Stanley, I am going to kill you when we get out."

"*If* we get out. I think I'm gonna die."

"That will be $2.50," we heard the ticket person say to Paul. It took a long time for Paul to get the money to him. Like eternity in the back of that death chamber. We weren't moving.

"I think I'm gonna throw up," Billy whispered.

"Shut up. We'll get caught."

"I don't care. It's better than dying of taco farts in the trunk of a fucking car."

"One more, Stanley, and you are dead, dead, dead."

The car lurched toward the asphalt berms that flowed through the Vineland outdoor drive-in theater. It bounced over a few and came to a stop with the front angled higher than the back. We scrunched up together as we rolled toward the bumper. We heard the door open and slam shut. A key entered the lock and then twilight appeared, Paul staring down at us.

"Holy crap," he shouted, waving his hand in front of his nose. "What died in there?"

Like clowns exiting a car at the circus, the four of us scrambled out of the trunk and sucked in gallons of fresh, sweet air. Paul laughed hysterically.

I looked at Stanley, who was smirking and shaking his head.

"You think that was funny, asshole?" I asked.

"Yeah... I do."

Kenny tried to grab Stanley by his shirt collar. Stanley saw the move and ran away a few feet and stopped, laughing. "Gotcha guys." He put two fingers to his nose, Pepe le Pew style.

"Paul, next time we don't stop at Dairy Delight first and let him eat tacos," Billy said, still trying to clear the smell from his nose.

Paul's laughing died down as he got back in the car, slamming the door. "Come on guys," Paul motioned like a traffic cop. We got in. "Let's watch the movie."

"What's playing?" Kenny asked, jumping into the back seat.

"*Night of the Living Dead*," Paul answered. "Double feature with some other flick." I got in next to Kenny.

"Roadrunner cartoon?" I asked.

"Seems like it," Paul said.

"*Night of the Living Dead*," Billy repeated in a low voice. "Guess we shouldn't have taken that acid."

"It will be alright," I assured him. "It's all fake blood and stuff anyway."

"You going to cut the cheese anymore, Stanley?" Paul asked. "Cause if you are, you're not gettin' in the car."

"Naw, I'm done. Let's get some popcorn and Cokes."

"Deal," Kenny said.

That was a long evening.

The zombies looked pretty real to us, and the blood didn't look very fake either.

At least not on Purple Barrels of acid and some weed.

I felt squeamish for a week.

Laguna Beach

I peered out toward the ocean beyond the moonlit volcanic coral rock and noticed something lurking in the water. Cautiously, I stood up from our small fire and tried to focus on what it was. We were in Laguna Beach, off Cliff Drive, and I couldn't imagine what would be moving in the water. Even if it were a seal, which was quite common there, it would have been smaller.

It suddenly rose from the lapping surf, raised its arms and roared. Seaweed covered it while the arms waved in small circular motions. It walked toward us Frankenstein style – large stiff steps, and I admit, it scared me shitless. Stanley screamed something at it while I looked around for anything to fight it. Nothing near.

Kenny was on the other side of the cave throwing some sort of rocky sea shells toward it as it closed in on us.

We had dropped some "Orange Sunshine" about an hour earlier, and the speed in it, along with a judicious amount of LSD, had fully kicked in. Were we seeing things? Was this some sort of hallucination? A remembrance from some old B movie we'd seen as youngsters like *Creature from the Black Lagoon*? Whatever it was, it looked real to me. I was getting ready to haul ass out of there. Stanley and Billy were yelling at the thing at the top of their lungs. Things looked very bad.

Then… hysterical laughter echoed off the rocky cliffs.
What the fuck?

The creature turned in a stilted circle and fell on the sandy beach. Motionless as a rock.

Who the heck was laughing? Sounds like Paul to me. Then the creature sat up and started pulling the seaweed off his body and throwing it to the ground.

It *was* Paul. He got us. *Shit.* My heart was pounding, and I knew from the others' expressions that I was not alone.

"Paul, you asshole. Why the hell would you do that when we're all high?" Kenny screamed, frustration in his voice.

"I got you guys," he replied, laughing hysterically, shaking the rest of the seaweed off.

I shook my head. "That was totally uncool."

"Come on, you guys know it was funny," he finally spat out.

What could we say? It was funny. But we sure weren't going to let Paul know that. So we went back to sitting around the small fire and hanging out by the cave.

We could only get access to that part of the beach at low tide. The water inlet revealed enough coral so that we could walk on it to access a small sandy lagoon and cave. Offshore in the ocean in front of this area, standing as a lone sentinel, was bird-shit rock, as we nicknamed it. It was where all the seagulls hung out during the day, and judging from the "barks" we heard, it offered a resting point and home for seals at night.

That wasn't the first time we'd dropped acid. Especially Orange Sunshine. As for me, it really did open me and my consciousness up to different vistas and perspectives. But mostly, it was the trails - those swishing blurs of hands and fingers that happened when you were high - the funny thoughts, the way of connecting observations in different ways, that I enjoyed. And, of course, the buzz from the speed.

The Brotherhood produced that particular type of LSD out of Laguna, California - somewhere in the canyons. I guess they thought the name befitted a group of self-absorbed, drug-crazed dopers who made acid. I didn't get it. We went to the main house once, but I didn't pay much attention to where it was. What was unique about that particular LSD, as opposed to the Purple Barrels, was the amount of Benzedrine in the mix. Totally kept you awake and tripping.

So we sat around the fire and told tales, laughed, waved our hands around to see the trails they left in the atmosphere, and generally were having a bitchin' time. Then we noticed an old guy (probably younger than I am now) walking along the beach from the other side, ambling toward us with a huge walking stick (sort of like what Charlton Heston used as Moses), and then he sat down in front of the cave.

Curious, we all rose and walked over to him.

He raised two fingers in a 'v' shape. "Peace, brothers."

"Peace man," I answered. "What's your trip?"

"Life, man, life."

"You trippin'?"

"Yeah man. It's really cool."

He lit up a cigarette and motioned for us to sit down.

"Hey man, I got some heavy shit to tell you dudes," he started. "Been lookin' back at my past lives."

"Yeah?" we collectively answered.

He nodded. "Socrates, man. That's who I was. See it clearly man... through the haze." He gestured by sweeping his arm.

"No shit?" I said. Tilting my head and raising an eyebrow. "How come, when you have a past life, it's always someone famous? How come you don't come back as Joe Blow the camel jockey?"

"Don't know man. Who chooses who they are? I just know what I know, man."

"Well, I've got to let you know, man... you must be the third or fourth person I've met who was Socrates."

"No shit?"

I shook my head. He looked around at each of us, smiling. He had a peace sign handkerchief tied around his head, wild bushy caterpillar eyebrows, dark piercing eyes, and a full brown beard. A Cheshire cat smile with big white teeth was his most prominent feature.

"Want to ask me anything?"

We Crusaders looked at each other, shrugging our shoulders.

"Not really," Stanley answered. "What would we ask?"

"Life, man. What is it all about?"

Paul squinted "You know?"

He pointed toward his head. "For sure, man. It's all right here."

"So what is it all about?" I asked.

"Love, man. It's about love, and brotherhood, and getting along."

We sat silent, waiting for more.

"Didn't you say you were Socrates?" Kenny finally asked.

"Yeah, man."

"Then what about Socratic thinking, you know, like the guy mentions in *Zen and the Art of Motorcycle Maintenance*?"

"It's all about love, my brothers. All else is cosmic noise."

We looked at each other, dumbfounded. The guy sounded like a bad version of Donovan at a peace rally.

Kenny winked at us. "So no *this* or *that*, versus *this* and *that*? No cosmic observations about the universe and how it works?"

Deer-in-headlight eyes stared up at us.

"Yeah. Well, we've got to be going now," I said, standing up. "Tide's coming in and we need to get over to our car."

The guy raised his hand again with two fingers extended. "Peace, man."

"Yeah, yeah," we replied as we left.

His smile followed us as we made our way to the beginning of the coral reefs, which were faced by cliffs that rose a hundred feet. The tide had come in. Waves were breaking against the cliffs. We could see the cold black ocean running over the coral, curling back in angry white foam. Waiting for short lulls, we had to time our climbing to get through them, scrambling over the coral rocks. A difficult feat if we'd had all of our senses. We didn't. We were still trippin' on acid. All of us got wet.

"Whoa, what the heck was that all about back there?" Stanley finally asked as we walked up the sloping walkway that lead to Cliff Drive.

"Who knows," I answered. "Looked like some crazed serial killer. We've got bigger problems. Look at the fog coming in."

Within minutes we were surrounded. Thick Laguna Beach fog. Paul was the only one who had a license. We had borrowed my dad's car, a '61 Lancer station wagon, to drive down there. Now we had to drive back.

We piled into the light-blue wagon and started up Coast Highway. Slowly. We found Highway 133 in the fog only because of the theater we'd just passed, knowing it was the next light. Turning right, we passed downtown and headed north. Although it seemed impossible, the fog grew thicker and colder. *What the heck?* We were stoned out of our minds, and watching our hands against the bright lights of the car against the fog. And Paul couldn't see one foot beyond the hood of the car.

We stopped in the middle of the road.

"What are we going to do?" Stanley asked. "I can't see a damn thing."

"You don't need to, Stanley, I'm the one driving," Paul said.

"We can't just stop in the middle of the highway."

"Got an idea," Paul said.

He opened the driver's door and stuck his head out so he could see the middle line while driving down Laguna Canyon Highway. At less than five miles an hour.

"You're crazy, Paul," I said. "We're gonna get killed."

"I can see the stripes here. All I've got to do is follow them, and we'll be home."

"Or in a ditch if they stop," Kenny said.

We all let out a collective sigh. "Shit."

All I could think of is what would happen if a truck came the other way and slammed into the door. Fortunately, there were no other drivers on the canyon road dumb enough to be driving in that fog. We finally cleared the fog after about fifteen minutes of dead silence. Our highs were quite low by the time we reached the Santa Ana Freeway. The fog ended there.

About five miles north we stopped and got some tacos from Jack-in-the-Box, which were only twenty-five cents each - well within our budget, after gas money.

"What do you think are in these things, anyway?" Paul asked, munching on one of the dark-brown deep-fried tortillas that dripped with some sort of red sauce. "Doesn't taste like anything I recognize."

"No idea," I answered, chomping down on my second one. "But there must be some kind of meat in them... although I have no clue what kind."

"Maybe it's chicken?" Kenny suggested.

"Best not to ponder too much," Paul mumbled as he slurped some more of his tacos out of their wax paper envelopes.

Stanley decided to look in his and made a gurgling sound. "Don't look, dudes. You won't want to eat them." He tossed his two tacos out the window.

I was hungry, didn't look and finished my third one.

Paul laughed, threw the Dodge Lancer into first gear, and headed to the on-ramp toward La Puente.

We cruised home.

Still wondering why that guy hadn't been the reincarnation of some lowly Russian peasant.

Initiation II

"You sure about this?" Paul S. asked.

"Of course," Paul said, looking at Sandy and winking. "We wouldn't say it if it weren't part of the initiation, would we?"

Paul S. really wanted to become one of The Crusaders. We had tried everything to discourage him, including locking him in a garage while stealing bottles. But giving him his due, he was a persistent guy, and so we invited him to go to the drive-in with us.

Sandy sat in the front seat. Kenny, Stanley and I in the back. Paul S. opened the front door, stood outside and closed it. He shook his head, and leaned into the front passenger window.

"Like this?" he asked.

"Just like that," Paul said as he rolled up the electric window and caught Paul S.'s head poking in the window via his neck..

"What are you doing?" he screamed.

Paul started up the engine and threw the car into gear.

"Stop," Paul S. cried out, trying to extract himself from the window. It was pretty tight against his neck. Paul moved the car an inch. Paul S. screamed some more to stop, and then Paul placed it in park and shut the car down. All of us were laughing. Sandy reached over and lowered the window.

Paul S. rubbed his neck and muttered to himself something about being totally uncool. He got back in the car, huffing.

We figured that would discourage any more attempts to join.

Billy, Sandra and Ray

New neighbors moved into the house next to Stanley's on the corner of Dillerdale and Mayland.

Sandra and her husband moved in at the beginning of summer, 1967. She stood five feet eight inches tall, had beautiful golden blond hair, green eyes, a wide oval face and large luscious red lips. A few beats under thirty, we guessed. How would we know anyway? Referred to as full-figured, her top filled out anything she wore, and her hips matched perfectly.

They kept to themselves for the first month, and then she came around to introduce herself to the families in the neighborhood. Ray, her husband, followed and they became a staple at neighborhood parties.

Ray was a hard-looking Mexican, with chiseled features, piercing brown eyes and slicked-back black hair. He was very talkative and always bullshitting about himself and what he did.

Sandra volunteered once to take us to the beach. Stanley, Paul, Kenny, Billy, and I strapped down a couple of surfboards on top of her 1958 green Ford, piled in, and drove down to Huntington Beach for the day. She wore a bikini that left very little to the imagination and had us gawking the entire time we were on the beach.

It was as if she were completely unaware of her sexuality, and yet used it all the time. Whether she was aware of it or not, we certainly were. She was just plain beautiful. Enchanting.

Sexy. Vibrant. We constantly spoke of her when we were together, and not in a matronly or sisterly way.

Billy came over to my house one day to shoot pool. The table was located in my garage. We played a couple of games. Neither one of us was very good. He set down the stick and lit a cigarette, blowing a big cloud of smoke over the table.

"John... I've got to talk with you."

"Sure. What's up?" I set my stick up on the rack.

He took another drag, held it a little longer than normal, and let it out slowly, curling his tongue and making a couple of smoke rings.

"You know Sandra?"

I nodded, held my hands out in front of my chest and moved them in and out.

"Yeah," he laughed. "Well, I've been meeting her on her back steps the past couple of nights."

"No shit?"

"I shit you not."

"So what happened?"

He hesitated. His eyes blinked rapidly. His tongue licked his lips.

"We made out."

"No kidding?" That was exciting. We all fantasized about doing it, but here was Billy telling me he *did* it.

"She said she had a crush on me, and that what we did together would be special."

I smiled. "What else did you do?"

"Felt her tits." He laughed to himself. "Thing is, I want to do more, and she has all kinds of excuses for not letting me."

"Like what?"

"Like, ah, I can't go all the way because I can't get pregnant. It isn't fair to let you feel my tits under my bra, because you'll get frustrated and try more... stuff like that." He took another drag, dropped the butt and toed it out on the cement floor. "It is really frustrating."

"Billy, you got to feel her tits?"

"Yeah... only on the outside."

I thought about those tits. "Where'd you do it?"

"On her back door step. She blinks the back door light a couple of times. I hop over the fence and meet her there. Ray is usually out of the house or asleep."

I pushed my fingers through my hair. "I don't know, Billy, Ray seems like one crazy motherfucker to me."

"I was thinking that too. But damn. I think she really likes me."

He left and went home. Guess he needed to tell someone. It went on like that for at least a couple of weeks. Got periodic reports, but nothing substantial. When we walked by her house, she waved as if nothing were happening.

Damn, she was beautiful.

A few weeks later Billy called and asked me to come over. I pedaled my metallic-blue Stingray over to his house. He was standing by the garage, one foot against the door.

"What's up Billy?"

He pushed off from the door, motioned with his arm for me to follow and walked to the side yard, stopping. "I almost got caught last night with Sandra... by her husband."

"What?" The hair raised on the back of my neck. My stomach felt queasy.

"Yeah." He took a deep breath and continued. "For the past couple of nights we would go a little farther, you know?

I'd rub her tits, she'd rub my dick from the outside. Then two nights ago she took it out and gave me a hand job."

"No."

He nodded. "It was bitchin'. And then we made out for what seemed like an hour. I finally went home."

"So how'd you almost get-"

He waved his hand like a stop sign. "I'm coming to that, hang on." He paced around a few steps, seeming to grasp for words. "Last night I went over there again. She said she was going to give me a blowjob. Man, can you imagine? So she unbuckled my pants and pulled them down, and then pulled down my underwear. All of a sudden I heard Ray calling out to her and then the back door handle started turning."

"Holy shit."

"Holy shit is right. My pants were down to my knees... underwear hanging below my balls and the fucking door is opening. She stood up, pushed me away and blocked the door. I ran as fast as I could, pulled up my pants, hopped the fence and hid in the backyard. Heard all kinds of screaming and yelling."

"What happened?"

"Don't know. Don't know if he saw *me* either. I think he knew someone was out there. I finally went into my house and fell asleep. Man, it was totally scary."

I stood there staring at him, and his eyes showed it. Fear. Didn't blame him, either. As I mentioned, Ray was one crazy guy. Somebody said he was in prison once. We all believed it.

"Hey John... you got any downers?"

"Sure, at home. Want me to get them for you?"

"Yeah man. This shit is not good. What if he finds out?"

"He won't find out, Billy. Unless she tells him."

I could see that bit of information did not make him feel any better. Me either. She could give him up to her husband and Billy would be in deep shit.

Later that day, all The Crusaders met and Billy shared everything with them. Paul had heard from Kenny about Ray being pissed-off too, that his wife was seeing someone. He suggested it was one of The Crusaders. At least he thought so. How Kenny knew about it was a mystery at the time. But the fact was, Ray was looking to find out who was playing around with his wife. And Billy was scared he would find out it was him. Couldn't blame him.

Paul said he would go down and see him. We thought it was a stupid idea, but Paul insisted. He left and walked up to their house with Kenny.

"What do you want?" Ray asked.

"Just wanted to talk. That okay?" Paul said.

Ray studied Paul for a moment, opened the door and let them in. They sat in the living room.

"Look, Ray, I had nothing to do with your wife, and I came here to tell you that," Paul said.

"How do I know that?"

"I came here didn't I?"

"You know, I could just get my gun and take care of this," Ray said.

"You could," Paul said, "But it wouldn't change anything. I came here to tell you there was nothing going on between any of us Crusaders and Sandra. Period."

He paced the floor, knuckles crunched, and stopped.

"I guess your coming here... well... you wouldn't be here if you did do anything."

"That's what I was saying."

218

Kenny nodded in agreement.

Ray walked to the door and opened it. "Guess you guys better go now."

Paul and Kenny strolled past him without eye contact. He shut the door.

"Man, that was scary," Kenny said.

Paul nodded, his trembling hand reached for a cigarette. "No shit. Did you catch the gun reference?"

"He ever finds out about Billy... well," Kenny's voice trailed off.

"Let's make sure he doesn't," Paul said.

A week later a pounding on the front door woke up Kenny and family near midnight. Sandra was on the porch, bloodied and crying. Ray had broken a mirror over her head and thrown her out. They called the police. After taking a report, the police took her away. Not sure where. A month later the house was for sale and they were both gone.

Neither Kenny nor I was sure why she ran the two blocks to his house. Seemed strange.

But then again, you look up strange in the dictionary and Ray and Sandra's pictures probably showed up.

Playing Music II

We recognized very quickly that Chiquita Bananas was an especially stupid name. Luckily, we did not spend any money getting business cards. We knew where to get the good ones - with the pearlescent background and raised lettering. Just needed a good name, and we would have them in a week.

In the meantime, we practiced as often as we could. Only then, we would smoke some joints before practice, when we had them. Didn't make us play any tighter; in fact, it hurt. But being loaded, it sounded better to us, and after all, we were all about "us" at the time.

Before all the stuff happened between Billy and his wife, Ray came over to listen to us. We played two sets, and he really seemed to like what he heard. What did we care. He wasn't in the record industry.

But he surprised us one day saying that he got us a gig at a party in El Monte in two weeks. Problem was, we did not have a bass guitar or amp. We were cheating it with a regular guitar. Then a plan started to percolate within the group. A few days before, Bob S had come over to listen to us, and brought his bass guitar and amp to sit in and play. Only one slight problem. He could not carry a beat with the music even if it had a handle he could grab onto. It was weird, actually.

How could one person be so out of sync with the music?

We were nice, thanked him for stopping by, and let it go at that. But now, we needed the guitar and amp, and not Bob himself. What to do?

We decided to invite Bob to play with us at the gig, and had him meet us there with his equipment. Once there and set up, we asked if Jeff (who could play bass but had no equipment) could try a couple of songs, and then never let him back in.

The night of the gig came, and we showed up ready to play our first paid show. But we had a much bigger problem. One we were not aware of. We were at a dance party. And, we were not a dance band. We played some songs that you could possibly bust a move to, but most were not. Hadn't thought of that before. After five or six songs, Ray came up to us asking if we could play some music the kids could dance to, and we were flummoxed. What would we play?

I knew *Louie Louie*, and Kenny could sing it, so we tried that. The place was filled up within seconds with gyrating teenagers. Then we were out of dance tunes. The other band that was supposed to play showed up early, and Ray had them set up and take over. They were a dance band. Motown. Beatles. Stuff like that. We went out onto the dance floor and danced ourselves. Had a great time

After that experience, we realized we would need to change our sets to accommodate dancing, and got to work on it starting the next week. But there was a problem. Stanley needed a full set of drums. We still needed a bass guitar (Bob figured out what we were doing and stopped coming around), and we only had one amp for the guitar and vocals.

Undeterred, we continued to practice while trying to find the necessary equipment. We also came up with a name all of us liked and had those really cool pearlescent cards with the raised lettering made.

The Living End.

Weeks later, Kenny had arranged for us to play in West Covina at an outdoor venue sponsored by the city. There would be half a dozen local groups playing on the permanent cement staging area they used for those types of events. No money involved, but supposedly great exposure.

We decided to postpone the dance part of our act and concentrate on the songs we knew pretty well. Practice, practice, practice. And smoke, smoke, smoke some joints. Seemed like we were really making progress.

We drove to West Covina and waited our turn to set up. In the meantime, we smoked a couple of joints. Started laughing. The giggles. Not the best to have when you are about to play music.

Nonetheless, we set up. It was a beautiful spring day. Clear skies. Warm and breezy. After tuning, I looked at Kenny, who shouted one, two three, four, and we started with *The Last Time* by the Rolling Stones. Only something sounded really weird. The sound was totally off. An outdoor venue. We didn't know how to compensate for that. My guitar was really loud, Billy's barely audible, Kenny's voice mike was squealing with feedback, and Stanley was unable to hear anything behind us to keep a beat to.

In a word, it was terrible. And it took no more than a few minutes for the crowd to start letting us know it sounded terrible. We soldiered on, trying to compensate for the audio mistakes by using the volume on our guitars. But it was no use. By the next song, *Get Off of My Cloud,* the crowd was booing. And finally Kenny stopped singing.

"Let's get out of here," he shouted.

I felt terrible, knowing that we were much better than we sounded, but unable to do anything about it. We tore down, loaded our equipment into the car, and drove home.

Dejected.

No one spoke.

We'd been booed off stage. How humiliating was that? Maybe the pot heightened the feelings of worthlessness. Maybe we really were that bad. Maybe we had no business trying to be a band in the first place. Not even the thought of smoking pot helped alleviate the hopelessness and despair that permeated the car as we neared home.

Finally arriving, we unloaded and left everything at Stanley's garage and went home.

I walked into the house and immediately went to the piano in the den and started playing. It had always made me feel better. Like a meditation of some sort. I played and played for hours. Finally exhausted, I went into my room and laid down, looking back at the incident.

We have to prepare ourselves better, if we're to be a band. And we were a band. And we were pretty good. Not great. Just good. That was enough in La Puente and local environs.

I resigned myself to try harder and learn more songs. I knew the guys would agree. I also had an intuition of sorts. We'd need to cut down on the pot - at least while we practiced.

That would be a little harder to convince them that it was necessary.

A year later, we had a new lead singer, Julio, because Kenny had moved to Anaheim. And we had a new drummer, Bernie, because of Stanley moving to Diamond Bar.

We rehearsed twice a week, and were getting very good. Dance songs, different riffs on the songs we knew, and Julio was a fantastic showman as well as a singer.

We kept the band name, The Living End.

Our first paid gig was to play at Edgewood Junior High's yearly dance. My Alma Mater.

We arrived early that evening. Performed a sound check, made sure everything worked correctly, and practiced a couple of songs. We sounded tight. Clean and bitchin'.

Everyone changed in the school locker room into their outfits, which were simply a change of clothes - except for Julio. He had some sort of an Elvis style suit he wore, which showed off part of his chest. As to his chest, he was the first person I had ever met who looked like he was wearing a sweater with his shirt off. He had to shave a circle at the bottom of his neck and tuck in the hair around his collar.

The auditorium filled with pubescent teenagers, girls on one side, guys on the other. We started with *Ain't Too Proud to Beg* by the Temptations. Julio gyrated and started to whip the crowd into dancing mode right away. Forty-five minutes later, we were through with our first set of songs. Three more to go.

Outside we smoked while waiting to reappear for the next set.

"Julio, you were fantastic man," I said.

"Thanks man. Fun gig, you know?"

I took a drag and blew it out while I spoke. "We only have enough material for one more set. What do we plan on doing, playing the first set again in a different order?"

"Seems like it will work to me," Julio said, smiling. Turning to Bernie he said "Can you slow down the beat a little? We raced through too many songs. If we slow it down, we can stretch them out."

Bernie nodded as he munched down some Cheetos.

"Got any stash, John?" Julio asked.

"Yeah, but I think we should wait until near the end before smoking any. Been through this before."

He nodded, finished his smoke and snapped the butt with his finger into the air. "Let's get this next set going."

Bernie had slowed down the beat, but we had run out of songs again and repeated a couple of numbers during the third set. Shit. What were we going to do?

We sat outside, and that time I passed around a few doobies. Then it hit me. Paul and I had been to the Shrine Auditorium a few weeks earlier and seen Iron Butterfly. We had played their signature song as a goof a couple of times at band practice. Why not, it might work.

Sharing the idea with the band, they lit up. Of course we could do it. Make it an epic effort. We ran over who would do what, and then finished the joints and went into the auditorium.

Julio asked for everyone's attention - he was very dramatic about it.

"I have a surprise for you. A special song we have been working on and never performed before. Are you ready?"

Half-hearted "yeahs" bounced back.

"Are you ready?" Julio shouted.

This time a more boisterous response.

"YEAH!"

Julio looked to me, and I started the riff on my keyboard that defined *In a Gadda Da Vida*. I also played the bass with my left hand. The auditorium was silent while they listened to the intro, and when the bass kicked in followed by the drums, they exploded with enthusiasm and started dancing. The entire high school basketball floor was shoulder to shoulder, a wave of bodies moving rhythmically to the music.

After about twenty minutes, I nodded to Bernie, who started on the drum solo. The rest of us walked outside, laughing. That was too easy. We smoked a couple of joints, waited until we heard Bernie go into the end of the solo, and returned, picking up the slack.

Forty-five minutes later, we ended the song, Julio pulling a James Brown act and falling to the stage on his knees, and the crowd erupted in applause. Lasted about four or five minutes. More, more they shouted.

The curtains closed, and we high-fived each other. *Fucking far out.*

We played often after that gig, having fun and enjoying the camaraderie of being in a band together. And always hopeful for those groupies that never appeared.

Except for Julio. They always showed up for him.

However, the band eventually broke up.

Mainly because of what happened to me.

Burned, Again

"You score, Kenny?"

"Yeah man. Got some heavy acid from Bernie up in the heights."

"What kind, man?" I asked.

"Some sort of Orange Sunshine."

"Scratch?"

"Five bucks a tab."

"Seems kinda steep."

"Said they're double tabs."

"Cool. Let's drop 'em now."

He unrolled the tin foil and pulled them out. Looking at the little orange tab, I was getting a little suspicious.

"Kenny. These look like baby aspirin."

"Naw, man, they're the real deal."

"I don't know."

"Come on man, let's just take them and start trippin'."

They tasted like.... baby aspirin.

"You sure Bernie sold us some real shit?"

"Of course. He wouldn't burn us."

"Taste okay to you?"

"Not sure, man. He said it was different from regular Orange Sunshine."

"I think he burned us."

"What are you talking about? If he did he'd screw himself with the whole pot deal. He can't get it if we put the word out to George."

"I know. But shit, Kenny. This sure tastes like... baby aspirin."

"Let's see if we get high before we jump all over him."

"Always the optimist."

"Not really. It's just that I can't believe he would burn us like that."

"Like your brother?"

"Yeah," he laughed. "Like that."

"Well, if he did, he's screwed."

Hours passed while we walked home from Valley Boulevard, getting more pissed by the minute.

Never got high.

Then again, we didn't get headaches either.

We did have George cut off Bernie's supply of pot.

That felt good.

Cousin Jeff

About once a month I would hitchhike to my "cousin" Jeff's house off Workman Mill Road and spend the weekend there. His grandparents liked me, and were cool about me staying. Ever since we met two years earlier we had become best friends.

We would hitch up to watch the 'classic cars' cruise Whittier Boulevard near Bob's Big Boy or go to the recreation center, which was off Painter Street in downtown Whittier. They held dances every week. Jeff had a friend who let us in for free.

We were two surfer guys, long hair, tall, good looking, and always had a good time dancing, since most of the girls were also in pairs. We would be loaded on pot, thinking we were funny as heck, and charming to boot.

Actually, we were.

Jeff wasn't really my cousin, but we told everybody we were because we looked so much alike. Especially after we got the inevitable question from girls: "Are you two brothers?" No. "You sure do look like you are." That's when we came up with the cousin idea.

Worked every time.

We met girls all the time, and would go over to their homes and see them, but generally speaking, nothing would happen except to make out. Jeff was a lot more experienced than me. Meaning, he said on a few occasions that he got laid.

I had my doubts.

One summer, we were in Lake Gregory. We'd met two really beautiful "older" girls - they drove and said they were in college. We dated them a couple of nights in a row, got drunk, smoked pot, and made out. The last night they were there, we met them, and they drove us to a remote spot in the mountains near a water tower. Drinks flowed, and so did the pot, and I was pretty wasted.

The one girl took Jeff outside the car and grabbed a blanket. The other girl, the one I was with, took me around to the back of the station wagon, put the tailgate down and laid out a blanket.

We continued to make out, but my mind was racing. *What was going to happen? Was I finally going to have sex?* Excitement and fear rose like battling sentinels throughout my body.

The kissing became more passionate, and finally she took off her pants and underwear, pulled mine off too, and positioned me on top of her.

I was too loaded to get hard.

And then the fear of not getting wood took over, and it was a hopeless cause.

She tried to help, but it just wouldn't work.

She dressed, was nice enough about it, and we smoked some more dope. Jeff and the other girl came back, looking disheveled, and they took us home to our cabin.

I made a promise then and there that if *ever* I had a date again, I would not drink.

Jeff told me he got laid.

I lied and said I did too.

Employment

In addition to our illicit activities, I generated money from somewhat more legitimate endeavors. I had a paper route for years. It was a free paper I delivered once a week, and then once a month I went door to door collecting money. It was not particularly profitable, but the income was steady. I needed it to supplement the money I had to pay back for the various screw-ups my parents constantly accused me of.

I always had the grass cutting job at home for a dollar, and we (usually Paul or Kenny and I) would sometimes wash neighbors' cars for a buck.

My first paid job was at the Toot-N-Totem Market, the equivalent of a 7-Eleven. It paid very little, and I had to work in a frigid cooler restocking beer, milk, and cokes all night until closing. Did I mention it was frickin' cold inside that cooler?

But it helped supplement The Crusaders' drinking.

At least once a night, I would add a six-pack of beer to the trash that was taken out and put in the dumpster. After closing, we would fish it out and go to the school to drink.

I found out a lot earlier, I did not like drinking. It might have been due to throwing up near the beginning of our trying it after two cans of Colt 45. I'm not sure. But I would rather toke a few joints than drink. The others loved it, and were happy to drink my share of the spoils.

Paul got a job at another branch of Toot-N-Totem, and the booze supply to The Crusaders doubled overnight.

Jeff had a buddy in Pico Rivera who sold pot for one-hundred dollars a pound. Billy, Paul, and I scraped together the dough and bought one from him. We hid it in Billy's parents' Ford station wagon and drove it back to La Puente, paranoid the entire drive. We made sixteen lids out of it, and quickly sold them for ten dollars each.

We were dealers.

And we had money to pay for gas, go to concerts, date girls, and buy more and better drugs.

The trips back and forth to Whittier continued for a few months until we found out George was also selling lids - bigger than ours - and the pot was better. So we made a deal with him to buy pounds wholesale (only paying one-hundred and twenty dollars each) and that ended the Whittier runs.

Billy had somehow found some guys in LA who would sell him jars of reds (1,000 to a jar), wholesale. I think he met them through his connections on Olvera Street. At the time, I had no interest in reds unless I needed to come down from the speed high on acid. Billy thought he could sell them and bought a jar and started foiling them - putting four in aluminum foil packets. He would sell these for a dollar. Not sure how profitable it was, but he always had money from that point forward.

Maybe too much, as it turned out.

Guy got a job in a gas station and worked nights. He would use the mechanics' bays to work on his cars. Not sure how much he made, but it was not relevant. His father owned the hardware store, and he always seemed to have money.

Modified PE

"Hey guys, I've got my mom's car. You want to go to the beach?"

Stanley and I were walking on Barrydale when a car pulled along next to us and followed until we stopped and looked to see who was talking. Jeff, a freckle-faced gangly kid we knew from a few blocks away, sat in an idling 1965 two-door Dodge Dart, teeth flashing like a Cheshire cat.

"You sure it's okay?" Stanley asked.

"Of course. I've got the car, don't I?" he said.

It was about six in the evening. Daylight savings was over, and we knew our parents wouldn't be expecting us home for a couple of hours.

"Can we make it there and back by nine?" I asked.

He nodded and opened the door. "I've done it lots of times. We'll be back way before then."

Stanley and I looked at each other, shrugged and jumped in – me in the backseat and Stanley in the front. Jeff punched the car and took off toward Hacienda Boulevard, radio blasting. The windows were down, it was a nice fall evening, and the wind blowing through our hair coupled with the scents of the last remnants of summer all blended in to make it a fun and exciting evening drive.

As we started up the mountainous road in Hacienda Heights, Jeff seemed to have everything under control. I was sitting forward with my hand on the back of Stanley's bucket sea. Jeff started to take the turns slightly above what even I thought was a safe speed.

"Maybe you should slow down a little, Jeff," I suggested.

"You want to get there and back in time, don't you? Besides, I have to have the car home before ten."

The radio was playing the Mamas and Papas *California Dreaming*, and all appeared fine. But I was still anxious. There was no reason to be. I just felt uneasy. I didn't say anything more. Just swallowed those feelings down as I clenched the rear of Stanley's seat a little tighter.

Suddenly we came to a sharp turn, and Jeff over-steered to the right.

I screamed automatically. "Jeff!"

He spun the power-assisted steering wheel to the left and grossly overcorrected, causing us to skid sideways. When the tires finally grabbed the asphalt road we were heading directly into an orange grove. Gaining speed faster and faster.

"Slow the fuck..." My voice failed. The fully leafed orange trees sped by us on the left and right as we barreled between them on the dirt. Everything was surreal. Time seemed to take on a new characteristic, as if we were moving in a sort of slow-motion. Like swimming underwater. No sounds. Trees whizzing by.

Then, up ahead, I saw a large palm tree racing toward us. We sped closer and closer until it filled the windshield. A loud crash followed. My hand pushed Stanley's head into the dash as I flew over and toward the windshield, trying to protect myself with my arm as I crashed through the glass. I stopped moving when my pants belt hit something and yanked me to a stop. I just laid there.

What had happened? My senses didn't comprehend where I was. I gazed around in a fog. The palm tree was pushed into the hood almost to my face. Glass was strewn everywhere. Then I looked down and saw wetness all around the car. Gas?

Holy shit, I thought, as panic started to grip me. I pushed myself back into the car, crunching the glass with my hands, and landed in the back seat.

"Open up the fucking door, Jeff!"

Nothing. I looked over and Stanley was lying with his head against the dash, the bucket seat pushed forward against him, motionless. I shook Jeff's seat.

"Open up the door," I screamed as I tried to reach the handle around Jeff. No luck. Finally he seemed to snap out of a stupor and pulled the handle, opening the door. He rolled out onto the ground. I quickly followed by pushing his seat forward and bolting out. My head ached, and I could feel wetness rolling down my face. I turned back into the car and grabbed Stanley by the collar.

"Come on, Stan, get out of there." He wasn't moving. "Stan," I screamed again, yanking on him, "we've got to get out of this fucking car, now!"

He shook his head and said something incomprehensible, but that was enough for me. He was alive. I pulled on him, and he groggily slipped over the center console and out the driver's door, hitting the ground.

"We've got to get away," I screamed. "I think the car's leaking gas."

We limped and dragged ourselves to the other side of the asphalt road behind the palm tree and sat on a grassy berm. Two cars stopped on Hacienda, about fifty yards away. The drivers said something to one another. One of them nodded and sped away. Other cars started to stop.

I looked at my arm, the one that I used to try and protect myself going through the windshield. There was a two-inch gash with a bone sticking out. Blood was dripping from my head and into my eyes. I pulled off my white shirt and pushed it onto my head to try and stop the flow. I could barely see. Jeff looked over at me and Stanley, who was still in a daze.

"We've got to get out of here," he said in a low whispered voice.

"What?" I asked incredulously.

"We've got to get away, man. I stole my parents' car."

I couldn't speak. I just stared at him in disbelief.

"What the fuck are you talking about?" Stanley finally asked.

"My parents don't know I have the car. I don't even have a driver's license."

"Look at my fucking arm, Jeff." I held it up with the bone sticking out. "I can't go anywhere." My white shirt was now soaked with red. A man was hurriedly walking toward us.

"Okay, we'll have to say someone else was driving..."

The rest of what he said was a blur. I guess I was getting light-headed from the loss of blood. The man reached us, a nice looking businessman about forty and asked if we were okay. I was shivering, probably from shock. He looked down at me, took off his suit jacket and gently wrapped it around my shoulders, touching them and telling me I would be okay. I started to cry.

Stanley and Jeff were huddled a short distance away, cooking up some sort of plan. I didn't care. The next thing I remember was hearing a siren. Red lights were flashing from the fire trucks as they stopped and ran out to check the car for a potential fire. An ambulance soon followed, and two young paramedics started working on me, asking what hurt and where. When they finally loaded me onto the stretcher, I looked around and watched as people whispered and pointed at me, concern and worry etched into their faces.

On the way to the hospital, the paramedic sitting with me leaned in and started whispering.

"I heard the story your two buddies were giving to the police. If I were you I wouldn't get caught up with their lies. The one guy's foot was broken, probably caught behind the brake pedal. If the police ask you anything, just moan loudly and tell them you can't remember."

"Okay," I said.

"You'll be alright. I've seen worse." Then he smiled.

The police did ask me about it and I moaned, told them I didn't remember, and they left the emergency room quickly. Dozens of stitches on my arm, head, neck and shoulders soon followed, and my parents finally got to the hospital to take me home. What surprised me was that I needed stitches on my back. Apparently I'd hit the rear view mirror bracket as I flew through the windshield.

After a few weeks my back started to really hurt, and I was not able to participate in regular physical education, or PE as the coaches called it. So I was relegated to the remedial PE until I was better. *Remedial PE? That was for the retards and wusses in school.*

Bassett High School was a hub school for the entire San Gabriel Valley school district. So all special education students were bused there, where special classes were created in one location. Hence the remedial PE class.

All I did was sit around on the bleachers and watch them in their wheelchairs and walkers on the basketball court, thinking how unfair it was that I had to spend fifty minutes in this class doing nothing.

One day, I was walking down the hall and saw a couple of seniors teasing two of the guys in wheelchairs.

"Hey, retards, why don't you watch where you're going in those fucking wheelchairs," one of them snarled, pushing the kid on the shoulder. They laughed as they walked away down the hallway.

I didn't think much about it until my PE class later that day. I saw the one they pushed sitting near the bottom corner of the bleachers, alone. His head was bobbing with his hands covering his eyes. I was sitting above on the bleachers and walked down the stairs over to where he was sitting in his wheelchair, and saw his eyes were reddened around the edges, tears running down his cheeks. I stood there. Tears started welling in my eyes, and I forced myself to hold them back. He looked up at me, embarrassed, grabbed the joystick that controlled his chair and spun it around so I couldn't see him.

Something changed in me, then and there. It was subtle. Not anything conscious. But nonetheless, I realized something that hadn't occurred to me before. He was a person, just like me. He had feelings. He hated being picked on. And he couldn't do a thing about it.

I knew what it was like to be picked on. I'd been experiencing it most of my life. But I could at least... I don't know. I could at least get away from it. He couldn't. They couldn't. I looked around and saw all of these young teenagers, boys and girls, playing in their wheelchairs, and others struggling to take some steps with their walkers, and I could no longer hold it back--I broke down crying. Couldn't help it.

I ran away to the back of the handball courts and squatted with my back against the cement wall, unable to comprehend what was wrong with me. Why I was crying like such a pussy. I pulled out a cigarette and lit it up. It tasted awful. I took another drag and threw it away. I couldn't get the image of that boy, a boy my age, sitting in that wheelchair, crying.

I steeled up as much as I could, went back in to PE, climbed the benches to the top and just stared at them all. I had to do something, but what could I do?

Physical therapy followed shortly after the accident, and I found myself lying on my stomach for hours at a time at the doctor's office with hot bags of sand pressing against my back. *Heck, I could just be lounging on the hot sand at the beach and getting the same thing.* But the truth was, my back hurt. Even walking caused me to cringe in pain.

I found myself thinking more and more about the incident in the hallway with the fellow in the wheelchair and wracking my brain to come up with something. What? I didn't know. I knew I couldn't say anything to the older guys, or else I would also get my ass kicked, which had happened already numerous times. They were jocks, and although I was in top shape, surfing, walking and running all the time, I was still Lurch from the Munsters to all of them, and skinny as a wet kitten.

Next time I was in class, I walked up to a group of kids in the gym.

"Hey, what's going on?"

"What do you care?" one of them replied.

"I was just asking."

"Nothing," another said.

"What are your names?"

One of them finally volunteered. "Jimmy." The others just stared in another direction.

"Well, Jimmy, you want me to throw the basketball?"

"What?" His look relayed his disbelief in my suggestion.

"I saw the coach throwing you balls last week, and wondered if you wanted me to throw you some."

He looked at me suspiciously. "Oh, I get it, so you can laugh at me when I miss it?"

"Look Jimmy, I just asked if you wanted me to throw the ball, that's all. If you don't," I shrugged, "then what the fuck."

He looked at his buddies and they all seemed to have the same thoughts. What's this long-haired surfer/hippie guy, who shouldn't be in our class in the first place, trying to pull off here? Why is he even talking to us? I could see it in their faces. Jimmy licked his upper lip and finally looked back at me.

"Okay." He pushed the joystick backward and spun toward the court. I went over, grabbed a basketball and stood where the coach had been the week before. Jimmy positioned himself left of center court and about five feet from the foul line.

I bounced the ball up and down, listening as the echoes reverberated from the walls. "Ready?" I yelled. He faced me and motioned with his arm. I bounced the ball again and then threw it toward the floor, calculating that it would bounce pretty close to him. He just sat there and watched it pass him.

"Did I throw it wrong?" He shook his head and eyed me cautiously. "No."

"Do you want me to try again?" He nodded yes.

I ran, grabbed the ball and went back to my position, bouncing the ball a few times before bouncing it toward him again. This time he pushed the joystick forward, moved about two feet and grabbed the ball with both hands after the bounce. He tossed it back to me with authority. Looking toward the sidelines confirmed we had about ten wheelchairs lined up watching the action. I bounced the ball and shot it toward him, this time a little to his right. He whizzed the chair over to it and grabbed it. A slight smile crossed his lips. He tossed it back.

"Want me to throw it a little harder?"

"Whatever."

Okay then. I bounced it a couple of times and threw it lower. It jumped off the floor and was going to go past him from behind. He yanked back the joystick, causing the tires on the wheelchair to spin around before grabbing traction, and stopped the ball with his body. Then he did something I wasn't expecting.

He started to bounce the ball with his right hand while pushing the joystick in his left, heading toward the hoop and backboard. He reached it, sat back and tossed the ball – through the hoop. I stood amazed. His buddies started cheering. "Way to go." "Good shot." "Great job, Jimmy."

He turned toward them with a look of triumph, smiling. I ran, got the ball and returning with it said, "You're a pretty good ball player, Jimmy. Any of your friends over there play?" I jerked my head at the cheerleaders.

"Most of them do." He raised his shoulders. "Some don't, I guess."

"Think they'd like to join us?"

The bell rang before he answered. I had to get to my next class and left, tossing Jimmy the ball as I did. He caught it and smiled. I only had PE three times a week, so it was two days before I returned to class. Jimmy was sitting, talking with the others as I approached.

"Want to throw balls again?"

"Can we play too?" one of the others asked.

"What's your name?"

"James."

"I'm Scott," another volunteered.

Soon all of them introduced themselves. We organized it so they would be in a semi-circle. I would bounce the ball to one, they would shoot it back; then the next one and then the next. Their friends started watching from the sidelines. I noticed some of them could not move their arms very well. But their eyes were full of life and enthusiasm. Pretty soon we had advanced to run-ups toward the hoop with a few of them. They gave everything they had to catch the ball and toss it up through the hoop. An idea was percolating in the recesses of my mind. *Maybe we might be on to something?*

A couple of weeks later I approached the coach.

"What if we were to put on some sort of exhibition match before the main games in the gym?" I asked him. "You know, to show off how good these guys are?"

"Are you kidding?"

I was startled by his response. "No. I just thought . . ."

"Don't think," he continued. "No one wants to see a bunch of retar..." he checked himself, "handicapped students throwing balls. It's a stupid idea." He'd emphasized the handicapped part of his sentence in a mocking sing-song tone, and the disgust in his demeanor was palpable. He was a jock, and didn't give a shit how they felt. They were just retards to him. Just like the other jocks.

After a few months my back started to feel better. I could skateboard with the guys, and the doctor told me I would be able to go back to regular PE in a few weeks. That also meant I would be signed off to surf again. Life appeared to be heading back to normal. However, one incident did happen in school that I was not planning on -- during driver's education. Due to some new law, everyone had to take driver's education to get their learner's permit. And here's the rub: it was given by this same coach -- Jock City in the flesh.

He relished showing dead people killed in auto crashes, and judiciously showed movies of them. *Sadistic bastard.* Anyway, I breezed through it, and the final day they handed out a test to take. I took two. On the first one, I wrote my name and gave the correct answers. However, on the second one I gave the name of Alfred E. Neumann, and proceeded to give answers that were sure to let him know what a dickhead he was. I handed them in.

A few days later I was called into the principal's office and was met by my mother and father, staring daggers at me. *What is going on?* I sat down and the coach showed up. Now I was getting a little antsy. What followed was their telling me how they figured out that it was me who turned in the phony test, because the pen marks of the second one (Alfred's) showed through on the first one, mine. Shit. They pulled a Perry fucking Mason on me. I was trapped. My mom just stared at me, shaking her head.

I figured the less said the better, so I just didn't talk. After several attempts at getting me to admit my culpability, they suspended me for a week. This was the second suspension that year. The first time I wouldn't get my hair cut. Fortunately, my parents backed me on that one.

There wasn't a chance in hell they would back me on this.

I continued going to physical therapy. After finishing the myriad of chores my parents thought up to keep me busy and punished for being kicked out of school, I would go over to Paul's or Stanley's and hang out. One day, Tony Tearso came over to pick up Stanley's older brother Paul in his 1965 metallic-green GTO. He'd just had a 427 dual quad engine with a four-speed Hurst shifter installed. And just for good measure, he had added wide slicks and a nine-inch Ford rear axle gear box. We stood around, oohing and aahing, when Paul A., Stanley's older brother, came out to get in.

"Will this thing scratch out?" Kenny asked.

"You assholes fuck off," Paul answered, and then started laughing.

Tony put the car in gear, turned around in the street and then revved up the engine. Finally, when it sounded like five-plus-thousand RPM, he popped the clutch and the rear tires started burning, and the straight front axle of the car flew up about two feet. He made the end of the street in a second, let off the gas, and the front end plopped down. Grayish rubber smoke and two long black lines were left in his tracks. He turned the corner and floored it while Paul stuck his arm out the window and flipped us off.

That night I laid in bed, trying to get to sleep, when an idea hit me. I noodled on it from every angle I could think of, and when I finally felt it would work, I slipped into sleep, knowing that there was a way to make my new friends in modified PE cool.

I relayed my entire idea to the guys in PE, and they were excited as hell. In fact, I'd never seen them so enthusiastic. We picked out an area behind the handball courts where I had broken down crying when I first met them. I paced it out and laid down tape. We tried a couple of tests, and it worked. All was set.

The next day I started the rumor that everyone had to be behind the cement handball courts at lunch time. Rumors travel fast in high school. Everyone probably thought it was a fight, which will always draw a much bigger crowd than any other type of rumor. Especially girl fights. Anyway, when noontime arrived, we had quite a crowd, including the jocks.

"Hey everyone," I started. "We're going to have drag races here today between all the guys in wheelchairs. They'll start down at the taped line, and the finish line is here." I pointed. "We'll start with Scott and Bruce."

"What are we doing messing with those retards?" one of the jocks asked.

"Hey, shut up," one of the bigger girls said. 'That's not nice." They responded to the admonition with a scowl.

"So we'll have the first race," I continued, "starting in five, four, three, two, one... GO!"

Scott and Bruce were ready. They each had a different color paper with a number on the side of the chairs, and actually looked pretty cool. They both pushed their joysticks forward with a start. The front wheels of their chairs lifted off the ground and they hurtled forward. They raced toward the finish line, one a little ahead, then the other. When they finally passed over it Bruce was ahead by a hair. All my friends started cheering, which I had already coached them to do. It was contagious. More of the students started clapping and making noise. The jocks just stood there, staring.

"Okay then, Bruce won that one. Now on to the second heat -- Jimmy and Kelly. You guys get into position."

They did, and now the students were getting excited, crowding in around the track. They lined up and started working the onlookers, moving back and forth to the start line while they waited. Kelly was a little more affected with cerebral palsy, and sort of had a crunched-up arm pushing his joy stick. But he was dead serious and focused.

"Five, four, three, two, one... GO!"

They both pushed full power to their chairs and the front ends lifted off. Kelly's tires started spinning, making a squeal. The crowd loved it. They were cheering them on. "Kelly! Kelly! Kelly!"

They were neck and neck, and when the finish line was crossed, it was Jimmy who won. Roars enveloped him, and people came up to congratulate the winner. The smile and gleam in his eyes let me know I had hit the right notes. The kids were treating him like a normal kid. Even the jocks were looking and talking back and forth, pointing, this time without even a hint of malevolent intentions.

We had two more races that day before lunch period was over.

The next day as I was walking, I noticed a lot of people saying hi to Kelly and Jimmy as they wheeled down the hall.

The races continued - every other day, coinciding with our PE classes. Pretty soon the whole school was showing up. Money was exchanging hands, little signs appeared with the kids' names on them, followed by "You can win it," "Go big guy," stuff like that. The event had exceeded even my wildest expectations.

Dickhead coach showed up with the principal in tow a few weeks later. I didn't notice them, but Jimmy did. He tried to warn me, but he just couldn't catch my eye. I announced the next race and who would be in it. Suddenly I turned around, saw them, and knew from their piercing scowls that I was totally fucked. Turbo fucked. I continued with the countdown and the two kids took off. None of the students had seen them, and they cheered them on to victory. But it was no use. They approached me. The principal said: "I'll see you in my office, now." The shit-eating grin on the pock-marked and tanned face of the coach, beaming "gotcha now, asshole," was the icing on the flattened cake that framed the whole moment.

Two hours later my mom was in the office to listen again to their version of what an absolutely incorrigible and unrepentant student I was; that I had no potential in high school and was a totally disruptive influence -- even on the poor special education students. They felt they had no choice but to suspend me permanently, and assign me to the continuing education school that had just opened up called Nueva Vista.

My mom took me home without a word spent between us. I knew she was mad. In fact, I was hoping she would start yelling at me so I could tell my side of the whole thing. But she didn't. Her version of mad was the silent treatment.

Once home, she told me to go to my room. I heard my dad's car pull up, and she met him on the porch. There was mumbling, and a "What?" burst from my dad. I was hoping he would yell at me too. But he never came into the room. I just sat there, wondering what they were going to do about it – and me.

When dinner finally arrived, the family sat around the table, and my siblings were just dribbling conversation right along as if nothing had happened. My mom and dad averted my pleading glances. After dinner my dad ordered me back to my room. My brother Patrick walked in behind me.

"Are you on restriction?"

"Don't know."

"Dad and Mom seemed really mad about something. What'd you do?"

"Nothin' you little kiss ass. Now get outta here."

He scrambled, after flipping me the bird, and I plopped on my bunk bed and stared at the metal triangles on the underside of the upper bunk. I reviewed what I did and why I did it. They say no good deed goes unpunished. I understood what was meant by that now. I was hurt, and bewildered by the principal's response, and felt that if he really knew why I had done it, he would have understood. But I was never going to tell him why. He could kiss my ass.

But a bigger problem loomed before me. And it scared me. One of the main reasons I liked school was because of my friends, and The Crusaders. Now, I would be going to a different school where I knew no one. The thought of it was overwhelming. I needed to get out of the house and get a smoke. But there was no way I could do that now. Dad would beat the crap out of me if I tried to leave.

Dad finally opened the door and poked his head in.

"The school just called."

"This late?"

"Apparently they want to make sure you don't miss anything important in your education. You are to report to Nueva Vista tomorrow morning."

What could I say? I just nodded and continued lying there. Dad peered at me for a few minutes and then closed the door. I knew he was disappointed in me. So was I. He'd told me many times how he had to quit school at sixteen in Staten Island and help support the family. He thought I could do better. But better than what? Remain in a school full of petty administrators? Sadistic coaches? Maybe going to a new school would help. Maybe I would find somewhere I'd fit in.

Indeed – no good deed does go unpunished.

A few weeks after the accident, my dad came into my bedroom and sat at the end of the bed. .

"Your friends came up with quite a story about that accident of yours." He raised and shook his hand dismissively before I could answer. "Oh, I understand you don't remember anything about it, but I thought I'd share what they said."

He pulled out a cigarette and lit it, blowing the bluish smoke out, slowly.

"Seems you guys met an older fellow at Food Giant. Everyone seems to forget what his name was. This fellow said he had a driver's license, so Jeff told him his mom's car was in his garage and that they could take that out for a spin."

The Crusaders

He inhaled another lungful and bit his lower lip after the exhale.

"So it seems the *four* of you went over to Jeff's, got the car, and decided to drive it to the beach. This mystery man lost control of the damn thing, and then you had the accident. Any of that ring a bell?"

"Not really Dad."

"I didn't think so," he said with a half laugh. "Anyway, the police just shook the real story from that Jeff kid, and Stanley finally broke down and confirmed it. Seems Jeff's foot slid under the brake pedal on that turn and got jammed on top of the accelerator. He broke it trying to get the car stopped. He also broke his nose on the steering wheel." Thin lipped, he looked at me.

"I, I don't remember, Dad," I lied. He knew it too.

Standing up he gave me a final stare and walked to the door. He stopped and turned.

"Good thing you didn't remember and tell that BS story to the police." He took another drag, exhaling as he continued. "Seems their insurance company cancelled their car insurance and are refusing to pay their medical bills, except for yours, of course, because you didn't lie to them."

He continued holding my eyes, and I could swear I saw the makings of a smile. He swung around and left.

Jesus Christ, I thought. *That was close.*

I remembered that paramedic looking down on me, putting his hand on my shoulder the entire ride to the hospital; his whispered words of caution to just shut up and moan.

What a great guy.

I guess there are times when a good deed doesn't get punished.

But not very often.

249

Right at the Light?

Located just south of downtown Los Angeles, the Shrine Auditorium was a great venue in the late 1960's. Paul was still the only one who had a license and car, so he would be the driver when we went there.

The building itself was designed for concerts with a huge stage. Styled with a Moorish facade, it had two levels with a stage at the north end on the bottom floor. As well-designed as it was, the sound wasn't really very good - it echoed and was always too loud. Built in 1920, and rebuilt in 1926 after a fire, its stylistic and beautiful architecture, with parapets on the roof and archways on the outside, became the place for music, concerts and bands.

And it was the place to go if you were under-age and wanted to see groups with a minimum of hassle, especially when stoned on acid.

The more popular places, like the Whiskey and the Rainbow up on Sunset, were too hard to get into, and the bouncers were sticklers about age and drinking. Not that we drank at all. But it was the attitude of the door bouncers. Not very cool. We were pain-in-the-ass kids to them.

We did put up with their bullshit one time when we wanted to see The Byrds at the Whiskey a Go-Go, and it was bitchin'. Smelled like a frickin' bong in there that night. We were expecting the police to show up at any time. Thank God they didn't -- maybe they liked The Byrds, too.

Our first concert was The Turtles at the Carousel Theater in West Covina, a theater in the round.

My parents drove us there. We were fourteen. It was all very proper. The kids were dressed in suits and dresses, Ed Sullivan Theater style. The Turtles dressed in suits. They played on the circular stage, and after each song we clapped. Not too big a deal.

However, I did get very tired of listening to *Happy Together* from that day forward.

Months later Stanley came over and told us The Doors were playing there. It was 1966. The Doors were huge. *Light my Fire* was on every radio station. We were going. Still none of us could drive, so a couple of our parents took us. We dressed up in our coolest Nehru jackets, slick tight pants and Beatle boots. Lights out. Anticipation. The Doors finally came on stage to a roaring crowd. They each faced a different direction on the stage, facing out, with the stage slowly turning around.

About thirty minutes into the set, Morrison was taking drinks out of a bottle, and then we saw him flip a handful of something into his mouth and chug down a big gulp from what looked like a Southern Comfort bottle. About fifteen minutes later, while playing *The End*, he suddenly fell down on the stage. Out cold. The lights went out while the other band members kept playing the music. We could barely see a bunch of stage hands carrying him out. The band played for a few more minutes, and then on the overhead PA system they thanked us for coming to the concert. *What the fuck was that? A forty-five minute concert?* We thought about asking for our money back, but the fact we were out on our own and having fun, no matter what else, was worth it.

Another reason the Shrine was the place to go was economics. We'd have to have money for gas to get there, eat, buy some weed and acid, and after these necessary expenses, there was not much left over. So we'd get one of us in the front door, and the rest of us would be let in by him through the rear fire door. It worked perfectly every time.

Iron Butterfly, Canned Heat, Fleetwood Mac, Jefferson Airplane (before they went Starship on us) and dozens of others played there, and we were listening to them on Orange Sunshine, Purple Barrels, Pink Ozzly , plus various amounts of speed and weed.

Stoned out of our minds one night, we waited until almost all of the cars were gone before we started on our journey home.

"Which way home, Paul?" I asked.

"Dude. I'm not sure," Paul replied.

We both started giggling.

"What are we going to do?"

Paul furrowed his eyebrows while pulling the car out of the parking lot, craning his head back and forth. He gunned the car and pulled up next to a Japanese guy standing there.

"Ask that guy," he said, putting the car in park.

I opened the door and ambled over to him.

"Sir, do you know how to get to the freeway?"

"Turn light at the light."

"Excuse me?"

"Light," he exclaimed, motioning with his right arm.

I tried not to break out laughing. "We need to get to the Harbor Freeway."

"Yes, yes. Turn light at the light."

"What about the San Bernardino Freeway?"

He put his hand on his hip, shaking his head.

"Turn light at the light over tear."

"You sure?"

He nodded, motioning with a sweeping movement of his arms, shooing me away.

"Go, go."

I walked back to the car.

"Well?" Paul asked.

"Turn right at the light."

"That doesn't seem right."

"I know, but the guy said 'turn light at the light,'" making quoting gestures with my fingers for emphasis.

Paul put the car into gear, peeled out and headed for the light on Figueroa. Once there, we turned right, and lo and behold - there were three signs there - Harbor 110 North, Harbor 110 South, and San Bernardino 10 East.

"The dude was right," Paul laughed.

"Yeah. I thought he was goofin' on us."

"Turn right at the light," Paul snorted, with a slight Asian accent.

"Right at the what?" I asked, winking at Paul.

"The liiiiggghhhhttt," he shouted, busting out laughing at finishing the "t" in the word.

Acid and pot had a strange effect. Sometimes. Funny thing is, we still use that saying to this day.

"How do we get there?"

"Turn right at the..."

We became concert groupies - going to as many concerts as budgets would allow:

Devonshire Downs - Various Groups
Monterey Pop Festival – Jimi Hendrix, Jefferson Airplane
San Bernardino Civic - Jimi Hendrix, The Doors
The Forum - David Bowie, Vanilla Fudge, Average White Band
Pasadena Civic Auditorium - Various artists, including The Kingsmen and Ventures
La Puente High School - Paul Revere and the Raiders
El Monte Legion Stadium - Sam the Sham and the Pharaohs
Long Beach Auditorium - The Beach Boys
Lakewood - The Righteous Brothers

Fun times.

Once we drove up to Hollywood, specifically to the Whiskey a Go-Go, and snuck in to see Crosby, Stills, and Nash.

That was turbo cool.

We tried to get into the Rainbow on Sunset, but it was impossible. The bouncers were too good. We were too loaded.

Later that night, the riots started. Not sure what was happening, but the police were kicking the crap out of the long-haired kids on Sunset. Police vans, riot cops. A real bad scene.

We got out of there.

Back to the safety of the burbs.

MLK

The news was on our TV when I walked into the house. Looked like dozens of reporters at a news conference.

"What going on, Dad?"

"Someone just shot Martin Luther King."

"The civil rights guy?"

Dad nodded and motioned me to be quiet.

The news said he was shot at a motel in Tennessee, and then rushed to St. Joseph's hospital.

"Is he going to die?" I asked.

My dad shushed me with his hand again. I remembered seeing the riots in Selma on TV. I knew there were problems in the South, but it also seemed to me that they permeated the whole country. It's just that the South was the focal point.

George Wallace was some politician from the south who every time he opened his mouth, the news media jumped down and choked him with his own words. Neither my dad nor mom cared for him. I was ambivalent -- simply thought the guy a jerk.

There was no real racism in our area to speak of. At least none I saw or was aware of. Everyone was equal, as far as The Crusaders and I were concerned. But I remember a few contentious incidents.

In physical education, PE for short, there was this jock coach that thought he was Gomer Pyle, USMC. He would take roll call before class yelling last names first, then first names. We'd have to shout back "here."

One of the black kids in class was named Guy Black.

Good Times, Bad Times

Since the sixth grade I had a crush on Nancy. Blond, cute in a Doris Day sort of way, as tall as I was, and smart. But she appeared to have absolutely no interest in me, even as a friend. She lived on my way home from Edgewood, and I would try to talk with her on the way home, but it was obvious that she would like me to be anywhere except trying to speak with her.

That was okay, I was not easily discouraged.

By the time we were in ninth grade, I was considered a hippie/surfer guy, and the divide widened between Nancy and her group of nerds and me. It was okay, because I had met Mary in Lake Gregory, and felt that even though she was miles away in San Bernardino, at least I had a girlfriend.

Then I met Nancy's younger sister Cherie. She was a cute, smaller version of Nancy, yet nothing like her. Devious, outgoing, and a pot smoker. We started talking at J & M Donuts one day and hung out a couple of times.

I invited her to my house (when I knew my parents were not going to be there). She knocked at the door. I opened it, and she looked beautiful: tank top, jeans, and sandals.

Invited her to my room to smoke a joint, but when we entered she leaned in and kissed me. Not the pressing kind, her tongue searched out and found mine. We made out in my bed (lower berth of a bunk bed) and, although scared, I moved my hand on the outside of her top. She didn't move it. *Good*, I thought. I made it to first base.

I explored around the outside some more and finally asked her to take her top off (assuming she would leave her bra on).

She got up, and proceeded to take off ALL of her clothes, slowly, looking at me the whole time. She stood there, looking a bit sheepish, and devilish at the same time. She pulled me up from the bed and started undressing me.

Although some awkward moments ensued, I was no longer a virgin after that day.

We met a couple of more times in the playhouse in my backyard and walked everywhere holding hands. I was in heaven. A good-looking girlfriend. No longer a virgin. New definitions for me.

A few days later, I was meeting Stanley and Paul at J & M Donuts in the early afternoon. School was closed for some reason or other. I was early, and walked into the patio area to find Cherie holding hands with some other long-hair guy from Torch Junior High. Laughing. Smiling. Having a great time. Until she saw me.

She pulled her hand out of his and stared at me, a half-smile gracing her face. I walked up, said hello, and she introduced me to the fellow. Although putting on a good face for the occasion, I was devastated. I had actually thought we were an item. I quickly excused myself and ran home, plopping on the bed and crying. When I turned over and laid on my back, I started to wonder why I was so hurt? I divined no immediate answer to the question but did swear an oath to never be with Cherie again. We were through.

Which was kind of stupid, since she had apparently already made the decision she was through with me and was working on her next conquest.

Felt good to think it was *probably* my decision. I figured she was a slut anyway, based on how we started having sex. Then a horrible thought gripped me: *Was she on the pill?* Didn't know. And quite frankly, didn't care. I dismissed it as quickly as it appeared.

John O'Melveny Woods

Then I felt a smile take over my face.
At least *I* was one of her conquests.

And . . . at least I was no longer a virgin.

Palm Springs

The newspapers announced that a music festival would be held in Palm Springs, California. Lots of famous bands would be there: Canned Heat, Steppenwolf, Jefferson Airplane. Everyone in La Puente was going, including all the beaners like Danny L (who technically was not a beaner), Mike B, and Raul G, who technically were. My cousin Jeff was meeting us there, bringing with him a contingent of hippies from Whittier. We rode there in the Crusadermobile, and left the morning of the concert.

Arriving in Palm Springs about 4 pm, we found that everyone was converging near the Tahquitz Indian Reservation where South Highway 111 turned and headed east. Plenty of parking. Hundreds of cars -- looked like a love-in with Detroit metal. They were parked in long rows, like a car show, and everyone was walking down those rows scoring drugs, meeting people and flashing two-finger peace signs. Tie-dyed shirts, Levi's, huarache sandals, long hair, mustaches, and beards, if you could grow them, rounded out the dress code of most of the kids. Even our beaner friends were wearing the official outfits, although they looked ridiculous with their slicked-back greased hair. No matter, all was peace and love.

Aromas of incense, patchouli oil, pot, and cigarettes floated through the crowd like a heavy fog in San Francisco. Grateful Dead and Led Zeppelin blasted out from car stereos.

As the blue sky dissolved into twilight, word went out that the concert had sold out. *Shit. All that way.* Word also started spreading that we were going there anyway and see if we could get in - without tickets. Sounded like a plan to us Crusaders.

Some invisible universal force caused all of us to gather around 6 pm outside the venue, like lemmings. Police were scattered around the fences that separated the concert from the outside world. Kenny, Billy, Paul, and I blended in with the crowd, loaded on pot and Orange Sunshine LSD, having a good time. We strategized about how to bypass the police to get in. We had done that at Devonshire Downs a few months earlier. Didn't seem that difficult.

Then it started.

Someone threw a bottle at a cop, and hit him in the chest. The police started kicking ass on the kids - nightsticks started flying and slamming into people. Screams and commotion followed. People scrambled toward us from the front of the pack. We backed up, quickly, instinctively. This was bad, and we didn't want to be anywhere near the trouble. Peace and love were nowhere in sight, replaced by panic and pandemonium.

Bullhorns shouted for us to disperse immediately or face arrest. The police started methodically walking toward us, shields in one hand, clubs in the other, pushing us back into the main street. Paul suggested we get the hell out of there, since acid and violence did not good bedfellows make. So we hauled ass back the five blocks to the car area. People trickled in with tales of pig brutality. Tear gas. Whatever. What did we care? We were there for the good times and camaraderie anyway. Hours later, wrapped in sleeping bags near the Merc, we fell asleep. First light woke us up the next morning.

"Hey man, you dudes been to the falls?" a gruff looking hippie with a three-day-old beard and unwashed brown hair said as he ambled past us.

The Crusaders

Paul rubbed the sleep out of his eyes. "Naw, man, where is it?"

The hippie pointed toward the mountain behind the savings and loan building parking lot.

"See that peak?" he said. "Follow the trail behind this building toward it. Then after, I don't know, maybe thirty minutes, you'll find a big pool of water. Ice cold and deep blue." He looked over at the rising sun. "Feels good in this heat."

He looked as though he was going to say more, seemed to check himself and walked away. Suddenly he stopped and turned. "You got any weed?" We had. Kenny tossed him a joint. He lit it, inhaled deeply and held the smoke. "There's two more pools of water higher up. They feed into the main one through the waterfalls. Peace bros."

We thanked him and flipped the peace sign back at him and decided to go to the falls straightaway. The heat had already started to beat down on us.

First, we made sure we had some pot, a bottle of water, some candy bars - all the necessities for an adventure into the unknown. Then, full of bravado, we ventured toward the trail into the desert. We passed a few stragglers coming back who confirmed the story. "Yeah... there was a big pool of water there. Yeah, people could swim in it." We were heartened by those reports for good reason. We'd already run out of water.

Forty-five minutes later, we rounded a large rock outcropping and found the oasis. Tahquitz Falls. It was better than advertised: a fifty-foot waterfall cascading into a deep blue pool of water. In the middle stood a large rock the waterfall pounded upon before splattering into droplets everywhere. People were swimming, climbing up to the top of the waterfall and jumping off into the cool fresh water below. Guys and girls were sunbathing.

Naked.

I did notice something curious to me.

Seemed like most of the hippie chicks were not that good looking. Not ugly, either. They didn't shave the hair under their arms or on the legs, or anywhere else it grew. They seemed to relish dirty, matted hair. And . . . they almost always smelled like patchouli oil. Not very appealing. I suppose they thought the same about us guy hippies. Don't know. But tits are tits, and it was fun looking at them. Couldn't see much else through the bush.

We Crusaders stripped down to our skivvies and jumped in. Spent most of the day splashing around in the crystal clear, ice cold water, smoking joints and speaking of peace and love to the majority of morons who were there and thought themselves intellectuals. Tolstoy. Che Rivera. Stalin's utopia. I doubted most of them could even pass a high school equivalency exam. But they were convinced they knew how to right the troubles of the evil capitalistic world. Harmless enough, and it passed the time while I tried nonchalantly to watch the naked girls without them knowing it. The girls knew, of course. It was a game.

While schlepping back we ran into a good friend, Craig T, a high school acquaintance who we met through Stanley. We'd had some fun adventures with him in the Crusadermoblie - smoking pot, going to the movies, stuff like that - and we really liked him. Tall. Lanky. Good looking. He was on his way to the falls. We promised we would catch up later at the car encampment.

Later never came.

We heard sirens that afternoon. A police helicopter roared overhead and raced toward the mountains.

Craig had climbed to the top of the falls, lost his balance and fell head first onto the large rock the waterfall splashed against. Someone jumped in and pulled him out. Paralyzed and almost dead, he spent a year in the hospital and then another in the rehab center. The result was his being a paraplegic and what you could only charitably refer to as a little... slow.

We left Palm Springs not knowing what had happened until a few weeks later. Tragic. Craig was a really nice guy. Sometimes you're dealt "aces and eights" for no apparent reason.

God bless him.

Our Music

Eight-track tapes had finally made their way into our lives. That meant we could listen to music in our cars. We also had FM radios at home, and we would listen to KNAC 105.5 Long Beach, which played cool music you would never hear on AM radio.

Whole albums could be listened to with no commercial interruptions. Disc jockeys like Jim Ladd would speak to us in low, drug-like whispers when naming the groups. It was pretty damn cool.

In our cars, we could then listen to Led Zeppelin, Pink Floyd, The Who, The Grateful Dead, and Jimi Hendrix. I had installed a light bar in my dad's Fiat that pulsated to the beat of the music on the tape being played. Blue, green, yellow and red lights. I also installed an echo-chamber box. Only problem with it was when the car went over a bump - it sounded like a car wreck from the spring coil bouncing in the little box. Oh well.

The point is that eight-tracks and FM radios in our cars allowed us to listen to music we never would have known about. And our tastes progressively grew and changed.

Crosby, Stills, Nash, and Young were on our radar.

Blind Faith.

Cream.

All of these, coupled with the drugs and lifestyle changes that we were making, brought subtle yet distinct changes to our mode of thinking and appearance.

Not bad, not good.

Just different.

Different enough to think we were independent and not part of the establishment.

Mary II

Our love affair was still going strong - at least as far as love letters were concerned. I kept my promise, and she hers. We wrote each other religiously every week.

I would share everything that went on, and she would reciprocate. It really felt like we were in each other's lives. I was only able to call once a week, because it was long distance. My parents' rule, since they paid the phone bill. But she was never far from my thoughts (except, of course, when Cherie showed up), and I still felt I loved her very much. I did not share with her about my taking drugs. Somehow I knew she would not approve.

Tragically, turns out I was right.

One day I received a strangely shaped card from the same address as Mary, but different handwriting. An invitation from Mary's mother. Her parents were planning a surprise sixteenth birthday party and invited me to go. I had recently gotten my driver's license and had shared that with Mary, who must have relayed it to her parents.

My parents agreed to let me take the blue Lancer to San Bernardino for the occasion, a forty-something-mile drive. Same distance as the beach, which I had already driven many times. The party was a month away. And, I had to keep it secret from Mary. That was difficult for me to do.

On the drive to San Bernardino I envisioned what I would say, how I would surprise her, how I might hold her in my arms and kiss her. A year had elapsed since we had seen each other. I tried to remember her scent from the country club.

These thoughts and more consumed me so that by the time I arrived, I was a somewhat nervous wreck. I had agreed to meet Mary's mother outside the American Legion Hall where the surprise party was taking place.

Mary's dad brought her to the venue, and when she walked inside everyone was there, except me. She started hugging and thanking her friends. I stepped into the room and said, "Happy Birthday, Mary." She looked shocked, and then came running over and hugged me, tears falling down her cheeks.

Her eyes searched mine. "How did you get here? How did you know?"

"Your mom sent me the invitation, and I drove here all by myself."

She kissed me, grabbed my hand, and introduced me to her friends, who were too numerous for me to remember all of their names.

The party ensued. Food, songs, dancing. All was well. I was more in love, if that were possible.

Later that evening I noticed a couple of her long-hair guy friends were whispering to each other, leaving the room for a few minutes and returning, laughing. A familiar smell accompanied them.

Pot.

While Mary kibitzed with a few of her girl friends, I moseyed on over to these guys and asked what was up?

"Nothin', man. Just enjoying ourselves."

"Cool," I responded. "Thought I smelled something 'familiar,' that's all."

They looked at me suspiciously. "You get high?"

I nodded.

"Want to toke with us?"

I looked around, seeing Mary still yakking away with her friends. "Sure, if we can do it quickly."

I followed them to the outside of the American Legion. It was dark by then. Out came a joint. I had taken two hits when I heard the door open and spun around to see... Mary staring at me with a look of horror on her face. She quickly slammed the door.

I excused myself, rushed back into the hall and searched for her. Her mom was getting ready to light the cake. No Mary in sight. Finally, her mother brought her out of the kitchen, the candles were lit, and we all sang. Her eyes averted every glance I gave her.

When the song finished and candles had been blown out, I walked up to her.

"Mary, I can explain about-"

"I don't want to talk about it, John. You're nothing but a dop--" She checked herself and walked away.

I felt like crying, shouting, running away, screaming, begging, and a host of other feelings all at once. *What was the big deal? A few tokes on a joint? Why was she acting this way? What about our love? Our commitment to each other?* It was no big deal, as far as I was concerned. We Crusaders did it all the time.

Mary must have said something to her mom, because not only did she go frigid on me, she finally approached me and relayed that Mary had asked that I leave the party.

What could I do? I left.

The drive home was longer than I could have imagined. The darkness of night, driving down the freeway alone, enveloped me and seemed to amplify my feelings of pain, hurt and rejection. I just could not comprehend how such a quick and immediate reversal of feelings - of cutting me off without giving me chance to explain, had occurred.

But then again, what could I possibly explain?

I *was* smoking pot. It was her party. I was her invited guest. And I guessed that she was disappointed, hurt maybe, in my choice to do that. I felt bad. Terrible.

But again, what could I do? The damage had been done.

It was the last time I saw or heard from Mary.

Nueva Vista

Located on Willow Avenue near Amar Road, Nueva Vista High School was Bassett High School's answer to what to do with the miscreants they were unable to deal with.

I was one of them.

Made up of temporary buildings laid out in a hodgepodge arrangement on an acre of land, there was little else to distinguish it as a beacon of lower learning. I guess it could also be called higher learning, based on student profiles. Referred to in the pejorative slang as 'continuation school,' it was also known as the final home for losers and druggies who couldn't make it anywhere else. That was not completely true. But almost.

To be perfectly honest, most of the guys at Nueva Vista - and they were all guys, no girls - were drug-toking and needle-shooting fuck-ups. As it turned out, the school district only got money from the government when kids were IN school, so it was the only place they could send them with any hope of getting paid. Unlike me, however, who also happened to be a drug-taking hippie, those kids never had any intention to excel in anything other than the personal goal of getting more wasted than the day before.

Although it did have its share of people whose only goal was how much of their gray matter they could destroy in the shortest amount of time, there were others -- kids who could not endure the rules and regulations that Bassett High strictly enforced. In short, they were the mid-sixties non-conformists.

The Crusaders

I was squarely a part of both of these groups, *except* for wanting to destroy my gray matter.

Nueva Vista was headed by a very liberal and really cool principal. His philosophy was simple: here's what you have to accomplish to graduate. How you go about doing it is your business - completely up to you. Period. You also came to school every day. No exceptions. He surrounded himself with a group of teachers who held this same attitude except for one, Mr. Washington, who somehow must have done something wrong and been sent to Nueva Vista as a punishment. He didn't want to be there and he let us know it every day.

The others, including a very cool teacher named Mr. Dudack, were laid back and took the seriousness of the situation in stride.

They didn't.

What the school offered was something I had been craving since "leaving" Catholic School: mental stimulation with the added bonus of total freedom. No teachers bothering me and no one looking over my shoulder to see what I was doing. Nothing like that. I was in learning heaven.

By the end of my first few months there, I'd completed all the remaining lessons and tests for the eleventh grade, and dove in to get through the twelfth grade as quickly as I could. Additionally, I asked for more work. Mr. Dudack suggested that since they needed a new non-temporary building constructed, why didn't I learn to draw architectural renderings, and then design it. I studied relentlessly for weeks, drawing every day, learning three-dimensional drafting, and finally designed the entire building with specifications. I soaked up and enjoyed every minute of it.

They used my drawing to build it.

Days at Nueva Vista were an adventure, and really helped me not to miss my friends, of which there were none to be found there. Mr. Dudack would organize field trips to the mountains and beaches, and the least loaded of the school's population would end up going. I always went. Not that I wasn't loaded once in a while. But I didn't overdo it.

One memorable trip we took was to Mount Baldy, about an hour's drive from town. We all, and I mean students and teachers, dropped acid once we started up the mountain. It was snowing and cold. We got so high that we couldn't leave before five hours had elapsed. I took off into the snow, fell down into it, started freezing and then had some interesting thoughts. *What if no one found me here? I could simply fall asleep and die. Who would notice I was not in one of the cars going back?*

Then I realized that I was freezing, panicked, jumped up, and barely made it back. And true to my thoughts, no had one missed me.

We returned to school about four that afternoon and most of us did not get to school the next day - including the teachers.

I mentioned Mr. Washington. He was a black ex-football player and was a big man - over six-feet-six inches tall and solidly built. And he was just a little bit slow. Not stupid. He looked like he had to search his brain for a correct response when asked a question. Maybe he had taken too many hits in football. Anyway, I didn't notice him much and was never in his class. But the word out on him was not good. He was always the target of pranks or worse. Kids were always goofing on him between classes

Four of the school's bigger fuck-ups went out driving with him. He was the driver's education teacher. They talked him into going to Huntington Beach, which was thirty miles away.

The Crusaders

They kept driving until he asked them to stop so he could go to the bathroom. When he came out, the car was gone.

They cruised the beaches for a couple of hours, and then came back and left the car a few blocks from school. Mr. Washington had to call the principal and be picked up. That was the first time I really felt for the man. He had such a downtrodden and defeatist look on him when he returned with one of the teachers that I made a promise to myself to do something nice for him.

When he passed me the next day, I made it a point to say hello to him. The first time I'd ever done that. He looked at me and tried to figure out *why* I did it. I didn't have time to explain that I was trying to be nice to him, and kept going. I do think he felt better.

Days later, he was showing a movie on the dangers of smoking, which included shots of black shrunken lungs being pulled out of corpses. *Ugh.* Anyway, some guys were smoking joints in the classroom while Mr. Washington was outside the building, and when he opened the door, a wall of smoke rushed out. He started screaming at everyone, and as they ran out the door, one of the guys slugged him. The guy had a ring on his finger. A small gash appeared to the right of Mr. Washington's left eye, and blood starting oozing out.

I stood dumbfounded, hardly believing what had just happened. Tears started coming out of his eyes, and he rushed to the bathroom.

I rushed after and caught up with the guy who hit him.

"What the fuck are you doing?" I asked.

"What do you care?"

I stepped in front of him. "You can't hit a teacher like that."

"Well, guess what, asshole? I just did."

I stood there, staring at his feeble attempt at a clenched-tooth smile on his pimple-ridden face. I didn't understand why, but I was getting madder.

"What the fuck do you care anyways, John," he continued. "He's just a fuckin' nigger."

I pushed him back into the building wall. "Try that shit on me asshole," I taunted him. "Come on!"

"What are you man, some nigger lover? He's just a fucking teacher, for chrisakes."

Venom was running through my veins. Something clicked in me that I hadn't experienced before. I wanted to kill the guy. Beat him senseless. But why? Was it because of what he did to Mr. Washington? Because he called him a nigger? Because the whole thing seemed so unfair and chickenshit? I pushed him back into the wall, hard, and started to walk away.

"Try that again asshole and you're fuckin' dead," I shouted over my shoulder.

"You're lucky, John," he shouted as he ran away.

Mr. Washington came out of the bathroom and walked to the principal's office. He returned about a week later with a bandage still on his head. His eyes didn't connect with any of the students, and he walked around stoop-shouldered.

The little weasel who hit him was snickering with his friends, if that is what you can call a group of druggies whose only common thread was to talk about doobies and drugs and where the next ones would come from. Any one of them would have sold the others out for a roll of reds. My stomach felt nauseous and I just wanted to get loaded and forget the whole thing. What a group of assholes.

I felt isolated at school. It didn't hold the same importance in my life as when my friends had been there. If it weren't for weekends with everybody, I would've had nothing to look forward to.

It must be pointed out that the principal of Nueva Vista and Mr. Dudack turned out to be influential role models for me. They showed me how you could be an adult and at the same time be cool and understanding. Something I had had no concept of with the adults in my life up to that point. They displayed integrity, inner strength, a sharp intellect, and wit.

And they got high.

Traits I promised myself to develop - including the getting high part.

Truth was, I didn't know if I would ever want to stop - or even be able to stop if I wanted to.

Unfortunately, I never had a chance to say goodbye to the teachers I had grown to care about.

Mouseland

Paul, Kenny, Billy, and I sat in the gondola after a thirty-minute wait in line. We floated through the tunnel that opened up to hundreds of stupid-looking puppets, with Winchell-Mahoney-looking mouths and strings animating their arms and legs. They were singing, "It's a small world after all...." Phony-looking houses, painted mountains and cartoon landscapes rounded out the look.

Was this really a good idea?

We'd decided to take our first trip to Disneyland on acid. Purple Barrels. We dropped in the parking lot and entered the Magic Kingdom. Kenny suggested the Small World ride. I had wanted to go to the new Pirates of the Caribbean ride.

We weaved our way through those damn little puppets in our small boat, each "land" becoming more annoying and louder than the last. When we were in "Latin America", the ride broke down. *Shit.* "It's a small world after all" in Spanish for the next twenty-five minutes. Finally they restarted the ride. I could not get the song out of my head.

For months.

Paul sat down near Tomorrowland. Said the whole ground was weaving and moving and wanted to wait a few minutes.

"Are you okay?" I asked.

"Not sure man. Really weird. Looks like the ground is melting or something."

"We'll be back in a few minutes. You gonna be okay?"

He nodded yes. Billy and I scurried over to the Pirates ride and went through it. Twice. The drop over the waterfall was scary. Those pirates looked real. So did the fire at the end. We discussed how they did it on the way back to Paul and Kenny. We had no idea.

Every year when we were growing up, my family went to Disneyland and met my Uncle Jerry for breakfast: Mickey Mouse pancakes. We had a room at the Disneyland Hotel. After a day at the park, we took the monorail to the hotel, took a nap, and went back for the fireworks at 9 pm. After spending the night, we would have another breakfast - Mickey Mouse pancakes - and leave for home in the afternoon.

I knew every nook and cranny of the Magic Kingdom.

I convinced the guys to go on the Matterhorn. We did. Big mistake. We all became nauseated. Almost threw up. I tried unsuccessfully to *not* imagine that on acid: Technicolor throw-up with trails following the chunks. *Ugh.* Then we ambled over to the 'Adventure Through Inner Space.' That was far out. Especially the big eyeball staring at us through the microscope at the end. The ride caused all kinds of philosophical conjectures.

"Maybe our universe is simply a drop of water in a glass... of people who are in a bigger universe? Not even aware of us?" We thought that was heavy. *Right.*

Went to Swiss Family Robinson treehouse, rode on the carousel, passed on the teacups, but rode Peter Pan twice each. It really felt like we were flying.

But still, that damn 'It's a Small World' song was pounding in my head. I asked the others. They were stuck with it in their heads too.

Paul's trip had morphed into a more mellow experience by then. So we sat through the Tiki Room parrots, ate at New

Orleans Square, and finished the evening on the train that circled the park. The dinosaurs looked pathetic. Probably worse because of the acid. It was a low note to leave on.

The interesting thing about our adventure was that every color, every sound, every theme was exaggerated - at least in our minds. It was a constant bombardment to our senses. Overload really. And nobody seemed to notice we were loaded.

Then there were the different characters running around. Chip and Dale? Pinocchio? We had our pictures taken with a bunch of them.

Weird.

We were tired, it was dark, we were starting to come down, and the fireworks were still a couple of hours off before they started. The vote was in. Let's go home.

"Maybe coming here on acid wasn't such a good idea," Kenny said.

Billy and Paul agreed.

I liked it. It reminded me of my childhood.

But . . .

For years, whenever anyone mentioned "It's a Small World," I cringed.

God forbid that they should play the darn thing.

Sister Debby

My Sister Debby was what my Mom referred to as incorrigible. She was always in trouble for little things, usually of her own making. Then again, so was I. But she was a girl. Different rules and expectations.

Once we were playing Monopoly, and I landed on Park Place and proceeded to purchase it.

"You can't do that, Johnny," she said.

"Sure can. Watch."

"But I need that. I have Boardwalk already," she pleaded.

That was the point of my strategy. "Tough luck, sis."

As I was counting out the money, she flipped the entire game board over, dumping hotels, houses and cards everywhere. Then she slugged herself in the upper arm.

"What the heck are you doing?" I screamed, feeling my neck and face burn with anger.

"Dad," she cried so he would hear her in the next room. "Dad... Johnny hit me and flipped over the Monopoly game."

She jumped up, crocodile tears flowing, red blotch on her arm forming nicely, and ran out the bedroom door and into the front room, proudly displaying what her big brother did to her.

"Johnny, what did you do?" he said in a voice I can only describe as "you are in deep trouble and don't even try and lie to get out of it or you will be sorry."

"She hit herself and flipped the board, Dad. I swear to God."

"None of that kind of talk in this house," he said, teeth clenched together while he spoke. "You go to your room now." It was not a suggestion.

Years later, Stanley, Paul, Kenny, and I were driving in the Merc when we rounded the corner of Mayland and there, on the corner of my street, were two big bare asses staring at us from the front yard of a neighbor. Paul flipped his bright lights on and off, and the two asses were quickly covered up with pants and running down the street.

Debby and her best friend Janet -- they were inseparable, and were also very anti-establishment. She wasn't really into drugs, but everything else was fair game. They would stay out late, sneak out the window, smoke cigarettes.

Janet's parents finally moved away to West Covina, and then to West Los Angeles, where they settled permanently.

After she left, Debby got wilder and more out of control. It had finally caught up with her.

Debby was sent to juvenile hall at my parents' request. I never really found out the reason why. Janet's parents stepped up and took her into their home in West Los Angeles. It was short-lived. They sent her back. Thereafter, she was sent to Saint Ann's in Los Angeles, an all-girl's private school run by nuns that in reality was a gilded prison that you could not leave or escape.

When I received my driver's license, ninety days after my sixteenth birthday, I drove my dad's Lancer every week to Los Angeles to visit her. What she really missed was In-N-Out burgers, fries and shakes. So, I would stop on the way, pick them up for her and her friends, and take them to the school. We munched the food down in the visiting room.

I continued going until my parents took away my car privileges. Occasionally, Paul would take me to visit her. I lost contact with her for a time after that.

Once Debby was released, or rather graduated, from the school, she was never the same.

She never forgave my parents for putting her in that school.

Angry, hateful, spiteful.

Couldn't blame her.

Although I couldn't relate to those feelings at the time, I soon would.

RFK

Robert Francis Kennedy addressed his supporters shortly after midnight on June 5, 1968, in a ballroom at The Ambassador Hotel in Los Angeles, California. Leaving the ballroom, he went through the kitchen after being told it was a shortcut, despite being advised to avoid the kitchen by his bodyguard, FBI agent Bill Barry. In a crowded kitchen passageway, Sirhan Sirhan, a 24-year-old Palestinian, opened fire with a .22 caliber revolver. Kennedy was hit three times and five other people were wounded.

George Plimpton, former decathlete Rafer Johnson, and former professional football player Rosey Grier wrestled Sirhan Sirhan to the ground after the shooting. Kennedy was first rushed to Los Angeles's Central Receiving Hospital, and later to the city's Good Samaritan Hospital, where he died early the next morning.

Sirhan said he felt betrayed by Kennedy's support for Israel in the June 1967 Six Day War which had begun exactly one year before the assassination.

So the Los Angeles Times reported on the incident.

I'd only seen my dad looking as sad one time before, when President John F. Kennedy was killed.

I felt sad too, although I didn't yet quite understand why. It felt like it was the death of a dream, a hope, a chance that things could change, that a politician really cared.

A tragic waste of a good life.

Bad Trip

"Are you sure they are expecting us?" I asked cousin Jeff.

"Of course, man. I set it up with them before they left."

I was skeptical. Jeff had a habit of embellishing what he did and did not do, especially where girls were concerned. The plan was to hitchhike to Newport Beach, where these girls from Whittier had rented a house about a dozen homes north of the pier. We had hitched about halfway there, somewhere in the middle of Orange County, and the rides were slowing down.

Jeff wasn't a Crusader, technically. The guys knew him, and he hung out once in a while, but always as an outsider. However, when drugs started entering into the picture, Jeff seemed to have great connections, and he was around us more after that.

"You sure we'll be able to score down there?" I asked.

"No problem, cousin," he said, followed by a wink and a smile. "I've got some friends who are meeting me there."

A few years earlier we had graduated from pot and pills to LSD - almost unceremoniously.

The first time we dropped acid, we were at Paul's house in the evening, which was unusual because Paul's parents were rarely gone. We were smoking pot and had scored a few tabs of Orange Sunshine from some friends at five dollars a tab. It was made by the Laguna Brotherhood, and was laced with some speed.

"Wanna try it?" Kenny asked.

"Why not," Stanley replied. We all concurred.

It was no big deal for any of us at the time. In fact, LSD wasn't even illegal. It crept into on to radar of The Crusaders gradually, seductively, and it was just a matter of time before we would try it. The Beatles had come out with their album *Sergeant Pepper's Lonely Hearts Club Band*, and despite their protestation to the contrary, we knew what *Lucy in the Sky with Diamonds* meant: LSD.

The funny thing about it was we weren't doing it to raise our consciousness as Timothy Leary proselytized, or even Muktananda, who advocated using it to get a glimpse of the end goal of meditation; rather, it was to get high, laugh, and see things in a different way. Our hands leaving trails as they moved. Colors more vibrant. Realizations about life with a humorous bent.

That night we dropped a tab each, and because speed was laced within, it kicked in pretty quickly. Subtle but fun. We were laughing, eating, and carrying on as if nothing were that different from a pot high. And to tell the truth, it didn't seem that different.

However, after an hour or so I walked out into the backyard and saw Stanley, lying on his stomach with his head under water looking into the pool. The underwater light was on, and the water glowed a vibrant blue. I walked over to him, got down on my stomach and put my head into the water.

I observed an unbelievable array of light, movement, and color all mixed into one bad-ass experience. I looked over at Stanley, smiled, and continued observing the ripples of light.

He reached his hand in and moved the water, intensifying the experience and speed of the ripples. Suddenly, I remembered I was almost out of breath. That was a conscious reaction, not autonomic. I lifted my head out of the water and realized Stanley had been in that position a lot longer than I had. I grabbed his hair and yanked his head up. He started coughing and gagging, while at the same time laughing.

"That was bitchin,'" he finally coughed out. "Did you see the trails in that pool?"

"Yeah, man. Far out."

"I'm going back in," he said, lowering his head into the chlorinated water.

Standing up, I shook off the water and walked back to the kitchen.

"We better keep an eye on Stanley," I said, nodding toward the pool.

"Why?" Paul asked.

"He's checking out the trails in the water, and almost drowned," I replied, water dripping from my hair.

"No shit, you can see trails in the water?" Paul asked.

I nodded as Paul and Kenny raced to the pool near Stanley, laid down and put their heads in the water.

"This is going to be a long night," I said to myself, laughing.

That was the start of our love affair with acid. It quickly became the drug of choice, and we dropped it every chance we could get it.

The next year was a blur of fun, great adventures and camaraderie.

Jeff and I arrived at the house the girls had rented late in the afternoon. It was a glorious Southern California summer day - wispy white clouds, an inviting deep-blue sky, with the sun warming the sand and air with piercing rays of light. Turned out this time Jeff was not lying - the girls were expecting us. We dropped our bags in an upstairs bedroom they designated for us and proceeded to plan out the major party they wanted to throw that evening.

"No problemo," Jeff said. "All we have to do is tell a few people at the pier, and the word will get around, and everyone will be here. I'll take care of it."

He left and came back within fifteen minutes.

"All set," he said. He motioned for me to come over, turned away from the girls and started whispering. "John, I scored this psilocybin and want you to hold it while I go out and score some beer." Handing it to me he smiled. "Supposed to be some good stuff. Wait until I get back and we'll drop it." I looked in the foil and saw two tabs.

"Okay, cuz. See you later."

By seven o'clock the place was crowded with people. Crowded? It was packed like sardines. Jeff hadn't come back yet, so I decided to take one of the tabs. I figured I'd get a jump-start on the trip, and he could take the other when he returned. The music started blasting *In a Gadda Da Vida* and the crowd was moving almost rhythmically to the bass riff. I was flitting around, as I tended to do at parties, meeting one person after the other with the usual patter associated with it.

"Hey man, what's up?"

"Dude, everything, man. What's up with you?"

"Not much, man."

"I can dig it, man. Heavy party going on here."

"No shit. You holding?"

"Naw man, too hot here at the beach with the man out there."

"Hey man, what's up?"

"Everything's groovy, man."

"Cool."

"Cool."

"Far out."

After about twenty minutes the music was getting a little louder, at least in my head, and I started to feel a little claustrophobic. It felt strange. Foreign to me. I needed to get some air. Walking outside, I noticed the swarm of kids extended for at least half a block in both directions. *This little soiree was going to get busted for sure.*

Shouldering my way back in, I made it upstairs to the room we were given and it was full of people. Then the music changed to *Sympathy for the Devil* by the Stones. Suddenly a feeling came over me, one I'd forgotten having had before. Fear.

I first experienced it when I gave a piano recital in front of my school in the fourth grade. I had walked up to the piano where I was supposed to give the opening note to the choir, but they misread this and stayed seated. Minutes went by. I sat there alone while the audience just stared at me, waiting for something to happen. Finally, the choir rose, got into position and stood there, but a sort of panic took me over, and I could barely hit the one note. I couldn't get down from that stage quickly enough.

That same fear started to engulf me then. My breathing was shallow, my heart raced, and a high-pitched noise started screaming in my ears.

"Pleased to meet you, hope you guess my name. But what's troubling you, is the nature of my game."

I went into a full-blown panic attack. I couldn't move. I just sat in the corner, scooted against the wall on the floor, and tried to reason myself out of it. *What is going on with me? Why am I so scared?* Images started turning diabolical, dancing throughout the room. The music seemed to grow in intensity as my head and heart were overruling my consciousness. I could not stop it. Nothing seemed real or grounded.

Hours passed in this state. Nothing had changed for me. Panic, fear, paranoia, unable to move. The bodies in the room started thinning out. My ghoulish images of imminent disaster did not.

"John?"

I looked up to see Jeff, standing at the door in his shorts staring down at me. "What's happening, dude?"

"I don't know, Jeff, it's fuckin' weird." My arms were wrapped around my legs, as I rocked back and forth, trying to hold on to my sanity.

He kneeled down to look at me. "You okay?"

"No, man, I'm not. That psilocybin shit was bad news."

"You didn't take the whole tab, did you?"

"What do you mean?"

"Dude, it was an eight-way tab."

"How was I supposed to know that, asshole? Why didn't you tell me?"

"I was going to when we dropped it."

Fuck. I had taken eight hits of a psychedelic substance, and it kicked the crap out of me. Then I understood what had happened, but it didn't make the experience any less real or disturbing. I swore at Jeff a few more times, followed by his apologies for not telling me, and I stayed in the room the rest of the night, awake and hanging on.

Morning finally came, accompanied by the golden rays of a rising sun and the accompanying warmth of the sunshine. I made my way to the ocean, walking along it and taking in big breaths of salty air. It seemed to help clear my head, and I started feeling like my old self again. But something was slightly different. I didn't understand what, but I still felt off.

Later that day, Jeff and I hitchhiked to his house in Whittier, and I continued on to La Puente. When I walked into my house, all seemed normal. Don't know why but I thanked God for that. I was dead tired, not having slept the previous night, so I went straight to bed and slept.

When I awoke, it all seemed like a bad dream. Although I remembered it clearly, it was more like observing a movie rather than being in it. I chalked it up to experience, a bad experience, and vowed never to take more than one hit again. And no more psilocybin.

A few days later we were at my house and decided to drive to see some friends whose parents weren't home. We dropped some Purple Barrels and took off. By this time, Billy Souza had his license and was using his dad's white '66 bug. On the way over there, I started to feel spacey again. The high-pitched noise returned, my heart started racing, and I felt claustrophobic in that little VW.

Panic set in. I wanted out of the car. Where? I didn't know. I screamed for Billy to stop the car, climbed out of the back seat and took off toward home, walking. It seemed everyone was staring at me as I passed the houses that all appeared the same. Sidewalks looked out of perspective. Sounds were piercing. Birds were chirping just to accentuate my fear.

I started running. Running away from what? It was inside me. I couldn't shake it. I was scared, more scared than I'd ever remembered being, and the only place I could think of to go was home, safety. I reached my house, raced in and shut myself in the bedroom. The hours passed. I started to calm down. My brother came in a couple of times, and I shooed him out.

What was wrong with me? Why had it happened again? Maybe I broke something in my brain? Maybe I fucked up really bad? I reached for my stash spot and took a couple of reds. *That will calm me down,* I reasoned. I took a breath, laid on the bottom bunk and tried not to think of anything. It was a fruitless task until I started feeling drowsy from the Phenobarbital kicking in. Finally. I started to relax and then drifted off into a fitful slumber.

Days passed and I made all kinds of excuses why I didn't want to drop any more acid with The Crusaders. I figured I needed a little time to let my almost-fried mind recover and repair itself. It was a thought, anyway. I still smoked weed, but even that didn't feel quite right. I found I didn't like the spaciness of the high. In fact, it wasn't fun anymore. Almost like I was not in control of my feelings. *Odd*, I thought. *This never happened before.*

I was over at Sandy's house. We were smoking some pot, listening to Jimi Hendrix's *Purple Haze* album, and we were having a good time. Sandy was like a sister to us, and her place was a cool and safe place to get high and just goof off. Plus her older sisters were absolute foxes.

We lit up some doobies, and after about ten minutes, the same sensation started hitting me. Panic, fear, paranoia. *What the fuck?*

"I've got to leave, Sandy."

"You okay, John?" she asked, concern in her voice.

"No, not really. I've got to get home."

I raced home, but couldn't get there fast enough. Once in my bedroom, I took some more reds, and laid down on the bed.

What is going on? Full panic mode ensued. Demonic images danced on the walls. *When is this going to stop?*

Then it started happening even when I was not loaded. Perfectly straight. Yet the high-pitched noise started in my head and my heartbeat started to race. I found myself taking more and more reds to stop the panic attacks, and it was affecting everything I did. Slurring my words, fogging my thinking, pulling away from my friends -- even my fellow Crusaders.

Months passed, and it didn't get any better. Fact is, the attacks grew in intensity.

After school one day I came home and my parents informed me that I needed to have some medical tests performed because I was acting... strangely.

I argued against them, but to tell the truth, inwardly I was hoping that maybe it was a medical condition that did indeed need fixing. My parents made a decision that would become such a turning point in my life that even I could not comprehend the full magnitude of it.

Ingleside

I woke up in a room. Small. Stark. A TV against the wall. Rails on each side of the bed.

And I couldn't remember a thing. Even my name. I laid on the bed, wondering where I was. A high-pitched noise echoed in my head. Straining to lift it up, I looked around. Nothing looked familiar.

Where in the fuck was I?

Two weeks earlier I had asked my mom, "Where are we going?"

"To the hospital."

"Why?" I asked.

"You need help, Johnny," she replied.

"With what?"

She kept driving, looking straight ahead, silent. My dad didn't look back either.

I admit I hadn't been feeling my usual chipper self for the previous few months. Acid trips were continuing with more regularity, and then I found myself counteracting them with downers, which also were growing in equal proportion. I wasn't sloppy or mean when I took the downers - quite the opposite. It was my normal reaction to just mellow out and not cause any problems at all. To withdraw into myself.

But I never knew when the infrequent high-pitched noise followed by sheer panic would start up, coursing through my body and electrifying every nerve I had with fear. It was a dictator I no longer wanted, but was forced to serve: ungrounded fear.

Car privileges had been revoked by my parents months before, and I was resigned to walk everywhere when Paul and the Crusadermobile were not around.

Word had spread of a huge party at Howard Feingold's house, so that Friday night I borrowed my brother's Stingray (without his knowing it) and pedaled the dozen or so blocks to Howard's house.

There must have been fifty people there, packed into a tract home and backyard very similar to my parents' house. Booze, pot and acid were freely available, and I partook of all but the acid. Unfortunately, most of the wine was Gallo red in gallon jugs. I drank way too much, and before I knew it I was starting to get dizzy in the house.

Howard and I got along pretty well after the fight we'd had years earlier in Edgewood Junior High over his girl's hair color, but that night he was being pretty obstinate. I accidently tripped over a chair, spilled some wine, and he told me to be careful -- he didn't want his parents knowing he'd had a party. I didn't respond quickly enough, or maybe he thought I didn't care (which was not the case), and he forced me to leave the house, pushing me out the door.

Okay. Time to leave.

I picked up the Stingray and started pedaling home, head slightly spinning, my balance wobbly, and steering in anything but a straight line.

Suddenly I heard a crash, broken glass, and then silence. I came to lying on the hood of a car, unable to grasp what had happened. I shook my head, pushed off the hood and stood up in front of the bumper. The car was parked. No one around. I looked at the Stingray and noticed the front wheel was bent, and the left headlight of the car was shattered. Picking up the bike, I walked the rest of the way home. My brother would bitch about the bike, but I could claim someone stole it and dented the wheel. I'd think about that. Right then, I needed to get into my bed and hopefully feel better. Nausea was sweeping over me like a blanket. I wobbled into the house, stumbled to my bedroom and plopped into bed.

The room was spinning. I held on, and all the prayers that were drilled into me over the years in Catholic school came out of my mouth by rote; each succeeding one getting more serious and earnest, followed by "Please don't let me die, God, please don't let me die."

Eventually I must have passed out, because I woke up to daylight and the fragrance of bacon and eggs floating in the air. My favorite. I rolled off the bed and noticed I'd changed into my pajamas. Strange. Didn't remember doing that. Shrugging, I walked out into the living room and stood, staring at my dad reading... the Sunday paper?

"Finally awake, sleepy head?" my dad said, not looking up.

"Yes... but when did we start having eggs and bacon on Saturday?"

My dad peeked over the paper and looked at me, perplexed. And then he smiled.

"This is Sunday, Johnny."

No shit? I rushed back into my room and tried to remember what happened to Saturday. No memories at all. I must have been really fucked up. Scary fucked up to miss a whole 24 hours. I made a note to myself to never drink again from that point forward. After all, I had promised God numerous times the previous evening (I guess I meant Friday evening) that if I lived, we had a deal. I had, however, purposely left out drugs.

I hoped God wouldn't notice that omission.

But I really think the tipping point, as far as prompting my parents to act, happened at Lake Gregory, where we vacationed as a family each summer. Paul, Kenny, and Stanley were sitting in the Crusadermobile in front of the penny arcade when I spotted them. Walking over, I poked my head in the passenger side window and asked if they had scored any acid yet. Kenny was motioning for me to shut up with his hands, eyes wide like saucers.

"Come on guys," I continued. "Are you holding or not?"

"Hey, John," Paul blurted out. "We were just saying hello to *your* parents..." He looked toward his driver's side window and jerked his head. I bent in and saw my mom and dad standing there, staring at me. *Shit, shit, shit.* I laughed, said hi to them and walked away, but I knew they had heard the whole exchange.

Four weeks later my parents informed me we were going to the hospital for some medical tests.

We pulled into a drab asphalt parking lot and stopped in front of a non-descript building. There was fog and mist that added to the chill and dreariness of the day.

The sign in front read "Ingleside Psychiatric Hospital."
What the heck is this all about?

With my dad beside her, my mom filled out the paperwork and, in a feigned and limpid show of support, tried to reassure me that these were just tests, and everything would be alright. I wasn't at all convinced. But what could I do?

To tell the truth, I was tired. Staying a night or two didn't seem all that bad. *Maybe I'll get a good night's sleep. Maybe*

I'll get some better drugs to help me sleep. At the time, I didn't give it much more thought.

That was a mistake.

Ingleside was headed by a psychiatrist named Doctor Walter Kempler. I learned a lot about him years later from his former wife, a coincidence that defies all logical explanation. But I didn't need her or her son (my then best friend Frank) to tell me that there was something seriously wrong with him. I learned it quickly enough on my own.

Tests filled up most of the following day - blood work, physical, thyroid, things like that. Innocuous enough by themselves. I didn't get to meet anyone else until later that evening, and a more motley group of miscreants I could not have imagined. It was as if the movie *Reefer Madness* had morphed into some Kafka'ish reality. My reality. The caricatures could not have been more startling.

Heroin addicts with loose-fitting suits of skin over protruding bones, potheads who didn't know up from down and couldn't care less anyway, speed freaks with sunken eyes and overly articulated arm and head gestures, paranoids huddled head-down in corners with eyes cast upward staring over their eyebrows. In summary, the dregs of the drug world. A three-ring circus of damaged teenagers, many of whom had made a seriously wrong turn somewhere and left their brains behind in the process.

And then there was me.

A Crusader. In a damn hellhole of losers and deviants. The thing of it was, my parents must have thought I was as bad as these poor souls, or else they wouldn't have brought me here. Could I really have been that fucked up? Seriously?

I picked up my sleeping pills from the nurse's station and crashed for the night. *At least there were better drugs in this place.*

Waking up the next morning, I realized I had no idea what to do next. *Will they come and get me? Do I just sit in my room and wait? Wait for what?* They didn't lock the door, so after dressing I wandered out into the hallway and told a nurse I was hungry. She directed me to the cafeteria where I was able to get some cereal and toast. After a couple of bites, another nurse came in and stopped me from eating anything more, stating that I had a treatment later that morning and could not eat anything.

"Coffee?"

"Oh," she said, "that would be okay."

"What kind of treatment?" I asked her.

"You'll have to discuss that with the doctor."

"How do I do that?"

"I'm not sure."

"Who is my doctor?"

"Doctor Kempler. He is everyone's doctor."

I meandered to the main recreation room. A thin, lanky guy came up to me. Said his name was Gary and asked me why I was there.

"Not sure, man," I said.

"You doing any drugs?"

"Some, nothing big."

His sallow eyes kept staring at me.

"Want some dope?"

"What are you talking about?"

He looked around, leaned in, licked his upper lip and whispered:

"You know, man, junk. I got some hidden in the back of this place."

"Fuck, no," I said, shaking my head. "I've got to go." And with that, I rushed back to my room.

297

What have I gotten myself into here? What were my parents thinking? What kind of help did they expect me to receive here?

An orderly found and took me to· an office to meet Dr. Kempler. Sitting behind a desk, he quickly glanced up and then back down from a manila folder with my name typed on the tab. Slightly graying short- cropped hair, square-jawed, and beady narrow eyes. Without looking up, he said that there were a number of things abnormal with my blood and thyroid, and that he was prescribing a treatment for me that should take care of it. He slapped the manila folder closed and plopped it onto the desk. He focused on me, looking grave, his head shaking slightly.

"Shouldn't take more than a couple of weeks," he added.

"What won't?"

He stood up and called for the nurse. "There is no other way," he cautioned. "I will call your parents and let them know."

About noon two orderlies escorted me to a small room with a couple of gurneys, and instructed me to get on one of them and lie down. *Okay, whatever.* I laid there, still. Olive green walls the color of split pea soup. I wanted this over so I could call my parents and have them get me the hell out of there. Fifteen minutes later another orderly came in and rolled me down a hallway and into a sort of operating room. Looking left and right I wasn't able to see any operating instruments, just a stack of equipment and a large overhead operating light with multiple bulbs. A nurse smiled as she stepped over me and wrapped my chest with a leather strap, cinching it tight. Then more straps over my arms and feet. *What the heck? What are they going to do?*

A man in a white coat inserted a needle into my arm and slowly pushed the green liquid in. At first it burned, and I said so. "Not to worry," he said, "you will be out quick enough." *Out quick enough?*

"Count backwards from ten to one," I was told. I started at ten, and then my body started to feel warm. Calmness started racing through my veins. "Open your mouth," I heard echoing in the background. I did. A rubber piece was put in, like the piece worn by football players when they were in the game. "Bite down." I did.

Then nothing.

Time flew by in a daze, because I had no concept of it. Every few days - I guessed they were days - I would go through the same routine: into the green room, lying down on a gurney, strapped in, mainlined with anesthesia, and finding myself waking up in my room. I would walk down the halls staring and yet not comprehending or recognizing people as I passed them. Meals would go by as if I were in a dream, watching myself eating but not really being a part of it.

One of the worst of the group of patients in the hospital was the heroin addict Gary, who had already tried to get me to shoot up a number of times. He was shooting up twice a day with a hidden package in one of the recreation rooms. I was sitting in a chair in the television room when he approached me, his head jerking up and down and looking around, paranoid style.

"Hey, man," he said in a lowered whispery voice, his body moving in quick cat-like jumps. "What the hell did you do?"

"What do you mean?"

He took a drag from the non-filtered camel cigarette he held with his yellow-stained bony fingers. "They're frying you, man. Big time." His head and eyes darted back and forth, never focusing on me.

"Frying?"

"Yeah man. You've been fried at least a dozen times since you got here. What gives?"

At first I couldn't comprehend what he was saying. All I could do was stare at him, cocking my head.

"What are you talking about, man?"

His eyes finally comprehended.

"Dude... they're using the electric shock machine on you."

"The electric shock machine?" My voice trailed off. My fists tightened until the knuckles turned white. *What is going on?* I ran to the nurse's station and told the nurse I needed to use the phone. She handed me one over the counter and turned to continue her paperwork. I started to turn the rotary dial and stopped. *What is her number?* I tried again and stopped. *Shit. What is it?*

Finally, I finished dialing and it rang.

"Sandy?" I muttered.

"John? Where are you? Where have you been? We've been worried about you."

"Sandy... I think... I'm in trouble."

"Trouble?"

"I... I'm not sure. Something about shocking me. I... I can't think straight."

"John, I'll call Paul. Where are you?"

"I think they may be trying to kill me."

"Who?"

"The people at this hospital."

"What's the name of it, John?"

"I don't remember."

"John... John?"

"Yeah."

"I'll have Paul call your parents."

"Thanks... Sandy."

Silence for a few moments.

"You... you okay?"

"I don't think so."

It was silent for a few more moments.

"Hang in there John..."

Tears started to run down my cheeks.

"Okay."

A dial tone followed. I hung up the phone and decided to call my parents. I could remember that number - Edgewood 44706.

My dad answered. "Hello?"

"Dad, it's Johnny."

"Hey, Johnny, how are you feeling?"

"I'm not, Dad."

"What?"

"I'm not feeling... anything. I think they're trying to kill me here."

"Hold on a second." I could hear him set down the phone and call out to my mother to come to the phone. He picked it up again.

"Hold on, Johnny, here's your mother."

There was some murmuring and she picked up the line.

"Yes, Johnny?"

"Mom, can you guys come and take me home?"

"We're waiting to hear from the doctor before we can do that," she replied as if she were answering a question about the weather.

"Mom... I... I... think they're shocking me with something here."

Silence.

More silence.

"What, Johnny?"

"I... I said they're using some sort of shock treatment on me. I... I can't think," I sobbed, unable to hold back the tears. "I'm not crazy, Mom. I just can't think!"

"Johnny, we'll talk to the doctor today-"

"Please... get me out of here."

In a businesslike tone she answered, "We'll see. Goodbye."

Dial tone.

I slowly hung up the phone and could see that the nurse overheard everything I'd said. I struggled out a smile and walked back to my room.

Ten minutes later two orderlies came for me again. "Doctor's orders," they said.

"No. I won't go. I'm waiting to hear from my parents before . . ."

They forcefully grabbed me and escorted me to the green room. I hadn't the strength or the will power to resist with any great force. There was no struggle left in me. Up on the gurney, strapped in, then the green 'happy' juice and waking up in my room.

The next day I was told to pack up my things. I was going home that afternoon.

Home.

Like a zombie, I went through the motions of packing clothes, stuffing them into a small suitcase and setting it down on the floor.

Lunch time came, and I met most of the other patients in the lunch room. Told them I was leaving. Gary the heroin addict said it was about time.

"What about you?" I mumbled.

"Me, I got it made here. Good drugs, no police. Three squares a day. I'm not going anywhere." He lit a cigarette, blew out the bluish smoke and leaned over to whisper. "They don't shock heroin addicts."

Home.

I tried to remember the details. Couldn't focus my mind and see them. Only a feeling came when I uttered those words. Home. It felt safe.

Tears welled up in my eyes. I fought to hold them back. I lost.

I was going home.

Whether they knew about it or not, on purpose or by ignorance, I was going home to those same people, my parents, who put me there in the first place.

Damn.

John O'Melveny Woods

The Crusaders
Part Three

1969-1970

"Pleased to meet you,
hope you guess my name.
But what's troubling you is...
The nature of my game."

Moving Away

Kenny's mom was planning to leave his dad. It was an open secret in the neighborhood -- how they didn't get along. Nothing violent. He just drank a lot, and she was tired of it. Got pretty mean when he drank. One weekend, while his dad was away on business, I saw the moving truck in the driveway, loading up. Kenny wasn't there. His mom said they were moving to Anaheim, and that Kenny would keep in touch.

I was still in a fog from the hospital. It had only been a couple of weeks since my parents came and picked me up. Paul and Stanley came over to visit, and I could see it in their eyes. They thought I was screwed up. Not exactly crazy, but from the effects of the shock treatments. In a *One Flew Over The Cuckoo's Nest* kind of way. Maybe I was. Maybe I'd finally crossed the line and fucked up so badly I was unredeemable. I didn't have the strength yet to care one way or the other.

I didn't get high or drink with them. At least for a while. Just didn't have the thought processes to deal with it.

After a few more weeks, I was feeling better and started to get out more, visiting the guys and starting to smoke some pot. Paul, Stanley, Sandy, and Billy seemed to be keeping an eye on me - I guess they were wondering what I would do... if anything. But being that I was not crazy, and that no more "crazy shit" would materialize, we fell back into our main Crusader routine: thinking up things to do that would be fun. Getting loaded. Doing deals.

One idea was to go see Kenny in Anaheim. Together, we planned out that trip.

The next day Stanley called us to come over and visit. A few minutes later, he drove up in his brother's VW.

"What's up?" Paul asked.

"We're moving to Diamond Bar. Dad just told us."

"No shit?" I said.

"Guess not," Stanley replied.

Billy was thoughtful for a moment. "Where're you gonna go to school?"

"Don't know yet."

I looked to Paul. "How far is that away from here?"

"Darn if I know. Maybe twenty miles."

"Any girls out there?" Billy asked.

Stanley shrugged and lit up a smoke. "Hopefully. At least more than here."

I smirked. "What, Joanie isn't working out?"

"Or in?" Paul laughed.

Stanley took another drag and blew out smoke rings. "Wouldn't you like to know. Anyway, we move in about a month."

First Kenny, then Stanley.

Kim had disappeared from our group. Not really, but we didn't see much of him. Not sure what happened. Did not see him even in school. He hadn't moved. He just didn't come around much anymore. It's funny looking back. We didn't even notice it. At least overtly.

That left Billy, Paul and me. And of course Sandy, who was an honorary Crusader anyway.

I found myself mostly hanging out with Sandy and Paul at Sandy's house during the following months, smoking pot.

It took a while, but it seemed that my memory started coming back.

At least what I thought I could remember.

Billy

"Pssst."

I stopped and looked around. Nothing. *What was that?*

I'd just left my house and was walking to Billy's. It was dark. We'd made plans to get together and smoke some new pot he had procured from some vato beaners in East Los Angeles. Part of a deal he was working on to sell the stuff in La Puente.

"Psssst. John," came a whispering voice.

I cocked my head to one side, trying to figure out where the damn voice came from. *Weird*. Licking my bottom lip for a moment, I finally shrugged and continued walking.

"Up here, man."

I turned around, leaned my head back and looked up. I made out a shadow in the tree. "Who's there?"

"It's me, Billy. Keep your voice down, man."

I strode directly under the tree. Billy was there, on the bottom branch, perched and hunched over like a vulture, his arms wrapped around his legs.

"What the heck are you doing Billy?"

He put his index finger to his lips. "Not so loud, John. They might hear you."

I shook my head. "Who might hear me?"

"The guys who are after me."

"Who's after you?"

Silence ensued while he craned his head left, right, and then down at me.

"I don't know."

I stared at him for a few moments. "You high?"

"Yeah man. Smoked some good shit." He lowered his voice and held a cupped hand to his mouth. "I think it had some PCP in it or something."

I thought about that. *Bad shit that PCP.* "You coming down?"

"Not 'til I know they aren't going to get me."

I laughed, softly. It wasn't a humorous one. "Okay then. I'll see you later, Billy."

As I turned to walk back home he whispered. "Don't tell anyone where you saw me."

"Yeah man," I whispered, not turning around. "I won't."

Phyllis

A year or so after the hook-up incident between Billy and the blond neighbor Sandra, Billy met Phyllis. It was while I was in Ingleside Hospital, so I have no details of how it happened - but I was glad it did. I can say that with no hesitation. I loved Phyllis. Not in a covetous or jealous way. Rather, in a true friendship way. Unconditionally. It was obvious she loved Billy. And I was glad for them both.

Phyllis went to Bassett High, transferring there from Torch Junior High. She lived up in the hills south of Valley Boulevard in a nice ranch-style house.

Slim, lanky, long light-brown hair, blue eyes, thin face, full eyebrows that curved around her eyes, thin lips and dimples when she smiled. Slightly creased chin. Not much of a body, small breasted, but shapely nonetheless.

She was always in a good mood. Fun to be around. Interested in what you had to say, and interesting to listen to.

Billy and Phyllis were inseparable. And she became an unofficial yet welcome addition to The Crusaders. In fact, she could hang around us even without Billy, which she sometimes did. She also became quick friends with Sandy, and would come over to her house often - with and without Billy.

She and Billy made love all the time. Or so it seemed to me.

As far as sex and girls were concerned, Billy was ahead of all of us. It was not only that Sandra incident. Girls seemed to find Billy wildly attractive and sexy. He was a good looking guy -- Italian or Castilian looking rather than Mexican. Like his dad, who was a complete whore and was constantly cheating on his mom - or so Billy told us. Girls were no mystery to him.

Many times I would come over to Billy's house, knock on the front door, and Billy and Phyllis would poke their heads out of his bedroom window, which looked onto the porch, and usually say, "We'll be out in a little while."

Phyllis was in tenth grade. Billy was too, only he attended Bishop Amat, so I saw Phyllis all the time. We became close friends, and it was nice to have another female friend in addition to Sandy, especially after what Cherie did to me. I could talk with Phyllis about anything. She would urge me on, to try again, to not give up with anything I attempted.

I also shared with her about my panic attacks. She said she understood. It seemed she really listened to me.

When I was asked to leave Bassett and attend Nueva Vista, I didn't see Phyllis as often. I missed her dearly.

Things went well for a year. However, we Crusaders started to notice changes in Billy - subtle at first. Stanley was the first to mention it, even though he had already moved to Diamond Bar. We all agreed but it was hard to pinpoint. He would take acid and just go into himself. Wouldn't talk. He started coming around less often. Already driving his own car by that time, a 1966 VW given him by his dad, he would go back and forth to LA. Not sure what he did there, but it involved drugs and he did not want to tell us about it.

I had been at a party in Crestline a few months earlier and opened the bathroom door. Billy was there with two other guys, heating a spoon and shooting up seconal. *Shit.* The whole scene scared the crap out of me - especially having sat through *Reefer Madness* as a young and impressionable teenager. Made up my mind back then never to shoot up anything. But there Billy was doing it. He asked if I wanted to. "No thanks, Billy."

Weeks later I went over to his house and The Doors' *Riders on the Storm* was playing. Loudly. No one was home but Billy. When he answered the door, I could barely hear him speak. It was then I noticed his eyes. They were detached, yet very focused on something; something not there. Reminded me of Vincent Price's eyes in *The Raven*. Spooky.

> *Riders on the storm.*
> *Into this life we're born.*
> *Into this life we're thrown.*
> *Like a cat without a bone, actor all alone,*
> *Riders on the storm*
> *There's a killer on the run...*

I sat with him awhile and we talked. About nothing, really. It was non-sensical. Unimportant. Shallow. Distant. He simply would not engage with me. On any level.

The Doors continued in the background. *Crystal Ship*. And finally, *The End*. He asked me to leave and turned up the volume after I was out the door. It was strange. Almost seemed as though we hadn't known each other the past six years.

Paul, Kenny, and Stanley, when he visited us from Diamond Bar, all gave the same report. Billy would listen to The Doors and basically ignore them when visiting. He stopped going to concerts at the Shrine and Pasadena Civic with us. He would only see Phyllis, who also was coming around less and less. We could see he was pushing her away too. *Why*, we wondered? What had happened? A bad acid trip? PCP?

Billy was still being entrepreneurial, getting reds from some vato gangs in East LA. Thousands of them. He would spend hours at home wrapping them with foil into four-packs and then wholesale them out to some barrio kids he knew, also in LA. Made good money at it. But we found out later he had a habit - of heroin - that took a lot of that money. Whenever we'd see him, even in his car, The Doors was always blasting in the background.

Paul drove over to his house and asked if anything was wrong.

"Why do you ask?" Billy responded.

"Nothing man...just... that we don't see you around much anymore."

"Been doing business with my hombres in LA, that's all," Billy said.

Paul nodded and lit a smoke, slapping the lighter shut. *Hombres?* "Cool."

Billy closed his eyes halfway and then slowly opened them wider.

"There is one thing," he finally said.

"Yeah?"

Billy glanced right and left. "I think... I think I may be becoming like that Mark guy, next door."

"What?"

"Yeah, you know that scary-crazy junkie that almost never comes out of his house? I was always wondering what the fuck was up with him." Billy shook his head.

"What do you mean, you're becoming like him?" Paul asked.

"Forget it, Paul. No big deal."

Billy walked back toward his house, stopped. "You know, Paul. I...have become just like him... in a way." He shook his head and appeared lost in thought, eyes unfocused. "I'll see you later, okay?"

He didn't wait for an answer. He simply walked back into his house.

People are strange,
When you're a stranger,
People look ugly,
When you're alone

Lost... at the Forum

Where is it, Paul?" I asked.

He looked around, seemingly perplexed. "Not sure, dude. Weren't you watching?"

"Hell, no," Kenny said, with a short laugh. "We were just coming on, man. You're the driver."

Kenny was right. Paul drove Billy, Stanley, Kenny and me to the Forum, a venue in West LA that held large concerts as well as basketball games. The parking lot was a 360 degree affair that circled the entire building.

"Anybody have any idea where the car is?" Paul eyed Billy, Kenny, and me.

Damned if we knew. We shrugged.

We had just seen Crosby, Stills and Nash, having dropped acid on the way to the show - this time Orange Sunshine with speed. When we exited the arena, we found ourselves in the dark. Under the floodlights in the parking lot, every car looked the same.

"What are we going to do?" Stanley asked.

"Well, I don't want to walk around all night looking for it," I said.

The rest agreed. We sat down outside and waited.

Silent and smoking.

Two hours later the parking lot was almost empty before we spied it. A blue Dodge Lancer. We had borrowed my Dad's car and forgot about it.

Oh well...

George

George became friends with us after we started Bassett High School. He'd gone to Torch Junior High with Sandy and Phyllis. Gangly, sandy-blond hair, gray eyes, thin-faced and a hint of a beard. He dressed neutrally, plain t-shirts and jeans. He was neither a hippie, surfer nor beaner.

He was a dealer.

George was a wise-ass. Always taunting people until they were about to hit him. And then he'd flash a wickedly charming 'melt your heart' grin, and would laugh it off.

"I was only kidding," he would say, or "Come on, you weren't taking me seriously, were you?"

It worked on us most of the time. Especially once he became the main pot distributor for Bassett High.

We weren't sure where he got the pot, but he always had dozens of lids to sell. We became fast friends with him, not *only* because of the pot; rather, we were just simpatico with him and his humor. Very Crusader-like.

This helped immensely with the vatos or beaners in Bassett High School who were legendary for being assholes. Hell, we were the only school ever to be kicked out of CIF sports because at one of the games, we lost, and then the vatos stabbed four of the other school's players.

They liked to smoke pot. They could get it elsewhere, of course. Many had direct connections with Mexico. But George seemed to have a better grade of the stuff, and they liked it.

Plus, George always delivered three-finger-high lids. A great bargain for ten dollars.

Why did this help? Because they wouldn't pick on us hippie-surfer types, who were friends of George's, for fear of him cutting them off their pot supply. Seems trite, but true. Drugs were barely entering the mainstream as far as kids were concerned. There were very few drug dealers. Those guys who bought it cared more about their supply of pot than their disdain for surfers or hippies.

We, on the other hand, supplied George with something he loved - LSD.

Very simpatico relationship, indeed.

One evening I was at a party near Sandy's house on the west side of Puente Avenue. No parents were home. Drugs, pot and beer were in abundant supply. I noticed George was getting stoned and sloppy, pissing people off with his comments and generally being his usual sarcastic asshole self.

But he was my friend. And dealer.

So I offered to walk him home after the party - about four blocks away. I was walking because I had lost car privileges again for some reason or other, and Paul was over at Sandy's.

We crept along down the street, George almost unable to walk on his own. I had one arm wrapped around him holding and guiding us both as we laughed and joked around.

A low-rider car edged around the street corner and was heading toward us. George looked up and saw it, and I could see in split-second clarity what George's mind was thinking of doing.

"Don't, George," I implored. Too late.

"Hey, fuck you Goddamn beaners," he shouted, raising his arm and proudly waving the bird.

Skidding tires ensued, and all four doors to the car flew open. My heart raced; my skin went prickly; and I felt blood rush to my neck and head. *I have to drop George and run. Now. Run, John, run.*

The four guys rushed toward us, and I realized there was no way I could get away. I had hesitated too long. Frozen with fear, I stood there observing what was sure to be a bad experience.

They stopped a few feet away. Stared.

"John, is that you?" one of them asked.

Didn't recognize the voice. I tried to focus on him. He moved into the streetlight.

"Danny?" I finally asked.

He walked closer to me. "What the fuck are you doing, John?"

I let George plop into the ivy next to the sidewalk. "Shit, Danny, it's this asshole George. He's the one who shouted at you."

It was Danny. We'd been friends since sixth grade. Around eighth grade he started dressing like a vato, although he was as Irish as a leprechaun.

"Shit man, we were gonna fuck you guys up good." He pulled a knife from behind and motioned to the other guys, who had belts and baseball bats in their hands. I could see Mike B and another guy I knew from school. They nodded acknowledgements to me.

"Sorry, Danny," I said, shaking my head. My hands were trembling. "Like I said, George is fucked up." I pointed to him lying in the ivy. "Looks like he's fucking passed out."

Danny put the knife away and smiled. "Fuck him. How about we give you a ride home?"

"Sure, Danny." I had trepidation but didn't want to offend him. Especially since he was then in a good mood.

We jumped into the car, me sitting bitch in the back seat, and they fired up the '53 Chevy. An eight-track blasted some old Motown tune, and we took off.

"Just need to make a quick stop before we go, John," Danny said, leaning over the front seat from shotgun. "Only take a few minutes. You mind?"

"Sure, Danny."

We drove south on Puente into El Monte, and then west on Valley Boulevard. Joints were passed around. Reds were dropped, followed by beer chasers. They were looking for a particular street. Mike Bruno pointed it out. They turned right and went two blocks. Slowing down, they turned out the lights, turned off the eight-track tape player, and silently cruised like a shark toward its prey, stopping behind a '58 Chevy parked on the street, lowered and almost sitting on the asphalt.

"That it?" Danny asked the driver.

He nodded.

"Okay then, let's go." The four got out of the car, this time grabbing baseball bats, and proceeded to pound the shit out of the car, breaking windows, denting every piece of metal on it, and causing a huge amount of noise.

I started to go into a panic attack. Reached into my pocket and swallowed another couple of reds, hoping I wouldn't blow it completely and run out of the car.

Lights went on in the house. They jumped back into the car, laughing. Shouting from the house followed. The driver peeled out from the curb, spun the car back toward Valley Avenue and pushed the pedal to the metal.

"That will teach those assholes to come into our turf," Mike said, laughing.

Danny nodded. "Next time, we'll do the same thing to them."

We reached Puente Avenue and turned north toward my house.

"John, I forget what street you live on, Cagliero or something?"

He'd been over to my house a number of times as a kid. But I didn't want him remembering exactly where it was. I told him I lived on Barrydale, one block over from my real street. My words were noticeably slurred, even to me.

"Man, you are fucked up," Mike B said, laughing and slapping me on the back.

We arrived about ten minutes later. He pulled up to the front of what he thought was my house. I got out of the car.

"See ya later, Danny," I said. "Sorry about George and his big fucking mouth."

"Tell him to keep it shut if he doesn't want to get fucked up," Danny said. "Let him know how close he came to getting the shit beat out of him."

"You know George," I said.

Danny shook his head. "Yeah," he said. "Hey, John, great seeing you, man. Tell Paul and the guys hi for me, eh?"

"Sure thing. See you guys later."

The rest murmured goodbyes, shut the door and took off. I watched the car disappear, and once out of sight I sloppily hopped a couple of fences to my street, scraping my hands in the process.

I was thinking about how Danny did not have a Mexican accent when we were kids, but it was very pronounced when he spoke to me then. *What the fuck is that all about?*

Then I thought a moment.

Do I have an accent too? Some sort of surfer or hippie deal going on? I'd check in with The Crusaders and see what we could come up with.

If I remembered it in the morning.

Gas Gods

"Jeff around?"

"Yes, John. He's in his bedroom."

Jeff's grandmother pointed in the direction of his door and I thanked her. I had driven my dad's blue Lancer to Whittier to pick up Jeff and go to the beach.

Jeff lived with his grandparents in an older Sears-style house in East Whittier. Never met his parents. Never knew what happened to them. Asked a lot about them, but Jeff would always skirt around the answer. I finally let it rest.

Opening the door to his room, I found no one there. *Odd. They said he was in here.* I sat on the bed and listened. I could hear some sort of breathing in the closet. Rising, I slowly ambled to the door and opened it. Jeff was sitting on his butt inside, almost in a fetal position, with a lunch bag in his hand. Eyes bright and red-rimmed. Bloodshot.

And the smell leapt out at me.

Gasoline.

"Shut the door, John, before they find me."

I pulled the door shut and squatted next to him. It was pitch black except for the light coming from the gap at the door's bottom.

"Who, Jeff?"

I could hear him taking some more inhales from the paper bag. "The gas gods."

"What?"

"I'm tellin' you, man. They're after me. I hid in here so they wouldn't find me."

"Jeff, what are you sniffing?"

"Gasoline, man... want some?"

"Nah." I thought for a few moments while he took a few more inhales from the bag. It was starting to get me high being cocooned in that closet.

"Jeff, I came by to see if you want to go to the beach."

"Can't man. They'd see me and then I'm fucked."

"Who'll see you?"

"Told you man, the gas gods."

I stood up and opened the door. "Dude, I gotta go."

"Hurry up and close the door, man."

I looked back at Jeff, huddled in the closet, and felt bad for him. Not sure why, but I did. "I won't tell them you're here."

"Thanks, cuz." He smiled and motioned with his free hand for me to close the door. I did, waited a minute and then left. His grandmother asked me why Jeff wasn't leaving with me. I made up some excuse about his not feeling well, and his wanting to be left alone.

I shook my head as I started the car.

The gas gods? How fucked up can you get?

I was soon to learn.

Patrick

It wasn't there.

I searched everywhere I could think in my bedroom, spots I would routinely use to hide my stash. Nothing. There was no escaping it.

Someone had found my stash and taken it.

Shit!

From the side of my eye I observed my little twelve year old brother Patrick sheepishly enter the room, watching me in my search.

"Patrick," I said. "You seen my bag of stuff that was in my drawer?" I continued rifling through the closet.

"No."

"You sure?" I turned and stared at him.

"Yeah, I'm sure."

He had found it. I sensed it. I strode to the bunk bed, sat down, patted the mattress beside me and motioned for him to join me. He did. Cautiously. Like a dog afraid to be hit.

"I really need that stash, Patrick," I said in a perfectly calm voice. "What did you do with it?" I smiled. A brotherly love type of smile.

"You'll hit me if I give them to you," he blurted out.

My smile widened. "No I won't, Patrick. But I need it back. They aren't mine. I'll get in a lot of trouble if I don't get them."

"Really?"

I nodded. "Really, Pat. If you just get it for me, I'll be on my way and we'll just forget about this."

"Really?" I could see he was thinking about it from all angles. A few moments passed. My smile continued beaming. Finally, he relented, letting out a breath and standing up.

"You need to get off the bed," he said.

I did.

He lifted the inside upper part of the mattress, and reached under it to retrieve a sock he had pinched in between the springs that held up the mattress. He handed the sock to me, again, sheepishly.

"Here."

Putting it in my pocket, I looked around and smiled. "Thanks, Patrick." I motioned for him to stand up.

I grabbed him by the front of his shirt, swung him around and slammed him into the wall, pushing him up after he hit. His feet were barely touching the floor.

"If you ever, and I mean ever, touch my drugs again, or if I ever even hear of you trying drugs," I motioned with my index finger in his face for effect. "I will fucking kill you, you understand? Kill you. I'm not fuckin' around here. Do you hear me?"

His eyes glassed over and tears streamed down his cheeks. He nodded. I threw him to the carpet. He was pitifully scared. I would be too. It was the most pissed off I'd been in years. I was ballistic.

"You better remember," I spat out as I left the room and closed the door

Hippies and Angels

For some unknown reason, Hell's Angels had a greater than deserved disdain toward hippies. Or anyone they considered might be hippies. And we Crusaders looked like hippies, although technically, we were surfers. A very fine distinction, but one we didn't want to try to explain if caught. I thought it might have had something to do with a lot of them being ex-servicemen. Anti-war protesters and anything associated with that movement didn't mix well with the military.

Don't know for sure. It was just a guess.

Didn't matter why. Whenever we saw a few motorcycles cruising together coming down the street, we vamoosed out of sight until they passed.

A few of our friends had already been beaten up pretty badly by some Hell's Angels, simply for looking like hippies. They put out an edict that any hippie they saw on the street would suffer the same fate. An ass whuppin'.

So we hid when they were around. No shame in it.

It was survival.

We were never caught by any bikers.

One Small Step

President Kennedy had promised that we, as a country, would rocket a man to the moon in the decade during which this book takes place.

My dad worked for Autonetics, the space division of Rockwell Corporation, the lead contractor for the Apollo program. He would bring home stickers that were used for the spacecraft. Very cool.

He couldn't say what he did. And we knew he was one of the few at the facility that had a top-secret clearance. I remember the FBI coming to the house to interview him and all of our neighbors. It didn't affect us much except on weekends, when he was sometimes called away to go into special areas that only he could enter.

As the Apollo 11 spacecraft flew nearer the moon, the buzz about it started to reach fever pitch in the press and throughout the neighborhood. Even with us Crusaders. Hell, we knew history was in the making - a man on the moon!

The night of the landing, July 20, 1969, we were all at my parents' house watching it live on TV. Or delayed live. Anyway, my dad was proud as a peacock at what he was witnessing.

I stepped outside for a few minutes to smoke. Paul and Kenny joined me. All we could hear were the echoes of everyone's TV's throughout the block - all watching the moon landing.

Dad yelled for us to come in.

There, on the television screen, were Neil Armstrong and Buzz Aldrin climbing down the ladder. And then Armstrong's foot touched the moon.

It's hard to explain, but at that moment I was proud of who I was -- an American; of who my dad was and his involvement in the whole affair; of the country I lived in; and of all the peoples of the earth.

But most especially, I was proud of my dad.

Meet the Doctor

"Hey, Johnny, we'd like you to meet our friend," my parents gushed as I walked in the door of our house.

"Sure. How are you?"

He looked to be the same age as my parents, square jawed, bushy eyebrows with deep brown eyes below them, thick mustache above thin lips. He rose to meet my outstretched hand.

"Your parents were just telling me about you, young man. Glad to meet you."

He returned the shake in a limp-wristed fashion.

"Same here." Turning my attention toward my mom. "When's dinner?"

"After Dr. Smith leaves," my mom replied.

"Doctor?" *I didn't know they had a friend who was a doctor.*

"Yes, John," he said in an even tone. "I was just telling your parents that I'd like to have you come down to the office and take a few tests, if you wouldn't mind. Nothing bad. I think you'd enjoy them."

I thought about that for a moment. *What kind of tests was he talking about? What was going on here? Why did he use the term bad?* After running it through my "parents are sneaky bastards" paranoia filters, I made a decision.

"Sure. Nice meeting you, Dr...?"

"Smith."

I nodded a smile, left for my room and changed clothes. I could blow him off later. Better to agree then and work out the way I would get out of it later.

However, later came within the week. After school I came home, washed up and was ready to get together with The Crusaders at Stanley's house. My dad came home early and both he and my mom came into my room.

Unusual.

"We made an appointment for you today for the tests Dr. Smith wanted you to take, Johnny."

I pulled on my Vans and looked up at them.

"There's nothing wrong with me, and I don't need any tests."

"Johnny," my mom said emphatically. "You told him you'd take them and we are going to drive you there."

"What kind of tests are they?"

"He didn't say... exactly. But the appointment is for 4:00."

"Okay, I'll go. But just give me the keys to the car, and I'll drive there."

"You're sure you will go?" my dad asked.

"I said I would."

They eyed me skeptically and finally relented with the keys and directions. I drove over to Stanley's house and shared with the guys what I was going to do.

"What kind of tests, dude?" Paul asked.

"They wouldn't say," I replied, lighting a cigarette and blowing crooked smoke rings. I hadn't mastered the technique yet. "So I'll just go there, get it out of the way and be back in an hour."

"You know your parents, John," Kenny said. "Seems kind of fishy."

"I know," I said. "But I met the guy at the house. He seems okay. I'll be back soon."

It took a while to find the office in a medical complex in West Covina. As I walked up to the door, I read the sign: Dr. Winston Smith, MD. Psychiatrist. I went on high alert. I started to turn around and leave and then abruptly stopped myself. *What do they think I am, crazy? I'm not! What did they tell this asshole about me that would cause him to think that? I started to get angry. I'll show them!*

"Thanks for coming, John," Dr. Smith started. "Is it okay if I call you John?" I nodded. "Please sit down." He looked up and gestured toward a leather chair in front of the desk. I promptly filled it.

What now?

I looked around the office. Large, modern fixtures, almost Jetson-like, dark walnut desk, and a dozen degrees on the wall. He stopped the shuffling of papers and folders on his desk, sat up in his chair and folded his hands together.

"John," he said in an overly earnest tone of voice, devoid of emotion. "Your parents are very concerned about you." He half-smiled, condescendingly. His eyes did not seem to match his facial gesture. "And from what they told me, I think with good reason."

"What did they say?"

"What do you think they would say?"

I squirmed in the chair. I hated it when people did that - answered a question with a question. Turning it on me. Reminded me of the times I was called into the school office. "Why do you think you are here?" Seems like it was used more often than not to get you to cop to something they didn't know about in the first place.

"That I'm an ideal son who never gets into trouble and gets straight A's in school?"

He slowly licked his lips. It seemed calculated. The precursor to a slight grin that followed.

"Well, the straight A's part is correct. I've been speaking with your teachers... but as to the other, well..." He shifted in his chair. "Why do you think you're always in trouble?"

"I've no idea." And I meant it. But more concerning to me was his speaking to my teachers. That seemed a little intrusive. In fact, it pissed me off.

"Well, I think you do, John. Your parents are concerned that you'll do something that will result in your getting in a lot of trouble. Can you see how they might feel that way?"

"No."

"I see." He stood silently and walked over to a file cabinet, opened the drawer and pulled out a folder. From over his shoulder he continued.

"How do you feel about your parents?"

"What do you mean?"

"Do you love them?"

"Of course. They're my parents."

He pulled out the papers he wanted and walked back to the desk, standing still and looking down at me.

"Do you love them?" He asked firmly with an expressionless face. He stared without blinking. I wondered how he did that.

I hesitated. I loved my dad, unconditionally. My mom, well, she was hard to make any kind of emotional connection with. About as emotionally available as a rock. I decided to hedge my answer.

"I guess so - especially my dad."

"Hmmmm."

He sat down and laid the papers on his desk, face down.

"John, I'd like to ask you some questions, based on the pictures I am going to show you. It's called a Rorschach test. Have you ever heard of it?"

Of course I had. It was designed to expose your innermost subconscious thoughts by your answers to the ink blot images. I wasn't an idiot. But clearly he -- and my parents -- thought I was mentally unbalanced. Or at least might be. But by that point, I'd almost had enough, and it was clear he was trying to use that Rorschach test to flush these supposedly crazy thoughts out into the light of day. What a joke.

"Yes, I am familiar with it," shaking my head *almost* imperceptibly.

He nodded. "What we're going to do is show you a series of ink spots, and then ask you to relate to me what they look like to you. In other words, what they remind you of, if anything. Do you understand?"

"Of course I do. Answer the first thing that comes into my mind after I see the picture, right?"

He nodded.

While he checked the order of the ink blots, I was running a different scenario in my mind. *What the heck does he think I'll say? That I'm scared most of the time because of a bad trip? That the panic attacks come without warning? That I am afraid I'll go crazy? That the psilocybin I took probably blew out all of my brain cells?* Well, I decided that I'd had enough and that I would give him what he -- and my parents -- wanted. A certifiable fucking crazy-assed son.

"Ready?" he asked.

I nodded.

He lifted the first one. "Tell me John, what do you see?"

"Nothing, really."

"Take your time."

Nodding. "No, I don't see anything. Looks like an ink blot to me."

Okay, I sounded objective to him. Now, I would start laying it on thick. Slowly at first and then lead up to a crescendo. For the next twenty minutes, I ratcheted up the descriptions of the images - in Technicolor - from my dog being run over to my mom being disemboweled by knives. Finally he stopped, half the pictures still face-down on his desk.

"John, I'd like to thank you for coming in today," he said. I could see a slight change in the way he looked at me, like he was observing a lab specimen he didn't quite understand. He stood up and reached out his hand. "I'll get back with your parents with my recommendation."

Returning the handshake, I was thinking what recommendation could he possibly come up with from that session? Anyway, I left his office self-satisfied, sure I'd fooled him into believing all that crap I had just laid on him.

The breeze through the windows on the drive home blew out the cigarette smoke and cloud of negative karma that Dr. Smith had tried to lay on me. It felt good. Upon reaching Stanley's, I told the guys what the doctor tried to do and how I handled it.

"He believed that shit?" Stanley asked?

"Hook, line, and sinker," I laughed, taking a hit off the joint that was passing around. "To tell the truth, I was surprised he didn't break out laughing and ask me if I was goofing on him. He was just a dead serious asshole."

"I told you about your parents," Kenny mentioned. "They set the whole thing up."

"My mom," I corrected him. "I'm sure it was all her idea. Anyway, no big deal. It's done. I'll see you guys later."

The following evening, my parents sat me down and said that Dr. Smith had called and asked if they could bring me down to the hospital for more tests.

"What?" I asked.

"He said there were more medical tests he wanted to perform."

Looking at my mom and dad, I surmised he relayed something of what I had told him, and that they were uncomfortable with the report.

"Mom, Dad, I was screwing with the guy. He's a shrink. I made it all up." I could see they didn't believe a word of it. Didn't care, really.

"Well," my mom said, "You can tell him all about it at the hospital. He wants us to be there tomorrow evening at 9:00."

"Shit."

"What did you say?" my mom asked.

"I said... shoot, Mom, that's what I said."

My dad's eyes were conciliatory, but distant. I could see he was not happy with either me or the situation. But the more important thought was why did the doctor want to see me again? And what possible tests could he need to run? He couldn't really believe what I told him?

Could he?

I started to get that high-pitched noise in my head that I knew preceded a panic attack. Quickly I excused myself and went to my room. I found my stash, pulled out a couple of reds and downed them. Lying back in my bed, I slowly started drifting off and forgot about the doctor, the hospital, everything.

Vietnam II

"What's up with your brother?" I asked.

"Not sure," Stanley confided in a low voice. "He's been acting really strange lately."

Some friends had dropped Paul off in front of Stanley's house. He brushed past Stanley, Kenny, Paul, and me sitting in the garage, without so much as a glance. Strange indeed.

He had been released from the Army a few weeks earlier.

The war had started blipping on our radar in a big way as we neared eighteen -- soon to be eligible for the draft. The first lottery was to take place that December. Protests were going full-blast across the country. But not very many in La Puente. In fact, none. Many of Paul and Kenny's friends had already been drafted. Kenny was Canadian. No chance he would go.

Every night on TV the news would show statistics of how many US soldiers versus how many of the enemy were killed. I remember coming home one night, stoned out of my mind, of course, and sitting with my dad watching Walter Cronkite mouthing away on the TV. Descriptions of villages destroyed, what the war was costing, and how Nixon was saying that he and Henry Cabot Lodge, Jr. were trying to negotiate a ceasefire because the one that Johnson had arranged before had fallen through.

My dad was watching intently. Images flashed of kids rioting in the streets and on campuses across the country. Marches with students holding signs chanting, "Hell, no, we won't go."

He shook his head. "You know, Johnny. Something is not right with this war. Just not right."

I'd never heard my dad say anything like that. But even in my stoned stupor, I realized that he, a staunch, dyed-in-the-wool Kennedy Democrat, had realized the madness of what was going on over there in Vietnam. It was an awakening for him -- and me. Because just then I realized that what all the protesting kids were doing was trying to save lives - on both sides - and when people like my dad started agreeing with them, it would soon be over. They, and the nightly news, were finally bringing the horror of war into living rooms. Middle America couldn't ignore it any more or pretend it was not happening.

I didn't care, because I had already made up my mind that if I had to go into the service, it would be the Air Force as a pilot. Forgetting the fact that, number one, I was probably a druggie that they would not take anyway; and number two, I had never even flown in an airplane; and number three, I probably would not be able to be dictated to by any authority figure without a fight. But aside from those small obstacles, I was ready to serve -- if I had to. But only in the Air Force. As a pilot.

I could have been delusional. Not sure. I also had the feeling that I would never have to go.

As I watched TV, a realization did hit me with the force of a sucker punch.

That is, dying in wartime, honorable or not, you are still dead. Dead is dead. No more dreams, no more hopes, no more possibilities. No loves. No family. Nothing.

Just dead.

Stanley called from his new home in Diamond Bar to share a story with me. The previous week, he and his brother Paul had had a fight, and Paul almost kicked the crap out of him for mouthing off. He then threw him against the wall and told Stanley that he was gonna kill him.

"So I tell him to cut the shit out," Stanley told me over the phone. "My mom jumps in and pulls us apart, and orders me... me, to leave Paul alone. And he started it, John."

I could hear Stanley take a huge drag from a cigarette and slowly blow it out.

"So anyway, my mom pulls me aside and tells me this story about Paul in Vietnam. He had this best friend, whom I knew about, that he met in boot camp. They ended up doing everything together, even shipped off to 'Nam together in the same outfit. Anyway, a year later they both received orders that they were to ship back home."

Stanley took another hit from his cigarette.

"Get this, John. The day before they are to leave, these snipers attack their base. Paul and his buddy are shooting at them, when Paul turns around, and his best friend has a third eye of red in his forehead. Dead."

"Mom says that is why Paul is so sensitive, and that I should cut him some slack."

"I agree, man. Can you imagine how that would feel?"

"Yeah, tough shit to go through."

"Yeah."

"He's going to go to chiropractic school and become a doctor," Stanley relayed. "Says that was all he thought about over there."

"Whatever, man. I'm just glad he came back."

"Me too."

When the Draft Board later held their first draft lottery on December 1, 1969, we were all sitting around the television waiting for each number to roll out. My number was 351. *Shit, Stevie Wonder was going to get drafted before me.* They were only taking up to number 80. My plans for the Air Force quickly faded, although they were probably a pipe dream anyway.

Turned out I would have much bigger problems to worry about.

My future freedom.

Crazy House I

I was startled awake by clanging noises in the distance. Blinking open my eyes, I was greeted by a stark off-white hospital room. Television centered on a dresser. Unoccupied hospital-style bed next to me. *Where was I?*

I sat up, hung my legs over the side and cleared my grogginess. It slowly started coming back.

The night before, my parents had delivered me to San Antonio Community Hospital at 9:00, as promised. I remembered walking down the long, shiny, tiled hallway toward the rear and coming to a door with a metal screen you could see through embedded in the window. My mom pushed a button, and it buzzed the door open. *Strange.* She signed me in at the front desk. My dad observed. After we'd said our goodbyes, a male nurse came and escorted me to a room at the end of another long, shiny, tiled hallway, and directed me to the bed I was sitting on. A female nurse came in and gave me a pill in a little white paper cup, watching me until I took it.

S*o what am I supposed to do now?*

Washed up and dressed, I walked out the door. I was at the end of a hallway. Maybe ten doors on both sides leading to the main reception area. I shuffled toward the counter where I had been checked in the night before and asked the on-duty nurse why I was there. She smiled as if she'd heard the question a hundred times a day and stated that the doctor would talk to me later about that. In the meantime, she suggested I should get some breakfast.

"Where?"

"In the dining room down that hall," she said, pointing.

Another long hallway. I walked into the room and found a buffet-style breakfast - eggs, potatoes, toast, orange juice and coffee. I piled the food high on my plate and looked for a place to sit down.

And then I saw her.

Hard to explain the action - or rather the reaction - I had upon seeing her.

She sat with her head slightly down, eating. Soft brown hair that fell to her shoulders. High cheekbones. Fair complexioned. Thin. Dressed in a tank top and jeans. She looked up at me and stopped chewing. Her eyes were a beautiful deep shade of green. They scanned me up and down, and then locked on my eyes. I wasn't able to move. Or speak. Or think.

It was an energy I had never felt before -- a kindred soul. A soulmate? I willed myself to walk toward her table. Her eyes followed me as I stepped closer and stopped.

"Can I sit down here?"

She nodded yes.

"My name's John," my voice cracked.

"I'm Shari," she said, smiling.

I hoped she couldn't hear my heart beating. It pounded in my chest and head. Scared. Excited. We finished eating, and she stood up.

"You staying here?" It was a stupid question. I didn't care.

She laughed. "Yes. I am staying here."

She said goodbye and left the room. *Why didn't I say more?* I felt like I might have just blown the most important moment of my life.

After breakfast, the doctor had scheduled some blood tests and an x-ray. That took a few hours. Always my questions of why I was there and when do I meet the doctor were answered by "all of your questions will be answered when you see the doctor." It felt like a never-ending loop.

At lunch I didn't see Shari. Waiting the whole time in case she showed up, I was more than disappointed. I was heartbroken. *How could that be? I spoke maybe a half-dozen words to her.* I didn't understand those feelings. Yet, I still felt sad.

After lunch, a male nurse informed me that I was to be in the doctor's office sharply at 2:00. Great. I could explain everything and get out of there.

Dr. Smith brushed past me in the waiting area and motioned for me to follow him. It was a much different office than his private one. Simple. Wooden desk, faded walls. Two filing cabinets. An old Sears lamp on the desk. Fluorescent tube lights overhead. He sat down and grabbed my file.

"John, I am sure you are wondering why you are here, yes?"

He didn't let me answer.

"Your tests indicated a great amount of repressed anger toward your parents and in general, and I suggested to your parents it would be important to get you into the hospital so we can deal with it, before it gets out of hand.

"We'll have your blood work back tomorrow, and see if you need any supplements for your thyroid. In the meantime, I have ordered that you start Thorazine immediately, and I'll prescribe something for you to sleep."

"Wait a second," I said.

"I am not done." His hand went up like a stop sign. "You will remain silent until I finish, understand?"

I did. He looked back down at my file.

"There are rules here, John, and you will follow them. No drugs will be tolerated or allowed. You will follow all of the rules, which the head nurse will give you. You are not to fight, raise your voice or cause any problems with the staff. If you do, you will be given more medication or restrained. You are to be in bed by 10:00 each night, and up by 7:30.

"And you will attend group sessions every day." He looked up at me, a different expression and aura than at his office. It was like looking into a stone wall. "Do you have any questions?"

I did.

"Did you believe me when I said all those things with the Rorschach test? Because I was totally bullshitting you."

"There is to be no swearing except in group. And yes, your answers were credible and taken seriously."

"I was B.S.ing you, for crissakes."

"Of course you were." He *almost* smiled, condescendingly.

Silence for a few moments.

"You don't believe me, do you?"

"I believe you need help, John. And we are going to provide it."

"Un-fucking-believable," I whispered.

"No swearing outside of group." He stood up. "In the meantime, you will find classes in the craft room every day, and you can watch TV in your room or in the lounge with the others. You are to be in group today at 3:00 pm sharp."

"You really don't believe me."

"Don't be late, John."

Twelve of us sat around in a large semi-circle in the therapy room. Dr. Smith sat across the circle where he could turn his body and face each of us. He introduced us to each other by name, stating that I was new and would be joining them for a while. Shari was there.

I was mid-circle. Shari was separated from me by a couple of people, and would be called on after me, judging by the way the doctor was asking people to speak about what was bothering them.

The first guy talked about how angry he was about his alcoholic parents. Doc thanked him for sharing and then on to the next. Parents treated him meanly, no one listened to him. Doc thanked him for sharing. Next guy spoke about how hard it was not to take heroin, and how his parents didn't understand him or his penchant for stealing things. Especially from them, no less. Thanks for sharing. Then it was my turn.

"John, since you are new, I wanted to say that you can feel safe in sharing any feeling you may have with the group. We all agree that nothing leaves this room, and that you are among friends. Is that okay with you?"

I squirmed for a minute, crossing and uncrossing my legs while I lit a cigarette and took a big drag, blowing it out slowly. The other eleven, including Shari, stared at me. I was scared, and angry at the same time. Also, I had taken my first Thorazine and was feeling a little light headed.

"I told you I was bullshitting you about that stupid test, and that is the fucking truth. I don't have any inner childhood bullshit problems, my parents don't beat me, nor are they alcoholics. I love my friends, and as far as I am concerned you can just fuck yourself. I want to get the hell out of here, now."

I crossed my arms and sat defiantly, staring at the doctor. For effect.

"Anyone have anything they wish to contribute to John's outburst?"

Shaking heads were their only response.

"I believe him."

I looked over at Shari.

"You do?" I asked.

She nodded assent.

The doctor took a big breath and sat there, furrowing his eyebrows and staring. Like a pious priest pitying a poor lost soul. "Thank you for sharing, John. You'll be able to leave when you are able to address your aggressive behavior. Not until then."

Then he called on the fellow next to me.

Shit.

That didn't go well at all.

"Mind if I sit down?" It was Shari holding her tray looking down at me. Smiling. Didn't even see her walk in for dinner that night, absorbed as I was in trying to figure out how to get out of the biggest jam I had ever gotten myself into. My heart raced.

"No. I mean yes." I stood up. "I'd like you to sit down."

She smiled and started eating. Small talk ensued. I thanked her for her support at the meeting. I found myself laughing for the first time since arriving in that hellhole. She was there because she kept running away from her parents. Her dad drank all day long, and her mom "ruled the roost" with an iron hand. She hated school - nothing relevant was ever taught as far as she was concerned, and she felt she just had to get away. After the third time, in which she hitchhiked to San Bernardino and was picked up by the Sheriff's department, her parents felt they had no choice but to get her some help. She wryly observed that if they had been on the receiving end of the help they sought for her, she wouldn't have had to run away.

I told her about my life: The Crusaders, living in La Puente, and the time passed too quickly. I was getting ready to leave for the recreation room, where Shari agreed to join me and have a smoke.

"Take it off," a snarly voice shouted from behind me.

We both looked around. *Who said that?*

A shaven-headed guy about twenty sat two tables over, staring directly at me, slightly foaming at the mouth. His eyes bulged; white surrounded the piercing dark focused pupils. They were a little further apart than seemed normal.

"I said take it off, now!"

I looked to Shari who shook her head, raising her shoulders up and down with hands up.

"Are you talking to me?" I asked.

He stood up. Short guy. Pale white. Almost like an albino. "Take off my mother's face now!" He gestured with a fork in my direction.

"I don't have your fucking mother's face on, asshole." I stood up and faced him, scared shitless. But I wouldn't look like a pussy in front of Shari.

"Take off my mother's face or I'll kill you," he spat out. Literally. Spit was flying from his mouth as he walked toward me.

"I warned you," he shouted as two male orderlies rushed in, grabbed him by the shoulders and sat him back down, telling him to calm down or he would have to see the doctor again. They forcibly restrained him in his seat. He turned toward me. "You take it off, hear me?"

"Let's get out of here," I suggested to Shari, who nodded. We walked to the rec room and sat down.

"I wouldn't pay much attention to him," Shari said. "He really is crazy, but seems harmless enough. Must be his meds."

"You taking anything?"

"Yeah, they have me on something or other to calm me down. Something else for sleep. But I don't take them."

"How do you get around that? They watch . . ."

"Under the tongue, silly." She stuck her tongue out and then tickled me. "Then I flush 'em."

We spent the evening chit-chatting. I had never been so comfortable with a girl before on that personal of a level. I had many friends who were girls, but none that I felt I could share intimate feelings with. Even with Mary in Lake Gregory, there was a certain distance between us. Shari said she felt the same way. I invited her to my room before lights out where we could have another smoke. I was secretly hoping to kiss her. I thought she felt the same way.

Minutes later, while sitting on the edge of my bed, I leaned over and touched her lips with mine. It was magical. In fact, I think a spark literally flew between us. Static electricity from the bed, I supposed. I pulled back. She moved her head toward me and continued the kiss.

"Take off my mother's face!"

We jerked apart and listened. It was a horrifyingly sick scream.

"I told you to take off my mother's face." The voice reverberated down the hall. We heard the slapping of bare feet as they came closer to the door.

I jumped off the bed and started to close the door. Too late. His arm came through. In it, a large carving knife. With all my strength I pushed the door against that arm.

"I'm gonna cut it off, hear me? Cut it off."

Shari got behind and helped push. He screamed. We heard footsteps scurrying down the hall, getting closer.

The door flew open, pushing Shari and me into the wall and then onto the floor. He came flying through, tackled from behind by two male orderlies. They grabbed his arm, extracted the knife and kneed his head against the floor, at the same time shouting for help.

One of them motioned with his arm for us to leave, which we did. Another two orderlies raced down the hall with a straightjacket and disappeared into the room. We hurried to the rec room, which was empty and dark, and sat down on the couch. My heart was racing. Not out of love, but rather fear. I was scared. My hands started shaking. Couldn't hold them still to light the cigarette.

I had really fucked up this time. Turbo fucked up. I was in a crazy house. I had no way to contact anyone. The doctor did not believe I was *not* crazy. And, I had met the woman I knew I would fall in love with.

After we said goodnight, I ambled lazily back to my room, closed the door, plopped on the bed and broke down and cried for the first time in years. My chest hurt. My heart ached. I felt abandoned by those whom I thought loved me. My parents. My friends. Totally alone. What had I gotten myself into?

And I didn't have a plan to get myself out of that damn crazy house.

I needed one.

Huntington Beach

The sky was blue, the waves were breaking at almost four feet, and the sun warmed the light-brown sands as Billy and two of his new friends from LA walked to the ocean's edge, smoking joints and laughing. It was near noon, and they decided to go swimming. Billy had left them for a while and gone into the bathroom on the way to the water. He came out glazed and glassy-eyed.

Billy stripped down to his surf trunks, and ran toward the water. He made a big jump, dove head first into it and hit a sand bar that had formed a few feet from shore. They heard a big crack and saw that Billy was floating on the surface, face down.

One of the guys started yelling for help. The other ran in and turned him over so he could breathe. A lifeguard had seen what happened and ran over while using his radio to call for back-up. He pulled Billy out and onto the sand. Started giving CPR. Time seemed a blur. Police. Ambulance. They found a needle kit and heroin in Billy's pants.

They put Billy into the ambulance and drove away.

Crazy House II

Life in San Antonio Hospital became bearable with Shari there. I fell asleep thinking of her, and woke with her still in my consciousness. We'd eat every meal together, go to crafts classes together, and spend every waking minute talking and just being friends. We were more, of course. I knew from the moment I met her that I would fall in love, and I did.

She did too.

We were an "item" in the hospital. All the nurses knew. Orderlies, too. I found I was less anxious to leave. I scoped out the entire place. It was about one-quarter of the ground floor of the hospital. All the windows were wired like the glass in the main entrance - no chance of getting out. No pay phones or ways to call anybody. I - and everyone else who was a patient - was locked up tight as a Scottish banker.

I found I was not as angry as when I first arrived. As if the hurt I felt was being supplanted by a new seedling of love. I thought it sounded sappy myself, but it was how I felt.

I didn't say much at group therapy for a couple of weeks. Didn't seem important to share anything with a bunch of messed-up kids who feigned caring in order to win points with the doctor.

"Anything to share with us today, John?" he would ask.

My response was curt and to the point. "No."

Shari came into the rec room, searched me out and rushed to sit by my side. She wanted to say something, but kept checking herself.

"What?" I asked.

She smiled and grabbed my hand, patting it slightly.

"The doctor says that I can leave tomorrow. My parents are picking me up in the morning."

That high-pitched noise started squealing in my head. Palpitations in my chest ran rampant. Adrenaline rushed throughout my body and the room started spinning. I was in full panic attack mode. I closed my eyes and tried to focus on Shari. She became a blur.

"John... are you okay?" I heard echoing in the background.

Jerking my hand away from her I clasped my head and moaned. "No, I'm not." A few moments passed before I looked up. "I'm scared, Shari."

She grabbed my thigh and squeezed. "We'll still be able to be together once you get out, John. I'll ask the doctor if I can come visit you here."

If I get out.

Hadn't made any progress since I entered, and was sure the doctor was not endeared to my monosyllabic responses to his questions, or the occasional one-fingered salute I gave him. And, at least so far, I had had no visitors. Shari leaned in and kissed me.

"I love you, John."

It was so sudden, I wondered if I heard it. I looked at her. Tears made little glistening tracks down her cheeks. She had said it.

"I love you too, Shari. And I'm glad you're getting out. Sort of."

We talked the rest of the day, and that night we made out in my room, until the head nurse knocked on the door and "suggested" Shari go to her room.

Her parents were there at 9:00 am the next morning. We'd had breakfast together, and it must have been the same feeling a convict experienced when the time came closer for the electric chair. Before we knew it, the time was gone.

She introduced me to her parents, who viewed me as some nut she met in a psycho ward, condescendingly smiling and nodding as she explained who I was, and that she wanted to come back and see me. I understood. Probably would have felt the same way as they did under the same circumstances. They disappeared down the hallway, and I had the sinking feeling I might never see her again. It felt awful. I felt empty. *What the fuck would I do now?*

Returning to my room, I laid in my hospital-style bed and stared at the popcorn ceiling, legs bent up and hands clasped behind my head. The room seemed empty. Stark. Cold. And then I started shaking.

I felt so alone. More alone than I had ever experienced before in my life. All those that I loved had abandoned me: my parents, brothers and sisters, friends. And now Shari. My throat hurt. Lips started trembling. I wanted to stop feeling. To run away from the huge sense of abandonment that coursed through my body.

Why did my parents do this? What had I really done that was so bad? Had I pushed them so far they could no longer love me?

Tears flowed down the sides of my face as I scrunched up into a fetal position and rolled to my side, hugging my arms around my legs.

Sobs erupted uncontrollably. I tried to stop. Couldn't. I hurt so deep within. I was angry and mad at the same time.

The room started spinning. Time slowed. The high-pitched noise filled my head. I could feel my heart race. The night seemed to have no end. I alternated between anger and panic attacks. I opened my stash of pills I had hid and prayed for sleep to rescue me from the pain.

It was not to come that night.

Lying in my bed the next morning, I started going over all that I had observed at the mental hospital. The groups, the comings and goings of the patients, who said what, who did what, and after a while I discerned a pattern. Slight, but nonetheless potentially viable.

A few weeks after any of the patients started sharing certain "feelings" in group, in a very specific way, they were eligible to go home for a couple of days. Then they came back, spent another week or two, shared how things were going better, and were finally released.

After running it through my mind until it was solidly fixed, I decided that it was the best plan I could come up with, and that I would put it into action that very day.

I finally had a plan.

"John, do you have anything to share with the group?" the doctor asked. He wasn't expecting an answer and had already turned his attention to my fellow nut to my left.

"As a matter of fact, I do."

"Go on." His professionalism kept him from dropping his jaw.

"I've sat here for these past few weeks angry at you, and the group. And I want to apologize for that." I took an appropriate pause, held back the beginning of some crocodile tears, and continued. "Last night... I don't know why... maybe Shari leaving, maybe... I just don't know, but it hit me like a ton of bricks. I realized I wasn't angry at you, Doctor, or you others in here.

"I heard you mention it last week. Displaced anger, I think you called it. I'm angry at my parents." Another pause for dramatic effect. Eyes down, rapidly blinking. "Not angry, really, more like... hurt."

I put my head in my hand and held it there. Dead silence. I didn't look up.

"John," the doctor started, clearing his throat, "I think that is a very important realization, wouldn't the rest of you agree?" Murmurs of yes, uh huh's and right on's followed. I kept my head in my hands, not moving. The fellow to my right reached out and touched my shoulder.

"You okay, John?"

"I think so." I looked up and had an appropriate mixture of humility and sadness I'd practiced in the bathroom mirror.

"I don't think I can say any more today."

The doctor nodded his head affirmatively. "That's fine, John. We'll talk again tomorrow."

"I... I'd like that."

The group ended about an hour later and everyone in it was exceedingly nice to me the rest of the day. Seeing if I were okay. Did I need anything? Want to eat with us?

I started being very social, extremely nice to everyone, and encouraging. Especially when the doctor was around.

Shari was unable to visit me for about a week. After five more sessions like the first, the doctor allowed me a visit from her for an hour, wherein I shared with her what I was doing. She laughed.

"They believe you, John?"

"Hell, I believe me. It's pretty easy. Say what they want to hear, put some emotion into it. Voila."

"How long do you think it will take?"

"Another week at most. I'll go home for a day, tell them I love my parents and see the error of my ways, come back to a couple more weeks of therapy group sessions, and he will write me out of this godforsaken hellhole."

"A hellhole that allowed us to meet." She winked.

"I'm thankful for that."

"I've missed you," she said.

"God, I have missed you too, Shari. Think of you every day."

"So you'll be free in a couple of weeks?"

"That's the plan."

She leaned in and kissed me. "See you then."

It actually went a little quicker than I had calculated. Less than two weeks later I went home for the day trip, was the perfect model of a son with my parents, kissed my little brother instead of hitting him, got along with my sisters, and did not try to see my Crusader friends.

When I returned to the mental hospital, it only took five more days before the doctor called me into his private office -- the one with the Sears lamp on the wooden desk.

On the other side of his desk, he explained that I had finally realized what my problems were, and had made great progress in addressing them. He was recommending to my parents that I go home, and then see him once a week for a few months. I thanked him, with humility, of course. That night I had my last dinner at San Antonio Hospital.

Next morning my parents were there early. I packed up all my crafts that I had made, said goodbye to everyone, and left with Mom and Dad, much the same way I had come in. On the way home I asked them to stop at In-N-Out for a burger, fries and a Coke.

They tasted great.

Like freedom tasted at that very moment.

Hospital Visit

I found out what had happened to Billy and visited him. He sported a halo that was screwed into his head. The name fit the appliance. It encircled the top of his head and had screws that went directly into his skull. It connected to his shoulders, to keep his neck straight. He was not paralyzed. But he could not be allowed to move or he'd risk permanent damage. He smiled when he saw me.

"What's up, Billy?"

"Not me, man...I've got to lie here for a while," he said, forcing out a short laugh.

I pulled up a plastic chair and straddled it, leaning my arms on the back.

"Heard what happened, man. Bummer, huh? You holding up?"

He moved his eyes over toward me. That's all he could do. "I fucked up, John. Almost killed myself. Fucking stupid."

I rubbed the side of my face, thinking what the heck I would say next. He did fuck up. And he was on heroin at the same time.

"You couldn't have known about the sandbar, Billy. It was just bad luck."

"Maybe," he said. In the silence that followed I heard the beeping of the monitor attached to his heartbeat and viewed his vital signs on the green screen. Up and down went the green lines.

"Paul, Kenny, and Sandy came in yesterday," he finally continued. "Told me that I could get a job with Paul and Kenny at the bakery. Turn my life around." He bit down on his lip. "I don't know, John. I have to do something."

"You going to do it?"

"I told them I'd think about it."

The room became peaceful. Billy exhaled a big breath.

Choking back a tear that ran down the side of his face, he swallowed. "I know they mean well. I know if I don't do something soon... I think I'll... I'll--"

"What Billy?"

"I've got to do something. That's all." He scratched his forehead through the wires. "Anyway, thanks for coming by."

"No problemo, Billy. Came as soon as I heard."

He let out a short laugh. "Yeah, I bet I'm all the talk of La Puente. Dumb-assed Mexican gets loaded, dives into a sandbar and breaks his neck."

"Never heard anyone refer to you as a dumb-assed Mexican, Billy."

"You know what I mean." He tightened his fists until his knuckles turned white. "Man, I could use a cigarette. They don't let me smoke in here."

"When do you get out?"

"Who the fuck knows? Doc says a month or so. Could be longer."

"Anything I can get you?"

"Naw... they keep me loaded. No pain or anything." He closed his eyes. "You seen Phyllis lately?"

The question startled me. "Hasn't she been here?"

He opened his eyes and blinked quickly. "We had a fight a few months back."

"No man, haven't seen her for a long time."

"Just wondering." He let out another breath, heavier that time.

I said my goodbyes and left after a few more minutes of talking. Drove home via the coast and then up Beach Boulevard. I had never seen Billy more hopeless. It was shocking.

Laid up in bed, metal halo screwed into his skull, and the fact that Phyllis was no longer in his life was, well, unthinkable. They were like the yin and yang of relationships. Inseparable. I wondered what Billy could have possibly done to break them up. Screwed another girl? Got loaded too much? Maybe it was the heroin use. It didn't make any sense.

I called Phyllis's number after I arrived home that night. It was disconnected.

Freedom

Things were all peaches and cream once I got home. I was still grounded, unable to use the car except to go see the doctor or drive out to see Billy in the hospital. I called Shari every day. That part was wonderful, although she kept wanting to run away and come see me. I guess some things never change.

I told her to wait until I could come and see her.

Missing the first appointment with the doctor really pissed my mother off. Called me irresponsible. I didn't care. I wanted to be home as little as possible. The problem was, Kenny had moved to Anaheim, Stanley to Diamond Bar, Paul was busy with Sandy, and Billy was in the hospital with a broken neck.

So I would either hitchhike, or Paul and I would drive to Anaheim and hang with Kenny, where we got stoned on pot and acid. Kenny's new friends were nice, but they were total stoners; hard to speak with using anything other than monosyllables.

"Dude."

"Dude."

"What's up?"

"Nothin' dude. You?"

"Nothin."

"High?"

"Yeah. You?"

"Yeah. Weed and whites."

"Cool."

"Yeah."

"Yeah."

"Acid, man, Purple Ozzly."

"No shit?"

"No shit."

"Holding any more?"

"Nope."

"Bummer."

"Yeah, man."

"Later, dude."

"Later."

That was one of our more cogent exchanges. *Jeez.*

Stanley was having the time of his life in Diamond Bar. A completely new set of women who did not know him. Dozens of girls going in and out of his life like a turnstile. Once they got to know him, things usually went downhill. Objectively speaking, he was a flake. Always asking them for money. Always either drinking or high on something or other. But before that they thought him cute, affable, funny, and charming, which of course he was.

He was a Crusader, after all.

We went to visit him quite often, and got loaded out there too. Seems there was no problem getting drugs anywhere we went. We Crusaders were drug magnets. Especially when anyone discovered we went to Bassett High and lived in La Puente. The school and immediate environs had a reputation.

We exploited that every chance we could.

One day, I went to Paul's house and noticed a slight dent in the front of the Crusadermobile. Don't know why I noticed it, but I did. When Paul shared with me what happened.

Two nights earlier, he, Stanley, Billy, and Kenny were in the car, sniffing Energine--what we called getting energized, while driving down the street in Hacienda Heights. Paul turned around to say something to Kenny, got distracted, and went over the curb and hit a block wall. Stanley started laughing and yelled at Paul. "Floor it and knock this motherfucker down."

Kenny and Billy agreed.

Paul floored the car, turned into the wall, and he was damned if it didn't start falling over block by block as they started moving down along it. Kenny and Billy were shouting "Wall, wall, wall, wall."

About two-hundred yards later, he turned back into the street and they continued on their merry way, still sniffing the Energine.

"No shit?" I said, looking at the car again. "Doesn't seem like much damage."

"Hell no," Paul replied. "This car is bullet-proof. But check this out, dude."

Paul went into the house, and came out with a newspaper. He opened it to section two and there was a picture of the wall he had mowed down, with a headline that read something like "Vandals Destroy Block Wall."

Paul beamed. "Is that cool or what?"

"Un-fucking-believable," I said. Looking back at the car I shook my head. *That thing is a tank.*

By the way, we did go through a short phase of sniffing Energine. Poured it in a brown paper bag and sniffed away. An unbelievable high. So unbelievable, that it ended up scaring us, it was so good. Lasted only a few months.

Mike, however, *really* liked it, and was always wanting us to meet him in Edgewood's field and sniff it with him. When we could not find him, it was a good bet we would walk over there and find him in the bushes, sniffing away.

Kenny had created a great network of friends in Anaheim. Drug connections, I should say. He was able to get 'keys,' kilograms of pot, and break them down into lids. We would bring them back to La Puente and sell them, usually doubling our money. A side business that kept us flush with dough and pot. We would use the excess to buy acid wholesale and sell it retail. Not as profitable as pot, but made our habits affordable.

I still had that damn doctor's appointment hanging over me. When unable to put it off any longer, I resigned myself to go and fuck with him one last time. I knew he and my parents could not put me in the hospital again, since I would not get hustled like last time. They could not legally force me to go. So it was relatively risk free.

My only concern was to be careful not to lose my temper with him. That, I did not know if I could do.

My dad let me use his car to get there.

Crazy House - Postscript

"Sit down, John," Dr. Smith motioned with his hand while he read something. I assumed it was a report from talking with my parents - although I had no way of knowing that. The office hadn't changed -- sterile with monotone furniture. He continued reading without any outward sign of emotion and then looked up.

"Seems like you may be having a difficult time transitioning back home after your stay with us," he said. His monotone voice grated on my nerves.

"What makes you think that?"

He set the paper down on his desk and leaned forward, elbows on desk, hands clasped. "Your parents feel that you are still having problems. I spoke with them, and they are worried about you."

"Can't imagine why."

I thought I detected an emotionless half-smile. He remained silent for a half-minute, not blinking. I still wondered, "How he was able to do that?"

"I thought we made great progress in the hospital, John. Do you feel differently about something since then?"

I leaned back in my chair and crossed my arms. Smiled. Stared back at him. It was time. I felt nervous and excited. But I would not be bullied by him again.

"I was fucking with you."

"Excuse me?"

"What part of 'fucking with you' don't you get?" I uncrossed my arms and sat straight. For dramatic effect.

"When I came in here originally, I really was fucking with you. I made up everything. Purposely." I laughed. "What the hell... do you think I really wanted to see my family cut to pieces? You can't be that fucking stupid. It was all a goof."

He stared silently. I was looking for any sign of emotion. None surfaced.

"But I guess you are. That fucking stupid, I mean. Cause you believed it, right? So you tell my parents I am crazy or some shit and get them to bring me into the hospital and lock me up. It took awhile to figure out how to get out, but once I did, I fucked with you again about those 'anger issues' with my parents." I used air quotes on anger issues, again for dramatic effect. "And again, you are so fucking stupid you believed it. How goddamn gullible are you?

"Anyway," I stood up and stepped sideways to the door. "I just came in to let you know, and hope to God you haven't tried to fuck up other people's lives by being a fucking idiot and misdiagnosing them."

"John," he called out. No emotions involved. He used that authoritative voice that annoyed me so much. "You need to sit back down here and we can discuss this."

I pointed my index finger at him. "No, you need to kiss my fucking ass and apologize for what you did." I put my arm down and grabbed the doorknob. "But I guess you're even too stupid to realize how stupid you really are. So I'll be going. And don't bother calling my parents again. There's nothing you or they can possibly do about me anymore."

I flipped him off and exited the door, slamming it. Felt childish, and good, at the same time. I drove my dad's car home, and went into the house. Dad promptly demanded the keys back from me.

Dr. Smith apparently didn't heed my warning not to call them.

Still, there was nothing he or they could do about it. Or so I thought.

Turns out I was dead wrong.

First Kenny

We were parked at a park in Baldwin Park, laughing and cracking jokes while smoking some doobies. Getting high. Kenny and Cheri H. were in the front seat of Kenny's car, while Billy, Mike and I left the car to sit on the wooden benches in the park. We stashed our weed down the sides of the back seat of his Ford until we got back.

Kenny and Cheri moved to the back and covered themselves with a blanket.

It was a cool crisp evening. There was a carpet of dew and mist that stretched across the grass, and there was no one else in the park except us. Quiet. Eerily so.

Twenty minutes later we noticed a beam of light sweeping across the jungle gyms and swings of the park, casting ominous shadows of their skeletons on the sand that was surrounding them. We turned, simultaneously, to find a police car stopped, doors opened, next to Kenny's car. The officers were standing outside of it, using a flashlight to explore the occupants through the windows.

My first instinct was to run in the opposite direction. A quick glance at Stanley confirmed he had the same idea. However, a second Baldwin Park black and white taxi with red lights flashing pulled up on the opposite side of the park and quashed that idea, quickly. Two doors popped open, and a couple of roving flashlights searched the park until they landed on us.

What to do? We were boxed in.

The officers next to Kenny's car shouted for them to get out. I watched as first Cheri H., then Kenny, exited the car and stood next to the policemen. The officers from the other police car cautiously approached us, flashed the lights in our faces and asked what we were doing there.

"None of your fucking business," Mike replied, laughing.

Wrong answer.

I discovered that when you wear a Saint Christopher medal, a white Penney's t-shirt, faded blue jeans and huarache sandals, and the other guy has a gun, billy club, and the legal authority to beat the crap out of you, it is futile to fuck around with them. However, it took me a few times to really confirm that. The problem was, that little noise was starting in my head again. And I was not near any reds.

"Smart-ass hippies, huh?" one of the officers stated.

They grabbed my shoulders and wrists and spun me around, forcefully pushing and dragging me toward Kenny's car. The other one then grabbed Mike. Billy was ordered to follow. I guess he looked small enough not to warrant the extra attention. We observed an officer getting out of Kenny's car, with our bags of pot in his hand. *Our* pot. One of them had weed, the other half a dozen rolled joints.

"What is this?" the officer snarled, looking grim as a reaper with a roguish smirk. He seemed to take a certain pleasure in dangling the baggies in front of our faces.

"Who the fuck knows?" Billy answered. "Never seen them before."

"Just keep it up, asshole," the cop replied.

"That's what she said," Mike retorted, catching our eyes and causing us all to laugh.

The six-foot two-hundred pound brute looked at his fellow officers and then spun his glare back to Mike.

"What the hell did you say?"

"Nothing," Mike answered, snickering.

He looked to Kenny. "This your car?" he asked as he scanned the registration and the driver's license in his hand, "Mr. R.?"

"Yes," Kenny said.

"What was that?" It was an order, not a question.

"Yes... *sir.*"

The officer dangled the baggies in his face.

"These yours?"

Kenny shook his head no.

"What do you think are in these?"

"No idea. I've never seen them before," Kenny answered, cool as a breeze.

"Then how did they get in your car?"

"Don't know. Maybe somebody put them in there," he added, looking at and nodding his head toward the other officer.

The officer who had been speaking looked to the others with a furrowed forehead. They nodded toward Kenny and Cheri.

"Okay, Mr. R., you are under arrest." Kenny's look was iced and cool. Completely dispassionate.

"You too, Miss H. You are under eighteen, and that means you, Mr. R., are in a lot of trouble."

One of the other officers grabbed Kenny's arms and pulled them back, handcuffing him around the wrists. "Miss H.," the first officer stated, "Will you turn around and place your arms behind you.

"As to you three, you weren't in the car, so I can't arrest you. But I will tell you this. When we come back here in an hour after booking these two, if you are still here, we'll take you in for vagrancy."

"How are we supposed to get home?" I asked.

"Ask your smart-assed buddy with the long hair," he replied, pointing to Mike. "He seems to have all the damn answers."

"What about my car, man?" Kenny asked.

"It will be towed and held for evidence," the officer replied, smiling devilishly.

"Shit," Kenny breathed.

We watched, solemnly, as they placed Kenny and Cheri into the back seat of the patrol car, slammed the door shut, and drove away. The other two officers waited until the tow truck arrived and started to pick up the rear end of Kenny's car. They gave a slight laugh as they left and walked toward their car.

"Remember what he said," one of them shouted over his shoulder. "You hippies got an hour to get out of here."

It was eerie watching Kenny's car towed away. Then the reality hit us all at once. It would be a long walk home from where we were. At least five miles. But we knew, no matter what, we did not want to be there in an hour, so we started walking.

I was scared. Billy and Mike seemed calm enough. But I saw Mike's hand shaking when he took a drag off his cigarette.

We suddenly realized just how terrible a situation we were in. Kenny and Cheri were on their way to jail. No money, to speak of. The car had been towed. We were out of weed, and our buzz had definitely been replaced by the stark fear of getting away from that park, and for that matter, Baldwin Park altogether.

Like I said, it would be a long walk home.

Jeff and Altamont

"What do you think, John?"

I looked at the 1963 Buick station wagon and couldn't believe my eyes. Jeff had driven it over from Whittier, having called and asked if I wanted to drive with him up north to a free concert in Altamont, California. "Sure," I said.

He'd pulled up in front of my house, the car being blocked by my hedge. I had already told my parents I'd be gone for a few days and packed a small duffle bag. They were not happy about it.

After trading niceties back and forth with my parents (Wally-style from *Leave it to Beaver*), Jeff looked to me: "Ready?"

"Yeah, dude. Looking forward to it."

We strode out past the hedge and there it was. The roof was hand-painted dark blue, with tiny white stars covering it. Not orderly stars in rows, but haphazardly painted five-pointed blobs that went every which way but straight.

The hood, sides and rear of the station wagon were covered with red and white spray-painted stripes. Not a line was parallel to any other. In a word, a piece of shit car painted like a nightmare version of an American flag.

"Well, John, what do you think of what I did?" Jeff again asked.

I'd hoped my mouth wasn't expressing what my thoughts were screaming at me. No frickin' way am I getting in that car and driving three hundred miles up the coast.

"You're kidding, Jeff, right?"

"Huh?"

"I mean, what the fuck do you think I think?"

"It looks cool, man. I painted it myself."

"No shit?... all by yourself?"

I slowly paced around the car. "It looks like a hippie-mobile screaming to every police officer from here to San Fran to pull us over and fuck with us, that's what it looks like." I glanced up at him. "What were you thinking?" I continued my inspection of the most amateurish paint job I'd ever seen. "An American flag, Jeff? You know how much that will piss everyone off?"

"I know man. It will be cool."

"It will get us thrown in jail."

"Come on. We'll get there and the car will be the talk of the town."

"We'll never get there, Jeff, because we'll either get shot at from some crazy veteran, or get fucked up by Hell's Angels who hate us in the first place, or busted by some anal-retentive cop who has nothing better to do."

"You're jammin' my buzz, John."

I stopped my inspection and faced Jeff. "Dude, we're best friends. I'm asking you to not go there in this car. I'm surprised as hell you got here from Whittier."

"Nobody was pissed off at the car, John. You comin' with me?"

"I don't think so, Jeff."

His demeanor changed. His hand stroked the back of his neck, seeming as if he were searching for the right words. "I was counting on you, man. Need some bread for gas to get there."

I pulled out ten dollars and handed it to him. "Take this. But I'm telling you, Jeff. If you're holding, I would leave your stash here."

"How can I do that and get high on the way?"

I laughed. Couldn't help it. It was an insane conversation.

"Okay, Jeff. Have fun. Call me when you get there."

"Okay, dude." He flipped the peace sign, opened the door and slid in behind the wheel. "Sure you won't change your mind?" he said, sticking his head out the window.

"Not in this lifetime."

"It's the Stones, you know."

I nodded.

He waved, started the car and raced off. I watched as it turned the corner at the end of the block and disappeared.

Jeff relayed later he was pulled over four times on the way up. He'd hidden his weed outside near the gas tank, so it never turned up when they searched the car and Jeff.

Made it to the concert at Altamont just before it started. He was there when the Hell's Angels killed a concertgoer.

Drove halfway back home down 101 until the car broke down somewhere near San Luis Obispo. He abandoned it and hitchhiked home.

Jeff loved the concert.

The car was never seen again

Then Paul

"Leonard B. is here, Paul. He wants to buy some pot," Sandy said as she motioned for Paul to come to the door.

A few weeks earlier, Sandy's sister Debby had been paid off in weed on a loan she'd made to some musician friend. Two pounds. Thirty-two lids at ten dollars each. Good as cash, as far as she was concerned. Paul had agreed to put out the word and help her sell them.

"Hey, Leonard, what's up?" Paul said as he walked out the door of Sandy's house.

Paul noticed Leonard was fidgety, constantly looking around. "Not much man. Brought a friend who is looking to score."

"Cool." Paul looked at the young woman. A short woman, dark-brown hair, pixyish nose and deep-set eyes. Although she looked Leonard's age, she seemed older. "You a friend of Leonard's?"

"Yeah."

"She's cool man. How much you got?"

Paul thought a minute and almost walked away. An intuition he would later regret not following. "What do you need?"

"I could use a couple of lids," the woman said. "Maybe more later."

"No problem," Paul replied. "Do you have the money?"

She pulled out twenty dollars and handed it to Paul. He walked into the house, grabbed two lids from Debby's room, came out the front door and handed them to her.

"Can I get more later?" she asked.

"Later today?"

"No, I mean later like next week." .

"Probably not. This is a special deal for Sandy's sister." Paul looked to Leonard again, who would not even connect with his eyes. *Weird,* he thought.

"Everything cool, Leonard?" Paul asked.

"Yeah, man." He ran his hands through his scraggly black hair and rubbed the side of his face. "We gotta go, man. Thanks for the score."

"No problem, dude. Let me know if you need any more."

He nodded with a half smile and walked away with the woman. Paul entered the house.

"What was that all about?" Sandy asked.

"Don't know." Paul shook his head. "Leonard's always been weird. Guess today's no exception."

"Who was that girl?"

"Friend of his."

"A girl?"

"Yeah, I know. Leonard with a girl. Anyway, we only have another ten lids and we'll be done."

A few weeks later, I walked over to Sandy's house just to say hello and hang out. My parents had taken the car away, and I was looking for Paul to get a ride to Whittier to see my cousin Jeff. Paul's Merc was in Sandy's driveway, so I ambled to the door and knocked.

Paul answered. "John," he said, breaking into a big smile. Pushing open the screen door, he walked out and put his arm around me. "I have some bitchin' news for you, dude. Un-fucking-believable, really."

We walked together to the front of his car. He turned toward me, still beaming like a lighthouse on a stormy night. "So?" I asked.

"So," he said. "I am going to be a father."

I thought about it for a moment. I could see he was aware of my disconnect.

"With Sandy. Sandy and I are going to have a baby."

I had a myriad of mixed feelings at that moment. I loved Paul. Was happy for him. Loved Sandy, and was excited for her. The thought of them together and having a family thrilled me. At the same time, a feeling of loss engulfed me. Would this hurt Sandy's and my relationship as friends? What about Paul? Where would they move? And a hundred other questions in the same vein.

"John?" Paul asked.

I shook out of it and hugged Paul. "Couldn't be happier, Paul," I said, patting him on the back. Pushing back, I could feel the tears well up and start to moisten my cheeks. "You and Sandy will make a wonderful couple."

"You okay?" he asked.

"Of course," I said, wiping the tears away. "Just happy for you."

And I was. And wasn't. I couldn't understand my inner conflict. Just that it was there.

Paul motioned for me to follow him into the house. "Come on in and say hello to Sandy." He turned and winked. "My future wife."

Following him into the house I saw Sandy and teared up again. We hugged, and we talked about how far along she was, how her mom was so excited, and how Paul's parents, although apprehensive about it, were backing them getting married. Sandy was barely seventeen, Paul was eighteen. Not a large age difference, but a critical one: it would be, legally, considered statutory rape in California if Sandy's mom wanted to make a big deal of it.

Fortunately for all, she really liked Paul.

Months passed, during which part of the time I was on an 'Irish vacation', as far as anyone asking my parents, in the San Antonio Community Hospital -- out of contact with everyone. Paul and Sandy had made wedding plans and were to be married within a couple of months.

Paul was outside of his parents' house, washing the Crusadermobile on a warm Southern California afternoon. Out of his peripheral vision, he noticed a car pull across the street and stop. *No big deal. Lots of cars stop on Mayland.* Unnoticed by Paul, another car stopped a half-block up the street. Two men exited the car and went into the backyard of the house two doors down from his parents.

Within moments he heard a walkie-talkie click, voices statically saying something about being in position. Two men quickly jumped out of the car from across the street and ran toward him. He dropped the sponge and faced them.

"Paul W.?" the taller of the two asked.

"What is this about?"

He heard his mother scream and turned. Out the front door of the house two men exited, holding small handguns.

"What's going on?" Paul asked.

One of the men pulled out a pair of handcuffs, grabbed Paul by the arm and spun him around.

"Paul W., you are under arrest. Anything you say can and will be used against you." He continued the recital and put the cuffs on Paul's wrists, which were then behind his back. His mother and father came out of the house, startled and scared.

"What is going on Paul?" his father asked.

"I don't know."

"Your son is a pot dealer, Mr. W.. He is under arrest for possession and sale of marijuana."

Paul had no idea yet what they were talking about. He hadn't connected the dots yet. They put him in the back of the car, gave his parents a business card, and told them he would be booked at Industry Sheriff's Office and transported to LA County Jail. His mother was in a state of tears. His dad stoic, reserved. Paul knew that look. It was not a good sign.

Hours later he was thrown into a holding tank in the City of Industry, after being booked, fingerprinted, searched, and photographed. A white bus with wired windows finally came and took him to LA County Jail, where the procedure was repeated, and then he was put into a cell with three other men.

Paul's long hair and sideburns did not endear him to his new cellmates. But his bulky body size did keep them away. By then he had figured out what happened. Leonard B. and that woman with him. He had also replayed in his mind what he told them, and realized he was in some serious trouble.

Should have trusted my intuition, he thought

A few days later, his parents bailed him out, and he was home.

Facing five years to life.

Then John

I couldn't catch the eye of anyone in my family as I entered my parents' house after a day hanging around with Paul, getting loaded. My parents had again grounded me from using their cars. This time it seemed like it might be permanent.

I stood in the front room and looked around. "What is going on?" I asked no one in particular, glancing at my brother for an instant and noticing he immediately turned away.

No one answered. I entered my room, threw my tanker jacket on the desk chair and thought about it. What *is* going on? Usually my dad asked me where I'd been.

That afternoon, nothing.

Debby was still gone, sent away to that Catholic girls' reform school, which was really a sort of juvenile hall as far as I was concerned. She was locked up tighter than Jack the ice cream man's truck.

Shaking my head, I ambled past the family through the living room into the kitchen to get something to eat. *Maybe they were giving me the silent treatment because of... what?* Couldn't think of anything so I pulled out the Wheaties box and started fixing myself a bowl. I noticed my mom had gone into the bedroom, talking in a whispered tone on the phone.

It was about four in the afternoon on a Saturday. There was a football game of some sort on the TV, but no one seemed to be paying attention to it. Patrick was looking at me out of the corner of his eye. When I caught him, he quickly looked back toward the game.

"Who's playing?" I asked, trying to make some conversation as I munched down on my cereal with milk and about a quarter-inch of sugar on the top. I walked into the front room and stood so I could see the TV.

"Don't know, Johnny," Dad replied.

Suddenly I noticed, through the patio door, a casually dressed man with a pronounced mustache in the backyard, skulking about. He had a gun attached to his belt. I lowered my bowl and stared toward him as he stopped, motioning to someone.

"Hey, there's someone in the backyard-"

Knock, knock, knock.

I whirled around toward the front door. My mom reached it and cracked it open. Muffled voices were followed by her opening it fully to reveal another mustached man dressed in dark pants and a khaki-colored shirt, gun riding high on his belt. This one had a Sheriff's badge hung around his neck, lying against his chest. He fixed his cold steel-grey eyes upon me.

Panic set in. *What was happening? Why were they here?* My eyes darted from side to side and rested on my dad as I rubbed my tongue against my suddenly dry upper lip. His eyes diverted downward and looked away as I felt my arm being grabbed and spun around, facing the stranger.

"You are under arrest for possession of marijuana," he spoke in a monotone and deep voice. The other man, also an undercover police officer, came through the back door and joined him.

They turned me around and started to place handcuffs on my wrists. *This can't be happening. Not to me. Why? Where did they find the pot? Who turned me in? Shit, I'm scared.*

"You have the right to remain silent. Everything you say...."

The room started spinning. His voice grew into an echo in the background as they marched me out the front door, down the walkway and toward their police vehicle. I looked around to hear hushed whispers and see neighbors gawking and pointing. All was a blur. A dream. A bad dream.

Did my family just turn me over to the police? Numbness swept over my body as a high-pitched noise started to rattle my brain. Tears welled up, trying to burst past my eyes. I struggled to hold them back. How could they do this to me?

Then I remembered something. I'd left a bag of weed tucked under my mattress a couple of days earlier. Was that it? Suddenly it became clear. They'd found it and turned it in. The police were called by my mom when I arrived home and they had come to arrest me. Shit.

It was quick, methodical, and effective.

I was caught, and couldn't get away. Trapped like an animal. I looked behind me. The traitors all peered at me from the safety of the porch. Anger quickly grew into a kind of rage and hate. It was palpable. As they pushed my head down and sat me in the back seat, I steeled myself and glared back at them, emotionless. The hatred and rage grew with each breath.

Betrayed by my own family. Who would I turn to? What am I going to do? Who could I contact? My Crusader friends? No... they wouldn't have the money to bail me out. Bail me out? Shit, shit, shit. The full impact of their Judas betrayal began to sink in.

I was fucked. No doubt about it. And at that very moment, I realized just what a jam I was in.

No one was going to come bail me out.

No one was going to help me.

I was totally alone and on my own. Scared shitless. Heading to one of the worst jails in the country.

L.A. County.

The Crusaders
Epilogue

"All in all it's just another,
brick in the wall."

John O'Melveny Woods

Kenny

At his arraignment, the presiding judge took particular interest in the arresting policeman's testimony. After listening to his answers, he interrupted the district attorney's questioning.

"Officer Smith," he started. "Is it your testimony that you approached the car and the suspect, Mr. R., and the young woman, were under the covers in the back seat?"

"Yes, Your Honor."

"Then how could you possibly tell what they were doing?"

"It was obvious what they were doing."

"Obvious to whom? If you could not actually see them, then it was only a guess on your part. Is that correct?"

"Ah... not a guess, exactly. It was years of experience . . ."

The judge raised his hand. "Hold it right there, Officer Smith. If you could not see any crime actually being committed, then there was no probable cause for you to ask them to get out of the car."

"Your Honor," the district attorney said. "I think that when you consider the evidence . . ."

"That's another point. If there was no crime in the first place, then all evidence gathered AFTER that point is inadmissible."

Silence enveloped the courtroom.

"Very sloppy police work. I will not have any of it in my courtroom." The judge looked at the officer on the stand, and then the district attorney. Shook his head in disgust.

"You can step down now. Mr. R., please stand up."

Kenny stood.

"All charges against you are hereby dismissed." He slammed the gavel. "Court is adjourned."

Kenny was called to meet with his attorney a few days later.

"They are planning on filing charges against you again, Kenny."

"How can that be? Isn't there some sort of double jeopardy involved?"

"Yes and no. Yes, if you are a United States citizen. No for you, since you are Canadian. They are really upset with what that judge did. Made them look like idiots. I think they are committed to rectifying that."

Kenny paced the office. "What can I do?"

"As weird as this sounds, you have two choices. The first, go back to Canada, hope they don't try to extradite you."

"I've never been in Canada. Lived I mean. My dad was Canadian. There is nothing to go back to."

"Here is the weird part. If you join the service, then you will be under a different code of laws, the military code of justice, and they won't be able to indict or try you again."

"No shit? Join the service?"

The attorney nodded.

Kenny joined the Marines.

Surprised the heck out of me. A Crusader in the service? Just didn't seem right.

He got through boot camp, and then was stationed at Camp Pendleton, where drugs were plentiful, and he was one of the main reasons for that situation.

Months later, he met a Captain who was on duty with him. He shared with Kenny how he was saved by a religious conversion. He and Kenny prayed, and Kenny's life changed from that day forward.

He gave up drugs, much to the chagrin and ire of his former customers.

Months later, he was in a major motorcycle accident that put him in the hospital with a serious head injury. Luckily, he was wearing a Helmet that he had just bought the day before. He was finally discharged, honorably, from the service.

Kenny became a cement contractor and ran a very successful business until his retirement in 2014.

He married Gayle, a school teacher. They have two great children, both in seminary school, and live in the foothills of San Bernardino, California.

They are active in their local church.

Paul

At Paul's arraignment, the judge spelled out the charges. He was being tried as a major drug dealer, because of the comments made to the female undercover police officer.

His attorney was negotiating with the district attorney, trying to work out a deal. Weeks went by. Finally, his attorney recommended Paul plead guilty, and not to worry - he had worked out a deal with the judge.

"Really? What deal?"

"Still negotiating. But very little time in jail."

Paul entered the courtroom full of apprehension. Sandy was five months pregnant. They were scheduled to be married in a few weeks. Although his job had no opinion about his being arrested, he still was worried about doing any time and losing it. His parents, Sandy and his attorney were present.

"How do you plead, Mr. W., to the charge of selling and possessing drugs for sale?" the judge asked.

"Guilty, Your Honor." He replied somberly. At least he intended his response to sound somber.

The judge picked up a paper report and read it. "I see here you are planning to get married in a few weeks, and you have a steady job." He looked directly at Paul. "Is this correct?"

"Yes, Your Honor." He tried sounding humble.

"I see." The judge scanned the rest of the sheet and then put it down. "It is the opinion of this court that the sentence shall be five years in state prison." Paul's heart sank. Sandy started to sniffle. His mother leaned into his father's arms for support.

Paul thought, somberly, *Guess I'll be doing a nickel.*

"Suspended," the judge finally continued. He looked again to Paul, and then cast his focus back and forth to Paul and Sandy.

"You have shown that this was a one-time offense, and it is of no use to the court to punish you excessively for it. And I am glad to see you have turned your life around, Mr. W." He turned his attention strictly to Paul.

"You will serve twenty-six weekends in a county jail. This should allow you to keep your job, and take care of your future wife. After that, you will be on probation for two years. If you complete this successfully, then all charges will be dropped and the case sealed."

He slammed the gavel and gave Sandy a quick wink. "Court is adjourned."

Paul received a draft notification. His probation officer called the board and told them he could not go because of his conviction.

Sometimes crime does pay.

Paul completed the twenty-six weekends, and the two years' probation. He and Sandy were married.

Both Paul and Sandy had religious conversions and started going to Calvary Church. They are active in church to this day.

They had three great children. He has held various jobs in construction and became a licensed contractor.

He finally found his dream job--manager of construction for a major contractor. He joined the carpenters union and worked at the construction company, supervising jobs throughout California, until his retirement in 2014.

Sandy and Paul designed and built their dream home in the foothills of San Diego, California, where they are basking in their retirement, enjoying their grandkids, and life.

Billy

Billy drove to Boyle Heights in East LA to score another couple of jars of reds. It had been six months since the accident at Huntington Beach, and he was almost as good as new, according to his doctor. He stopped near an open field, parked his Volkswagen and approached a darkly shadowed car.

After exchanging greetings, Billy leaned in the passenger side of the lowered car. The driver pulled a twelve-gauge shotgun from under his seat, aimed it directly at Billy and pulled the trigger. The blast pushed Billy back about five feet from the car and flat on his back, the top of his face and skull gone. Blood formed into a puddle surrounding his head. He laid there for more than twelve hours before the police discovered his body the next morning.

After an investigation that lasted for months, where the authorities learned that Billy had a few thousand dollars on him that went missing after the shooting, the LA police finally admitted they had no leads.

They never caught the shooter.

Stanley

Stanley graduated high school. He met and married Doreen, a wonderful girl who was also a Jehovah's Witness. They moved to Orange County and had two children.

Doreen became friends with Sandy.

Stanley went through various jobs, never able to hold them for long. He continued drinking and partying. The only reason a Jehovah's Witness can divorce another is for adultery.

Doreen divorced Stanley.

He continued drinking, and was employed in a wide range of jobs, including the construction industry.

Never married again that we know about.

He dropped out of contact with the rest of The Crusaders ten years ago.

Guy

Guy continued working in gas stations until he had enough money to move to Hawaii. He loved it there. Surfed, smoked pot, and hung out on the islands for a couple of years.

Came back, and he too had a religious conversion. Stopped all drugs and drinking.

Married, and divorced, with two lovely children.

He has worked for the school system for the past thirty years. Continues to attend church.

He finally married again, to a wonderful woman, and is very happy, living in Orange County, California.

Allan

After moving to West Los Angeles, Allan attended college and received his teaching credentials. He taught public school for a couple of years. Didn't like it.

Quit.

Allan joined the family baby furniture business. He and his brother Marty successfully ran it until their retirement.

Never married.

Spends his time between Los Angeles and Palm Springs.

Kim

Never heard from Kim again, even after searching for years.

Cousin Jeff

Jeff was arrested for the sale of marijuana shortly after he returned from Altamont. He spent a couple of weeks in LA County Jail. He was never convicted of any crime.

He went to real estate school, became a successful agent, and sold real estate in Orange County, California.

Years later he got involved with cocaine, and ended up becoming addicted.

An especially expensive addiction.

Lost touch with him after that.

Paul S

Worked for years with Paul and Kenny at the bakery.
Had a religious conversion.
Married.
Divorced.
Religious conversion waned.
Everyone lost touch with him after that.

Mike

Got into more drugs, especially acid.

Lost touch with him for years, after he left to hitchhike up to Monterey for a concert.

Kenny was driving back from Portland a few years ago and saw Mike hitchhiking. Barely recognizable. Picked him up.

He was completely stoned on acid and, in Kenny's opinion, out of his mind. Nothing coherent.

Let him out in Los Angeles, and never heard from him again.

Phyllis

Had a religious conversion, shortly after leaving Billy and learning of his death.

Attended Calvary Church in Orange County.

Kept in touch with Sandy for a few years.

After that, Sandy never heard from Phyllis again.

Mary

I had heard from a girl I dated many years after leaving La Puente that Mary had gotten pregnant shortly after her sixteenth birthday and married a jock from school.

He was abusive and an alcoholic.

Mary became an alcoholic too.

They finally divorced.

That was the last that girl heard about Mary.

Howard Feingold

Shortly after graduating from high school, Howard went to a Kibbutz in Israel for a summer learning program.

He was shot through the head by a sniper.

Patrick

My brother Patrick decided to go to seminary school and lived in Divine Word Seminary in Riverside, California. While in Riverside high school he met a girl and decided that becoming a priest was not going to happen.

He attended the University of San Francisco, graduated with a degree in Catholic Theology and has been teaching high school school ever since.

While teaching he met his wife Mary, a student.

They married after she graduated and now have three beautiful children.

He never touched or got involved with drugs.

John

I languished in LA County jail for six weeks before my Uncle Gerald O'Melveny in Washington found out about my incarceration and posted bail.

After being released in downtown LA with no money, I walked to Olvera Street where Billy's dad was working in the family store. He gave me ten dollars, wished me luck. From there I walked to Billy's grandmother's restaurant and had my first non-jail meal.

Uncle Jerry had arranged for me to live in a house in Los Angeles that was run by the Salvation Army and headed by Ed Boyle, a psychologist. The possession charges against me were dismissed. There was no way I could legally be connected to the drugs found in my room.

I spent almost a year at the house in Hancock Park and was heavily influenced by Ed Boyle and his program of self-responsibility. It turned my life around. And I also made another couple of lifelong friendships.

I also never drank or took drugs from that point to the present.

With these new friends I moved to Beverly Hills, played music and worked for a major law firm in downtown Los Angeles.

Shari ran away to join me. Some things never change.

Took her back home and eventually asked her to marry me. We were wed in a Catholic Church, attended by my parents and Crusader friends, moved to Buena Park, and we had a beautiful daughter.

Ironically, she was born in San Antonio Community Hospital, the same hospital where I met her Mother.

Two years later, Shari decided she didn't want to be married to me - or be a mother - and left to discover herself.

That created a dilemma. Suddenly, I was a single father. I quit the law firm and my dreams of becoming an attorney, and instead became an entrepreneur, founding several companies. They ran the gamut from a merry-go-round and pinball arcade, a tear gas company, and a manufacturer of ultra-light aircraft. Most of them were quite successful.

Life has a funny way of coming full circle.

In 1976, I met Frank, who was to become a lifelong friend. Frank's mom, Patricia Kempler, was to become the role model for the mom whom I never felt I had - a cool, hip, non-judgmental woman. She was living with Bill Duffin, a brilliant man who taught high-school science. Between the two of them, I had role models for the family I'd always longed for, and it gave me the tools I needed for raising my daughter.

Twenty years later, Patricia mentioned that her former husband, a psychiatrist who tormented her and Frank after their divorce, had died. She said she was glad about it. Mentioned to me numerous times how she thought the guy was a certifiably crazy asshole. But she had never mentioned his name. Until that time.

Electrified chills shot through my spine and body. I flinched.

"What was his name again?" I asked her. *It sounded familiar.*

"Kempler, the same last name I kept because of business. He ran a treatment center in the San Gabriel Valley."

"Would that be Ingleside?" I asked.

Pat was silent for a few moments, and frowned, biting her lower lip. "Yes, it was. How would you know that?"

Memories flooded my thoughts as I spoke. "My parents sent me there in 1967 for tests and treatments."

She stared, seemingly measuring her thoughts.

"He used shock therapy on me," I continued.

"Oh God," she said. "He was hell-bent on using that." She teared up. "Said every kid who was out of line should be zapped." She wiped her wet cheeks. "Christ, John, I had no idea."

"It's okay, Pat. I made it out okay."

"He was such a frickin' jerk. Used to send me dead animals in the mail after I left him."

She gave me a big hug.

It was never mentioned again.

I met Karen ten years after my divorce and remarried, gaining another wonderful daughter, Kristie, and loving wife. We lived in Palos Verdes, California and raised our family.

At forty, I had a mid-life crisis. This one involved my career. *What did I really want to do the rest of my life?* After searching months for an answer, it came to me.

I sold my printing company and returned to school to learn to write, and afterwards founded a production company: indieTV.com.

Karen and I were eventually divorced, remaining friends until her death from ovarian cancer in 2006.

www.KarenSueLanier.com

In 2001 I was diagnosed with pancreatic cancer. Traditional medicine offered no options. It was suggested I get my life in order, since I would be dead within six months.

Through a dear friend, Sheila, I learned of an alternative treatment available in Tijuana, Mexico, offered by Dr. Neil Norton of the Scientific Regeneration Institute. He was a protégé' and friend of Dr. Virginia Livingston-Wheeler, a cancer pioneer I had written a movie about and who had lived in San Diego, California. She died in 1989 of heart failure. Dr. Norton was a pioneer himself, having developed several therapies for cancer that were extremely effective.

After four years of treatments, I was declared cancer free and have been living a health-conscious life ever since.

Dr. Norton and I became great friends.

He died in 2010 at ninety-four years of age.

Of heart failure.

I miss him dearly.

www.drneilnorton.com

Through my two daughters, who are happily married, I have been blessed with five grandchildren, and also have three wonderful nieces and nephews from my brother Patrick.

I now write books and reside in Fairhope, Alabama, with my two loves - Judy and Daisy.

Final Thoughts

Funny enough, after all we had been through, I realize now that we Crusaders really didn't know each other all that well. At least not in an intimate way. We knew each other as brothers. We trusted each other implicitly. Without questioning or reservation. But discussing things about our hopes, our dreams, our fears? What we wanted to become when we grew up?

Never happened.

Brothers never talked about such things, and neither did we Crusaders.

Yet we cared about each other. Deeply. We could always count on each other. We were there for each other. But we never shared the really intimate things we felt. Girls. Fears. Loves. Hurts.

We'd talk around them, much like a cat circling its prey, jabbing close but not making a direct hit. Never got into anything "heavy, man."

No reason, really. It just never came up, and we never asked each other.

But we did have a rather connected intuition going among ourselves. A sort of inner knowing. When one of us was hurt, the others would try and cheer him up. Or get him into a chase, which would immediately take his mind off of whatever was bothering him and transfer it into getting out alive. That always worked. We seemed to know what to do with each other, at just the right time.

The Crusaders were a group of guys you just knew were your friends -- where you could be yourself, laugh, get into adventures, get scared shitless together, and laugh about it knowingly later.

We could talk about girls – liking them, not liking them, dumping them, and getting dumped (much more common). That was fair game, manly, and tolerated. But anytime someone, including me, tried to bring up something to do with "feelings" that were personal, it was always followed up with something like:

"What the fuck are you talking about? Are you some kind of pussy?"

And that would end that.

It wasn't malicious or even uncaring. Rather, it seemed to me that we didn't know what to do or say. We weren't trained, nor did we ever have role models of how to be sympathetic or empathetic. Our parents certainly never showed or talked about their outward feelings.

Why would we?

We did manage to get through all the noise, tumult, angst, and tribulations of the 1960's in spite of these shortcomings. For that I am grateful to my friends.

The Crusaders.

My Mother

I made a reference earlier in the book about my Mother and her being what I called anal retentive -- and somewhat emotionless. However, I don't think it fair to the reader, or my mother, ending this book without giving an explanation as to reasons why she may have been that way - some of which I discovered after her death.

When I was ten years old, I was sitting in my grandparents living room going through the family picture albums. I turned a page and there, in black and white, was a picture of a nun who looked exactly like my mother.

"I didn't know my mom had a sister," I said aloud.

"She doesn't," my grandfather replied.

Perplexed, I held the album up and pointed to the picture. "Then who is this, Grandpa?"

"That is your mother," was his matter-of-fact reply.

"Really?"

I ran across the street and shared with my mom what Granddad had just told me.

"It's true," she said. "I used to be a nun. Then I met your father."

And that was it. She walked away.

Holy moly. My mom a nun. How did that happen?

Looking back, her actions started to make more sense. Her insistence that I become an altar boy. How the priests, the church, and the nuns who were my teachers were always right.

How she would never side with me against them. The constant demurring to those in authority.

But then... a larger and more important question came to me: *How in the heck did dad hit on a nun?* When I was older I broached the subject with him.

"So Dad, how exactly did you hit on Mom when she was a nun?" I tried to hide my smirk -- and secret admiration.

"I'm not talking about it, Johnny."

"Come on Dad."

"Did you not hear me? Drop it."

So I did. Sort of.

Periodically, over the course of my life, I would bring it up again. And again. And it always ended with the statement, "I'm not going to talk about it."

Even on his death bed. Full of morphine. Dad remained true to his word. He never talked about it.

My mom, in her later years, tried to return to the Sacred Heart order from whence she departed almost sixty years earlier. We found letters from her to the convent after she died, along with a papal decree from Pope John the XXIII, giving her permission to leave the order for personal reasons.

The Sacred Heart order refused to take her back.

We also found a hand-written autobiography. In it, my mom wrote about how she was engaged to four different men during World War II. Each one was killed. Her parish priest, Father McIntyre, told her it was a sign from God to become a nun. Another sign soon followed. She was sexually assaulted by several drunk servicemen, became pregnant, and sent away to have the child. After that she did become a nun.

In spite of all that happened, I loved my mother and was by her bedside, holding her hand, when she died.

John O'Melveny Woods

'Crusader John' can be reached through the official Crusaders website:

www.TheCrusadersBook.com

Other books by the Award Winning Author:

Lost Tomb of Alexander
www.LostTombofAlexander.com

Return to Treasure Island
www.TreasureIslandBook.com

Jesse James Secret
www.JesseJamesSecret.com

www.TheSeekers.com

Made in the USA
Columbia, SC
31 August 2020